THE COMPLETE BOOK OF
ZINGERS

Diet 63

Pastor Ed,

Merry Christmas and many
thanks for all you have done!

May God Bless You & Your
wonderful family.

Wendell & Phyllis

"1990"

THE COMPLE

Zing

CROFT M

Tyndale House Publishers, Inc

TE BOOK OF

ers

PENTZ

Wheaton, Illinois

Front cover credits: Illustrations, Jared D. Lee;
woman on phone, John Moss; record, David DeJong;
mother and daughter, Robert Cushman Hayes.

Library of Congress Catalog Card Number 89-51899
ISBN 0-8423-0467-3

96   95   94   93   92   91   90
9   8   7   6   5   4   3   2   1

FOREWORD

I've always loved sentence sermons. I've used them often in my sermons, the weekly church bulletin, and the monthly church paper.

Sentence sermons carry a message with a few words. Often they are remembered more than the other spoken words.

Next to God's Word and poetry, I personally feel sentence sermons have a greater impact upon mankind than any other spoken word.

For years I've collected these quips. In 1962 Zondervan Publishing House published my book *1001 Sentence Sermons*. It went through several printings. Some years later, The Baker Book House reprinted it. It too had several printings.

After collecting more than four thousand of these, I began to sort them out and place them under certain headings. This took hundreds of hours of work. There could be many more headings. However, we tried to narrow it down to as few as possible.

Some are original. Others were found in newspapers, church bulletins and church bulletin boards. Still others were from speakers heard in person, on radio, and on television. It is impossible to trace where they all came from.

I'm only a compiler. I have no intentions of using anyone's material for personal gain or profit. The purpose of this book is to keep alive this material, spreading it far and near, so many may profit from it.

My special thanks to the various magazines and sources who provided this material. I wish I could thank each one personally. Of course, this is impossible.

Thanks to Mrs. Cindy Storms for her typing and assistance in preparing the manuscript for publication.

May God bless these simple sentence sermons and use them for the glory of God.

Croft M. Pentz

A

✦Ambition (see also Work)

Every person should take some time daily to look at the road map of his ambitions.

Easy is the enemy of ambition.

The father of success is work—the mother of achievement is ambition.

The ambition of many dieters is to be weighed and found wanting.

✦Anger (see also Temper)

I will not permit any man to narrow or degrade my soul by making me hate him.

An angry man is seldom reasonable; a reasonable man is seldom angry.

Don't be angry with the people who are smarter than you—it isn't their fault.

Speak when you are angry and it will be the best speech you will ever forget.

A man is about as big as the things that make him angry.

The greatest remedy for anger is delay.

Every moment you are angry, you lose a minute of happiness.

Anger is only one letter from danger.

When a person strikes in anger, he usually misses the mark.

A man is never in worse company than when he flies into a rage and is beside himself.

Some people are like buttons—they pop off at the wrong time.

An angry man opens his mouth and closes his eyes.

Anger is the wind that blows out the light of reason.

One load that is too heavy for anyone to carry—a grudge.

He who loses his head is usually the last one to miss it.

A fellow with the smallest mind is the one who is usually most willing to give someone a piece of it.

Hating people is like burning the house to kill the rats.

A chip on the shoulder indicates there is wood a little higher up.

When we give others a "piece of our mind," we have no "peace of mind" left.

Some people think they have dynamic personalities because they are always exploding.

Hatred is self-punishment.

The more you grow up, the less you blow up.

Rudeness is a weak man's imitation of strength.

Anger is an acid that can do more harm to the vessel in which it is stored than to anything on which it is poured.

Bitterness is self-cannibalism.

Never answer an angry word; it is the second one that starts a quarrel.

Those who look for opportunities to hate, miss many opportunities to love.

A grouch is a fellow who has sized himself up and then is sore about it.

When you give a person a piece of your mind, you lose part of yours.

Some Christians are like balloons—full of wind and ready to blow up.

The wind of anger blows out the lamp of intelligence.

When we discuss we show our intelligence; when we argue we display our ignorance.

Swallowing angry words is always easier than eating them.

Anger is a feeling that makes your mouth work faster than your mind.

An argument is the longest distance between two points of view.

The test of a man's or woman's breeding is how they behave in a quarrel.

Though vengeance may seem sweet, there still may be bitterness in the heart.

Unspoken anger is never regretted.

When anger rises, think of the consequences.

Despair could be defined as anger with no place to go.

Anger is often more harmful than the injury it has caused.

Anger manages everything badly.

No one is able to stand up indefinitely under the weight of carrying a grudge.

Steel loses its strength when it loses its temper.

People who fly into a rage always make a bad landing.

A believer at war with his brother cannot be at peace with his Father.

No matter how long you nurse a grudge it won't get better.

B

✦Backsliding (*see also* Sin)

Backsliding begins in the knees.

Backsliding is the easiest thing to do—you do nothing.

The devil will be satisfied with you if you are satisfied with him.

People seldom lose their religion by a blowout—it is usually a slow leak.

Backsliding begins when knee-bending stops.

Backsliders usually are guilty of criticism, condemnation, and complaining.

When we expect more of others than we expect of ourselves, we are in a state of carnality.

Samson was asleep when he lost his strength.

Still water and still religion freeze the quickest.

If people would do what they should, there would be no time to do what they should not.

Hypocrites are persons who aren't themselves on Sunday.

Church members are like automobiles—they start missing before they quit.

Some people who never consider walking in darkness sure enjoy a little stroll in the shade.

The backslider who turns back to the Lord needs the backing of the church.

◆Bible

Not all biblical promises carry an unconditional guarantee.

God's Word is like a highway sign. You don't have to pay any attention to it if you don't care what happens to you.

One truth from the Bible is worth more than all the wisdom of man.

The value of the Bible is not knowing it, but obeying it.

Love for the Author of the Bible is the best preparation for the Bible.

Knowing the Scripture is one thing; knowing the Author is another.

When you study the Scriptures "hit or miss," you're likely to miss more than you hit.

Voltaire boasted that his work would make the Bible extinct in a hundred years. Recently his ninety-two volumes sold for two dollars.

A Bible in hand is worth two on the shelf.

Keep your Bible open and you will not find the door to heaven closed.

The Bible is a telescope; it is not to look at, but to look through.

It is good to mark your Bible, but it is better to let your Bible mark you.

The Holy Scriptures teach us the best way of living, the noblest way of suffering, and the most comfortable way of dying.

The Bible is a window through which we look at eternity.

Bible verses will save you from spiritual reverses.

Knowing the Bible is of little benefit unless you practice it.

Should all the people dust off their Bibles, we would have one of the greatest dust storms of all time.

The best way for Christians to grow is to eat the Bread of Life.

Because there is dust on your Bible does not mean it is dry.

The Bible is most helpful when open.

To master the Bible, the Bible must master you.

Some people thank God for the open Bible who never bother to open it.

Knowing the living Word is the key to understanding the written Word.

The Bible, as it is, is for men as they are.

The Bible is like a compass—it always points the believer in the right direction.

I read my Bible to know what people ought to do and my newspaper to know what they are doing.

The Bible should more than inform us—it should transform us.

The blood of Christ makes us safe; the Word of God makes us sure.

The Bible is not only the world's best-seller—it's man's best buy.

Some of the Bible's most precious treasures are discerned only with tear-filled eyes.

The Bible was not written to teach science, but the Bible is scientifically correct.

The Bible is the only book whose Author is always present when it is read.

Carrying your Bible will never take the place of reading it.

You can remove the cinders of doubt from the eye of faith only by the water of the Word.

The Bible will never be a dry book to those who use it as a source of "living water."

The Bible doesn't need to be rewritten—just reread.

We must adjust ourselves to the Bible—never the Bible to ourselves.

Don't criticize the Bible—let it criticize you!

God's law lasts longer than those who break it.

Trying to do away with the truth of the Bible is like trying to mop the ocean dry with a sponge.

Too many study their neighbor's faults more closely than their Bible.

The devil is not afraid of a dust-covered Bible.

Some people have memorized the Scriptures without practicing them.

The Bible breaks hard hearts and heals broken hearts.

It is a great responsibility to own a Bible.

You can learn a lot from reading the Bible; you can learn still more by practicing it.

Other books were given for our information—the Bible was given for our transformation.

A Bible that has frayed edges usually has an owner that doesn't.

The Bible needs less defense and more practice.

A well-read Bible is the sign of a well-fed soul.

The Bible, like a bank, is most helpful when it's open.

The best thing to do with the Bible is to *know* it in the head, *stow* it in the heart, *sow* it in the world, and *show* it in the life.

A home without a Bible is like a ship without a compass.

The Bible reveals the wickedness in the heart of man, but also reveals the grace and mercy of God.

Using your Bible as a road map will keep you off the detours of sin.

Every Christian should own a *read* Bible.

The one who only samples the Word of God never acquires much of a taste for it.

The more we read the sacred pages, the better we know the Rock of Ages.

The Word of God, spoken with compassion, has converted more sinners than mere eloquence.

Rich treasures of God's truth are waiting to be discovered in his Word.

The signals of Scripture are meant for our protection, correction, and direction.

If you pore over God's Word, his cleansing power will pour over you.

Long-lasting relief is not found in a bottle but in the Bible.

C

✦Character (*see also* Reputation)

The best way to be somebody is just to be yourself.

A good man, like a bouncing ball, springs ever upward from a fall.

Big people are those who make us feel bigger when we are with them.

God does allow U-turns.

How a man plays the game shows something of his character; how he loses shows all of it.

Reputation is for time; character is for eternity.

Character is not made in a crisis; it is only exhibited.

Christianity isn't worth the snap of your finger if it doesn't straighten out your character.

So live that when people speak evil of you, no one will believe it.

Much may be known of man's character by what excites his laughter.

A man's character is like a fence; it cannot be strengthened by whitewash.

It is better to be short of cash than to be short of character.

A broken character doesn't knit easily.

A reputation once broken may possibly be repaired, but the world will always keep its eye on the spot where the crack was.

When we die, we leave behind us all we have and take with us all we are.

Character is what you are when no one is watching.

Character is like a tree and reputation is like its shadow—the shadow is what we think of it; the tree is the real thing.

You can easily judge the character of a man by how he treats those who can do nothing for him.

One may be better than his reputation, but never better than his principles.

Character is easier kept than recovered.

Good character is like good soup—it is usually homemade.

To change one's character, we must begin at the control—the center of the heart.

Reputation is the other fellow's idea of character.

A bad reputation is the easiest thing to get but the most difficult to get rid of.

God will use even the mistakes of those in authority over us to achieve his character in us.

Don't be a character—have it!

Reputation is what men *think* you are—character is what God *knows* you are.

Thoughts become actions; actions become character; and character determines our destiny.

Be what you wish others to become.

Reputation is what you are in the home; character is what you are on the highway.

Reputation is precious—character is priceless.

Resolved: Never to do anything that I should be afraid to do if it were the last hour of my life.

What you are determines what you do.

Your life is what your thoughts make it.

Character is one thing we build in this world that we carry into the next.

Character is the total of thousands of small daily strivings.

Too often in prayer we ask for a change in circumstances rather than in our character.

I can work out a good character much faster than anyone can lie out of it.

The best measure of a man's mentality is the importance of the things he will argue about.

A beautiful heart seems to transform the homeliest face.

Reputation is what people say about you on your tombstone—character is what God has written about you in his books.

You can no more blame circumstances for your character than the mirror for your appearance.

It is all right to spend money to make character; it is wrong to spend character to make money.

What you are when you are not trying to be anything is the supreme test of what you really are.

No man's character is better than his word.

Your character is built on what you stand for—your reputation on what you fall for.

The company we choose is always an index of our character.

Only you can change or damage your character.

Good will, like a good name, is achieved by many actions and lost by one.

A bad disposition has lost many a good position.

Character is developed by two small words—yes and no.

Character is like a window glass—even a little crack shows all the way through.

I am three persons: The person *others* think I am; the person *I* think I am; the person *God* knows I am.

Character is like the foundation of a house—it is beneath the surface.

It isn't your position that makes you happy or unhappy; it is your disposition.

Character is revealed by your actions in an unguarded moment.

A person's reputation is precious, but a person's character is priceless.

Our present choices determine our permanent character.

If you want to get a true estimate of a man, observe what he does when he has nothing to do.

A well-rounded character is square in all his doings.

Three essentials: a faith to live by, a self to live with, and a purpose to live for.

Some people are so busy *being* good they forget they should be *doing* good.

The need is not for more worship but to change one's life-style.

Your words may hide your thoughts, but your actions will reveal them.

The greatest treasure one may possess is good character.

A good test of a person's character is seen in his behavior when he is wrong.

Measure a person's character by how he treats those who can do him no good and how he treats those who can't fight back.

Character is the sum total of what a man is after he has won all, and it is the sole thing left after he has lost all.

Character is not an inheritance; each person must build it for himself.

When some people aren't acting like themselves, it's an improvement.

What lies behind you and ahead of you is not as important as what lies within you!

Glory is the shadow of virtue.

✦Children (see also Discipline; Education; Parents)

By the time the average teenager is able to work, he won't.

Children are often spoiled because no one will spank Grandma.

The most *juvenile* delinquents are the ones more than forty years of age.

Every child is a bundle of potential.

The character of our children tomorrow is shaped by what they learn from us today.

"Juvenile delinquency" is the result of parents trying to train children without starting at the bottom.

There are some children who should be applauded with one hand.

Anyone who sleeps like a baby doesn't have a baby.

Child training—parents are training their children how later to train their children.

The greatest aid in adult education is children.

It now costs more to amuse a child than it once did to educate his father.

The strongest faith is often found in a child's heart.

He who takes the child by the hand takes the mother by the heart.

Every child has the right to the affection and intelligent guidance of understanding parents.

The surest way to make it hard for your children is to make it soft for them.

Here's a way to punish your children: take them away from their grandparents.

Better to bring the children to church and hear them cry there than to leave them at home and later cry in court.

Kids never change. First they won't hang up their clothes; then they won't hang up the phone.

A tanker can spill six million barrels of oil, and nothing happens— a child spills a glass of milk and he is punished.

When a child gets off the track, he can be put back on by pulling a switch.

If you find your son going down the wrong track, perhaps you didn't switch him soon enough.

The way to tell a child is growing up is when he stops asking where he came from and starts refusing to tell you where he's going.

A juvenile delinquent sows his wild oats, and his parents pray for a crop failure.

It's hard for children to learn manners when they never see any.

The best thing parents can spend on their children is time—not money.

Another thing the modern child learns at his mother's knee is to watch out for the cigarette ashes.

No man really finds out what he believes until he begins to instruct his children.

Years ago the board of education was a shingle.

We need a child labor law to keep children from working their parents to death.

The best time to put the children to bed is while you still have the strength.

There is only one beautiful child in the world, and my mother has it.

A perfect example of minority rule is the baby in the house.

Children and canoes are alike—they go best when paddled from the rear.

What on earth will today's younger generation tell their children they had to do without?

Did you ever notice how your belief in heredity is reinforced when one of your children does something outstanding?

Children are creatures who disgrace you by showing in public the example you set for them at home.

When parents don't mind that their children don't mind, the children won't.

The one reason there are so many juvenile delinquents today is that their parents didn't burn their britches behind them.

Years ago when the son started sowing wild oats, the father started the thrashing machine.

The best inheritance parents can leave a child is a good name.

"Stay at home" parents seldom beget "go to church" children.

We recall when a wayward child was straightened up by being bent over.

The great man never loses his child's heart.

Children should be taught more about the Rock of Ages instead of the ages of the rocks.

It costs less to train one hundred children in Christian living than it costs to deal with one average criminal.

Teaching smaller children may focus on four-letter words such as duty, work, earn, give, and love.

The man who lets his children take second place to his work will live to regret it.

A child of five, if properly instructed, can as truly believe and be regenerated as an adult.

Many a woman who has low-rated her son-in-law has lived to brag about her brilliant grandkids.

Nobody bruises as easily but heals as quickly as a child.

Children are so expensive today only the rich can afford them.

One way to curb delinquency is to take the parents off the streets at night.

One way to teach children to count is to give them different allowances.

Rearing children is like drafting a blueprint—you have to know where to draw the lines.

Money may not be everything, but it keeps you in touch with your children.

One reason why so many children are seen on the streets at night is they are afraid to stay home alone.

The trouble with some of today's smart kids—they don't smart in the right place.

One way to correct your children is to correct the example you are setting for them.

Education is what the parents get when the children are home from school on vacation.

A little more spank and a little less Spock might be the answer to many of our problems at home.

Babies are angels whose wings grow shorter as their legs grow longer.

The simplicity of the child and the profundity of the sage must be combined to make a perfect man.

More twins are being born these days. Could it be that kids lack the courage to come into the world alone?

Every child should have the right and privilege to be brought up in a Christian home.

As boys grow, so grows the nation.

It is easier to build a boy than to mend a man.

Before I was married I had six theories about bringing up children; now I have six children and no theories.

Lead a child to Christ—save a life.

Many fathers are willing to give their children everything except themselves.

Television is an appliance that changes children from irresistible forces to immovable objects.

A child is easy to impress but hard to convince.

It's a shame that adults do not make friends as easily as children.

A child's love is the purest thing in the universe.

An unusual child is one who asks questions that a parent can always answer.

Parents don't bring up children anymore—they finance them.

It's extremely important that parents with small children save something for a rainy day—their patience.

Perhaps we wouldn't need to be worried about how our kids turned out if we were more concerned about when they "turned in."

So live that when people say your son reminds them of you, he will stick out his chest, not his tongue.

The parent who is afraid to put his foot down will have children who step on his toes.

Perfect age for children—when they are old enough to shovel snow, but not old enough to drive.

Ideas are like children—your own are wonderful.

The worst thing about growing old is listening to your children's advice.

The only thing that children wear out faster than shoes are parents and teachers.

The child who knows the value of a dollar will usually wind up asking for two.

Chances are you will be proud of your children if you give them a reason to be proud of you.

When adults behave like children we call them juveniles, but when children behave like adults, we call them delinquents.

Next year three and a half million kids will turn sixteen and seven million parents will turn pale.

School days can be the happiest days of your life, providing the children are old enough to go.

If you have given up trying to open something, tell a four-year-old not to touch it.

It's funny that the things your kids did that got on your nerves seem cute when your grandchildren do them.

To insure the education of teenagers, parents need to pull a few wires—television, telephone, and ignition.

Allow a pig and a boy to have everything they want and you'll end up with a good pig and a bad boy.

Keep out of your child's life anything that will keep Christ out of his heart.

Adolescence is when children start bringing up their parents.

When children fight and pout, bending them over sometimes straightens them out.

This would be a better world if more kids were raised *at* mother's knee and *across* father's knee.

At times children can either be a lump in the throat or a pain in the neck.

A child that is allowed to be disrespectful to his parents will not have true respect for anyone.

The quickest way to get a child's attention is to take a nap.

Children are not only deductible, they're taxing.

A sweater is a garment worn by a child when his mother feels chilly.

Summer is the time when kids are out of school, and moms are out of their mind.

A woman handles a child much better with one finger than a man does with both fists.

Some people really bring their children up—others let them down.

Great people never lose their child's heart.

Your children are not only heirs to your possessions—they are heirs to your values and character.

A boy becomes a man when he stops asking his father for money and requests a loan.

The behavior of some children suggests that their parents embarked on the sea of matrimony without a paddle.

Seventy-five million children between eight and fifteen years of age work in the labor forces of the world, and some of them never live long enough to become a teenager.

Children who watch television night and day will go down in history—not to mention mathematics, geography, and grammar.

One thing you can say about modern children is at least they're not childish.

Children may close their ears to advice, but they keep their eyes open to example.

✦Christian

There are only two classes of people—the saints and the ain'ts.

We may face situations beyond our reserves but never beyond God's resources.

Christians are born—not made.

A true Christian is neither ashamed of the gospel nor a shame to the gospel.

If men are so wicked with religion, what would they be without it?

You cannot become a saint by comparing yourself with a sinner.

Sinners hate Christians because they make them conscious of their sins.

The life that you live may disgrace the fact that you are a child of God, but it cannot erase the fact.

The Christian life is a pilgrim journey, not a sight-seeing tour.

If you would seek a life of great adventure, go outside your door and act like a Christian.

Many Christians have enough religion to make them decent but not enough to make them dynamic.

The gospel breaks hard hearts and heals broken hearts.

By nature most people are the same, but through the supernatural we are made different.

The true Christian is a person who is right-side up in an upside-down world.

Many Christians are convertible people—angels on Sundays and imps during the week.

Definition of a Christian: "Under New Management."

In the Christian life, any time you let up, you can expect a letdown.

A Christian is a person who makes you think of Jesus.

The greatest saints are made of the same material as the greatest sinners.

A Christian heart is a good thing, but much better is a Christian liver.

When a Christian is in the wrong place, his right place will be empty.

A Christian is a person who makes it easier for others to believe in God.

A true Christian is like the figure 6—upset him and he will increase in value.

Christians should outlive, outlove, and outlaugh anyone in the community.

The gospel is a delicious meal—not a bitter pill.

Well-balanced Christians not only know their faith, they show it.

If you can't hear God speaking, check the volume control of your conscience.

The Christian's heart is Christ's home.

◆Christian Living (*see also* Victory)

Christians always are just a half a step from hell.

When you do what you please, does what you do please God?

The old nature knows no law; the new nature needs no law.

Someone said Christianity is a crutch; well, so what—we are all cripples.

The middle of the road is often best, but the path is narrow.

Happy is the one who walks so close to God that he leaves no room for the devil.

I will place no value on anything I have or may possess, save in its relation to the kingdom of God.

Some Christians who should be on the front lines are still in basic training.

Thinking well is wise, planning well is wiser, but doing well is wisest.

Christianity is meant to be bread for daily use, not cake for special occasions.

The conversion of a soul is a miracle of a moment; the growth of a saint is the work of a lifetime.

Christians are people with an eternal destiny.

If it doesn't affect your hands, feet, and thinking, it isn't Christianity.

Christianity is a movement, not a condition; a voyage, not a harbor.

Live so that if people get to know you, they will get to know Christ better.

The church, rooted by God, can never be uprooted by man.

Skipping church is the beginning of spiritual decline.

A living church is one that remembers the past, lives in the present, and works for the future.

Sign on a church: Try one of our Sundays.

If you want to be there when the roll is called up yonder, shouldn't you be present when the roll is called down here?

Christianity: know it in your head; stow it in your heart; show it in your life.

Christians are models for Christianity.

Periodic Christianity is perpetual hypocrisy.

Christianity is not just Christ *in* you, but Christ living his life *through* you.

Living the Christian life is like shaving—no matter how well you do it today, it needs to be done again tomorrow.

The true expression of Christianity is not a sigh but a song.

Nature makes it impossible for man to learn the ropes without falling over them a few times.

You will shrink or expand to the size of your vision.

We may not always see eye to eye, but we should walk hand in hand with Jesus.

Feel far from God? Who do you think moved?

Your deficit is what you've got when you haven't as much as you had when you had nothing.

If you are where Jesus put you, he will meet you where you are.

One of the pastor's problems is to decide when a church member is dead enough for burying.

Christianity has not been tried and found wanting; it has been found difficult and not tried.

The real strength of a man is not physical but moral and spiritual.

God will not judge you for what you have done but for what you have refused to do.

To get nowhere, follow the crowd.

Christianity is a beggar going into business with a millionaire.

If Christ is kept on the outside, there must be something wrong inside.

Those who walk the closest and work the hardest are the best prepared for Christ's return.

Vacant lots and vacant minds usually become dumping grounds for garbage.

The rich are not always godly—but the godly are always rich.

God looks more where men look the least—at the heart.

Christianity will help us to face the music when we don't like the tune.

God has wonderful things to display if he can only get the showcases.

How to find Christianity? Turn right and keep going.

Christianity is not a cloak to put on—it's a life to put in.

Lord, when we are wrong, make us willing to change. And when we are right, make us easy to live with.

When I do wrong—it's me. When I do right—it's God.

In the Christian life, any time you let up, you can expect a letdown.

It's natural to be religious; it's supernatural to be a Christian.

When God takes your picture, he doesn't touch up the negatives.

Don't pray "Our Father" on Sunday and spend the rest of the week living like an orphan.

The closer we walk with the Shepherd, the farther we are from the wolf.

Wouldn't it be wonderful if we could forget our troubles as quickly as we forget our blessings?

Don't spend the last half of your life regretting the first half.

Those who live on the mountaintop have a longer day than those who live in the valley.

If you wait until every hindrance is removed before serving the Lord, you will never attempt anything for him.

If you think the world is all wrong, remember it contains people like you.

Some have to stay on the ground to hold the ladder of success for the few who climb it.

Jesus often spoke of Christianity as a banquet but never as a picnic.

Don't worry about your station in life; someone will tell you where to get off.

No one who ever followed Christ ever went astray.

Jesus is God spelling himself out in language that all men can understand.

The right road may be rough and steep, but the vision from the summit is worth all the effort.

Too many people are trying to shine for Jesus without burning for him.

The one thing Christianity cannot be is moderately important.

We have learned the golden rule. Now it's time to put it into practice.

Live where you are with what you have in the light of God's promises.

Three "bee-attitudes" from the bee: go straight, keep busy, and gather sweet things as you go.

Are you more like Christ today than you were yesterday?

The Christian life is like a reproduction, not the imitation, of Christ.

The Lord's yoke never fits a stiff neck.

David said, "Surely goodness and mercy shall follow me." What's following you?

If you have no definite plans for worship on prayer meeting night and next Sunday, reconsider your conversion.

It takes more grace to live for God than it would to die for him.

You can't win respect by demanding it.

Life's greatest tragedy is to lose God and never miss him.

The rewards are always at the end of the road. It pays to go all the way with Jesus.

It is not more preaching that is needed, but more gospel in the lives of Christians.

If your Christianity isn't contagious, it must be contaminated.

Obstacles are those frightening things you see when you take your eyes off the Lord.

The degree of your devotion to Christ is the barometer of your love for him.

◆Church

You can't hide from God by missing church.

The prayer closets of God's people are where the roots of the church grow.

Religious differences are not nearly so disastrous as religious indifferences.

The way to preserve peace in the church is to preserve the purity of it.

Some people who watch "Saturday Night Live" come to church "Sunday Morning Dead."

Satan has a reserved seat in many churches.

If there is a hypocrite between you and the church, he is closer to God than you are.

If your religion doesn't take you to church, it is doubtful if it will take you to heaven.

The trouble with most people is that they are looking for a church that doesn't hurt their conscience.

An ounce of church attendance is worth a pound of police court.

God made the Sabbath and blessed it—even the rainy ones.

Too many church members have been starched and ironed without being washed.

A Christian without a church is like a bee without a hive.

The task of the church is not only to get sinners into heaven but to get saints out of bed.

The church needs workers—not a wrecking crew.

Night owls may become bedbugs on Sunday morning, but this does not prove evolution.

Don't wait until you die to be brought to church.

If absence makes the heart grow fonder—some people really love the church.

One way to defend the church is to attend it.

When the church service is over, it is time for *your* service to begin.

The church has too many bystanders and not enough standbys.

It's easy to lose interest in a church in which you have nothing invested.

What kind of church would you have if every member were just like you?

Sign at church parking lot: Unauthorized cars will be spirited away at owner's expense.

A hearse is a poor vehicle to start attending church in.

The ecumenical movement suggests that some churches are losing their sect appeal.

If God stays at your house during the week, you ought to visit his house on Sunday.

We don't use people to build a great church—we use the church to build great people.

Some people have such bad nerves that they cannot sleep in church.

The world has lost its faith because the church has lost its power.

If you want to hear all about the problems of the church, ask someone who hasn't been to church in many months.

Some people would walk a mile for a cigarette, but cannot walk two blocks to church.

It might be profitable to cross blankets with toasters so people would pop up out of bed, especially on Sunday morning.

Why look for a perfect church? You would feel out of place attending it.

The church should be a living organism instead of a dead organization.

Which is worse—to be for what the church is against, or against what the church is for?

Some churches teach history, while others teach *his story.*

The gospel is not something only to go to church to hear—but to go from church to tell.

If the church were perfect, there would be no members.

Every church has all the success it prays and pays for.

Some churches have too many carnal shirkers and not enough Christian workers.

God put the church in the world—the devil put the world in the church.

If there were as many idle parts in an automobile as members in the church, the automobile couldn't run downhill.

Church-going and Sabbath-keeping are not religion, but religion cannot live without them.

It is impossible to build a great church on ignorances.

The church is no more to be blamed for bad people in it than a hospital is to be blamed for the sick people that are in it.

Every seat in the church is a love seat.

Church attendance—come early for a backseat.

In church you use to hear about do's and don'ts. Now you hear about dues and doughnuts.

The automobile does not take people away from church against their will.

A church is like a bank—the more you put into it, the more interest you receive.

Church members are often weakened by too much weekend.

God's house is a hive for workers—not a nest for drones.

If the church wants a better minister, it can get one by praying for the one it has.

Some people are regular churchgoers—they never miss an Easter.

It takes years to build a church—seconds to need one.

Some people attend church only three times: when they are hatched; when they are matched; and when they are dispatched.

The business of the church is not to furnish a hammock for the lazy but yokes for the drawing of loads.

A Christian outside a church is like an athlete without a team.

The world at its worst needs the church at its best.

The church is a place where we can admit our failures to one another.

A church cannot be built upon stumbling blocks.

Some people go to church to see who didn't.

Floating members make a sinking church.

The man who drives with one hand is headed for church—either by the way of marriage or for his funeral.

The church has three kinds of members: pickers, kickers, stickers.

Church sign: You are not too bad to come in, and not too good to stay out.

Don't stay away from church because there are hypocrites—there's always room for one more.

It's strange that nineteen drops of water keep twenty-one people from church.

The church exists for a double purpose—gathering and sending out.

The reason people miss church when it rains is the reason why we have church.

There is a shortage of engineers and a surplus of brakemen in our churches.

Spiritual headaches occur regularly every seventh day.

Some church members believe the word *parishioner* means a "parish shunner."

The empty-pew problem is not solved when the pew is occupied by a person with a wandering mind.

Having a gas station closed on Sunday is all the excuse some people need to skip church.

Go to church to worship, not to whisper—to commune, not to criticize.

Most people want the benefits *of* the church but refuse to be a benefit *to* the church.

A church all wrapped up in itself is a small package.

The less spirituality a church has, the more entertainment it takes to keep it running.

The church gives the people what they need—movies give the people what they want!

An avoidable absence from worship is an infallible evidence of spiritual malnutrition.

The man who hasn't been to church in thirty years is usually the one who says that modern preaching is behind the times.

Going to church via TV is like talking on the telephone with your best girl and wanting to hold her hand at the same time.

A church only grows as the members grow.

Some people refuse to come forward in church unless escorted by pallbearers.

If you make your church important, it is quite likely to return the favor.

Many people go to church praying that they will hear preaching that will hit someone else.

A church without a purpose is like a house without a door—it has no reason to exist.

The church is not made up of people who are better than the rest, but of people who are trying to become better than they are.

The church is God's workhouse where his jewels are being polished for his palace.

People do not miss church services because they live too far from the church building—it is because they live too far from God.

A caring pastor will build his church—a caring church will build its pastor.

Marks of a strong church: wet eyes, bent knees, broken hearts.

Some church members are like blotters; they soak it all up but get it backwards.

Another type of automobile thief is the man who steals the hour of the church service to go riding in his car.

The church is paralyzed with timidity and dying with dignity.

All communication from your church to unchurched people should emphasize your desire to do something for them, not for them to do something for you.

Weather or not, come on in!

The church is a workshop—not a dormitory.

◆Complaining

The squeaking wheel doesn't always get the grease. Sometimes it gets replaced.

Watch your attitude toward the thing that troubles you. Your attitude may hurt more than the thing.

Please don't pray for rain if you are going to complain about the mud.

Those who beef too much often land in the stew.

As a rule, you will find that those who complain about the way the ball bounces are usually the ones who dropped it.

The loudest boos always come from those in the free seats.

Nothing is more displeasing to God than complaining saints.

Some people seem to find their greatest satisfaction in life just standing at the complaint counter.

People make enemies by complaining too much to their friends.

Don't complain about growing old—some do not have this privilege.

Murmuring and complaining unfits the soul for duty.

The fellow looking down his nose at others usually has the wrong slant.

People who complain that they don't get all they deserve should congratulate themselves.

Putting your best foot forward does not mean to kick about everything.

He who harps on a certain thing may be trying to convince himself that he is right.

May you never complain without a cause and never have a cause to complain.

When a fellow is kicking, he has only one leg to stand on.

Spend your time counting your blessings—not airing your complaints.

Christians are like autos—when they begin to knock, there is something wrong inside.

People who get something for nothing often kick about the quality.

We often write our benefits in dust and our injuries in marble.

If Paul and Silas would have complained while in prison, would the Philippian jailer have accepted Christ?

Whines are the products of sour grapes.

In America there is much complaint with little suffering—in some countries there is much suffering with little complaint.

It is poor practice to try to tame a sour note by just making it louder.

✦Compromise

The world can never be evangelized by Christians who compromise.

Compromise is always wrong when it means sacrificing principle.

By adopting the gospel to the age, men have crippled the gospel.

Compromise is always costly—and sometimes fatal.

✦Conscience

Conscience is a small voice deep down inside where the acoustics are generally poor.

Never trust a person with a hardened conscience.

A gash in the conscience may disfigure the soul forever.

A good conscience is the looking glass of heaven.

Nothing is harder to bear than a guilty conscience.

For some, conscience is the fear of being found out.

Conscience is a still small voice—when it calls, often the line is busy.

A quiet conscience sleeps during thunder and lightning.

A guilty conscience needs no accusing.

Someone should invent an amplifier for the voice of conscience.

The longest distance for humans is from the head to the heart.

Conscience does not get its guidance from a Gallup poll.

A sanctified conscience is the holy whisper of God in the soul.

An imperfect conscience needs a perfect Guide.

The "little voice inside" used to be our conscience—now it's a pocket radio.

Have convictions but be sure your convictions are convictions and not prejudices.

A bad conscience has a good memory.

Conscience and the Holy Spirit are the two great prosecutors of the souls.

A clear conscience can only be destroyed by its owner.

Conscience is that thing that hurts when everything else feels good.

Better to lose a good coat than a bad conscience.

Conscience should always go to truth for instructions.

Many persons tune out the voice of conscience when money begins to talk.

When you listen to your conscience does it sometimes seem you are in the company of a total stranger?

In the courtroom of our conscience, we call only witnesses for the defense.

Conscience is what tells you it is wrong the moment after you have perpetrated it.

A man of integrity will listen to conscience.

Cultivate a clear conscience; it may be the best friend you will ever have.

When you have a fight with your conscience and get licked, you win.

Many people have a bad memory to thank for their consciences.

Feeding your conscience with excuses is like giving sleeping pills to your watchdog.

It is your conscience that tells you that your instinct could be wrong.

Conscience is like a piano—if you only use it once a year, you probably will not notice it is out of tune.

The best tranquilizer is a clear conscience.

Conscience is what makes a small boy tell his dad before his sister does.

What your conscience says is more important than what your neighbors say.

Make sure your opinion of others is not their opinion of you.

A conscience is like a buzzing bee—it can make you uneasy without ever stinging you.

An evil conscience cannot be cured by medication.

Some people say they have become broad-minded when they have only stretched their consciences.

Conscience is like a sundial—when the truth of God shines upon it, it points the right way.

Conscience gets a lot of credit that belongs to cold feet.

Happy is the man who renounces anything that places a strain upon his conscience.

Beware of the rubber conscience and the concrete heart.

Conscience doesn't necessarily keep us from doing what we shouldn't; it just keeps us from enjoying it.

So long as your conscience isn't ashamed to acknowledge you as a friend, don't give a rap for your enemies.

A clear conscience is the softest pillow.

Conscience is not only the greatest preacher who ever lived, he's the best friend you've ever had.

◆Contentment

Don't be a cloud just because you can't be a star.

Just think how happy you would be if you lost everything you now have, and then suddenly got it back.

A well-filled stomach is indeed a great thing—all else is luxury.

If your bell isn't ringing, your clapper is broken.

A great deal of what we see depends on what we are looking for.

Luxuries are great, but only after you have the necessities of life.

Don't forget that living with your neighbors is also hard on them.

It may be true that man does not live by bread alone—but look at those getting along on crust.

Poor indeed is the man who cannot enjoy the simple things of life.

Unless we find beauty and happiness in our backyard, we will never find them in the mountains.

You are only poor when you want more than you have.

Be content with your lot—never satisfied with your achievements.

If you are not happy with what you have, how could you be happier with more?

He who lives content with little possesses everything.

Contentment is not found in having everything—but in being satisfied with everything we have.

Cure for covetousness: think of something to give instead of something to get.

Happiness is not having what you want—but wanting what you have.

The secret of contentment is knowing how to enjoy what you have.

Most of us won't be content with our lot until it's a lot more.

A really contented man has his yesterdays all filed away, his present in order, and his tomorrow subject to instant revision.

Contentment is the power to get out of any situation all there is in it.

All the world lives in two tents—content and discontent.

The richest person is the one who is contented with what he has.

It is all right to be contented with what you *have* but never with what you *are*.

Contentment comes not so much from great wealth as from few wants.

When you can think of yesterday without regret and tomorrow without fear, you are near contentment.

Gather the crumbs of happiness, and they will make you a loaf of contentment.

A contented person is one who enjoys the scenery along the detour.

He who lives content with little possesses everything.

He is not poor who has little, but who desires much.

Earth has no sorrow that heaven cannot heal.

Content makes poor men rich; discontent makes rich men poor.

The key to contentment is to realize that life is a gift—not a right.

Some Christians are like kittens—contented only when petted.

Many people want what they don't need and need what they don't want.

If all of us had everything we wanted, we wouldn't have enough places to keep it.

If we cannot have what we like, maybe we can like what we have.

We have possessions without peace and comfort without contentment.

Contentment can stifle improvement.

Christian contentment is part of the learning process of becoming a Christian.

A Christian is one who does not need to consult his bank balance to see how wealthy he is.

✦Cooperation

A steering committee is four people trying to park a car.

Most people are willing to meet each other halfway; trouble is, most people are pretty poor judges of distance.

The greatest need today seems to be the key to fit the deadlock.

Cooperation can be spelled with two letters—WE.

Chance favors the prepared mind.

Man is a symphony, God is the conductor.

Unity among believers is found in their union with Christ.

God called his people to unity, not uniformity.

If we would only learn to build bridges instead of fences, we could charge tolls.

God's Spirit doesn't work where people are divided.

"A bone of contention" has no place in the body of Christ.

We must be in tune with Christ to be in harmony with one another.

A small river will carry a lot of water if it keeps running.

A dewdrop does the will of God as much as a thunderstorm.

Coming together is a beginning; keeping together is progress; working together is success.

We didn't all come over in the same ship, but we're all in the same boat.

If you don't believe in cooperation, look what happens when a car loses one of its wheels.

A river is powerful because many drops of water have learned the secret of cooperation.

Most people are lonely because they build walls instead of bridges.

Great doors swing on small hinges.

To be agreeable when we disagree is a goal most of us have to keep working at.

As spokes get nearer to the hub of the wheel, they become closer together.

The little wheels in the back of the watch are just as important as the hands of the watch.

He who will not follow and cannot lead should get out of the way.

Group harmony is seldom achieved without personal sacrifice.

Cooperation is doing with a smile what you had to do anyway.

You have a right to your opinion as long as it agrees with mine.

It also takes two to make up after a quarrel.

✦Courage (*see also* Cowardice; Determination)

The people to worry about are not those who openly disagree with you, but those who disagree with you who are too cowardly to let you know.

The real hero is the man who is brave when nobody is looking.

Courage is grace under power.

Have courage to let go of the things not worth sticking to.

✦Cowardice (*see also* Courage)

How many would go deer hunting if the deer could shoot back?

To see what is right and not to do it is cowardice.

A man who gives in when he is wrong is wise; a man who gives in when he is right is a coward.

Dishonesty is a coward's way of getting out of trouble.

One of the nice things about being a coward is that he seldom gets hurt.

The fear of God makes a hero; the fear of man makes a coward.

✦Courtesy

No one is too big to be courteous, but some are too small.

Nothing is as strong to win friends as courtesy.

Nothing costs as little and goes as far as courtesy.

We may disagree, but let's not be disagreeable.

Some feel courtesy is a man offering his seat to a woman after he gets off the bus.

A little oil of courtesy will save a lot of friction.

Courtesy should be in the curriculum of every Christian.

Some people need solitary refinement.

One can tell how much of Christ a person has by the courtesy he reveals.

The test of good manners is being able to put up pleasantly with the bad ones.

Life may be short, but there is always time for courtesy.

◆Criticism

People who try to whittle you down are only trying to reduce you to their size.

If you enjoy honey, don't kick over the beehive.

You cannot hold down a man without staying down with him.

People always emphasize the negative—no one puts up a sign: Beware—nice dog.

Medicine and advice are two things more pleasant to give than to receive.

To speak ill of others is a dishonest way of praising ourselves.

To find fault is easy—to do better is difficult.

One of the hardest things to take is one of the easiest things to give—criticism.

If you must criticize, try criticizing the fault instead of the person.

Don't mind criticism. If it is untrue—disregard it; if it is unfair—don't let it irritate you; if it is ignorant—smile; if it is justified—learn from it.

The harshest criticism, if cushioned with kindness and enthusiasm, becomes bearable and helpful.

Nothing quiets criticism like involvement.

If criticism could cause some to quit, the skunk would be extinct.

The unfortunate thing about constructive criticism is that nobody really appreciates it as much as the one who's giving it.

Most people don't object to criticism if it's favorable.

Our own faults are the ones we condemn most quickly in others.

The goal of criticism is to leave the person better than he was before.

Did you ever notice that knockers are always on the outside?

Those who can, do; those who can't, criticize.

It is far better to know our own weaknesses and failings than to point out those of others.

Many of the suspicions we have of others are formed from the knowledge we have of ourselves.

Give so much time to the improvement of yourself that you will have no time for criticism of others.

Some are farsighted enough to see the faults of others but too shortsighted to see their own faults.

Only he who is faultless has a right to look for faults in others.

We can often do more for other people by correcting our own faults than by trying to correct theirs.

Be quick to praise, slower to criticize.

Any fool can criticize when a man makes a mistake—and most of them do.

Lack of a good reason to criticize is the best reason for not doing so.

As long as you belittle, you will be little.

The most destructive criticism is indifference.

If people don't measure up to your standard, perhaps you should check your yardstick.

It is better to bite your tongue than to let it bite someone else.

The goal of criticism is to leave the person feeling he has been helped.

The person who has a true Christian spirit never takes delight in the faults of others.

It is better to say a good thing about a bad fellow than to say a bad thing about a good fellow.

Fault-finding is one talent that should be buried and forgotten.

Think of your faults the first part of the night when you are awake, and of the faults of others the latter part of the night when you are asleep.

Criticizing another's garden does not keep the weeds out of your own.

Two things can be bad for your heart—running upstairs and running down people.

The fault-finding member has the lowest job in the church.

The person who is always finding fault seldom finds anything else.

No one can improve his work by tearing down the work of another.

Never judge a man's actions until you know his motive.

The bore has at least one virtue—he doesn't talk about other people.

Do not criticize unless you have made an effort to do a better job and succeeded.

Some people look for faults as if there was some kind of reward for each fault they found.

What will fault-finding people do in heaven?

Before finding fault with another person, stop and count ten of your own.

A cynic is someone who knows the price of everything but the value of nothing.

You cannot whitewash yourself by blackening others.

You cannot carve your way to success with cutting remarks.

When looking for faults, use a mirror, not a telescope.

Some people get a lot of pleasure just from being shocked at other people's sins.

If you aren't big enough for criticism, you're really too small for praise.

You cannot build your mansion in heaven with mud you throw at others.

Those who criticize us are the unpaid guardians of our soul.

If it is true what they say about you—do something about it. If it is not true, forget it!

A critic is a legless man who teaches running.

It is easy to make a mountain from a molehill—just add more dirt.

Count your blessings—your critics are keeping track of your mistakes.

Look over your own faults, and soon you will overlook the faults of others.

Some folks who are inclined to criticize their neighbor would do well to step aside and watch themselves go by.

When you weigh the faults of others, do you put your thumb on the scale?

When I am right—nobody remembers. When I am wrong—nobody forgets.

The imperfect person is always looking for a perfect pastor.

Blaming your faults upon your nature does not change the nature of your faults.

We see the handwriting on the wall, and all we can do is criticize the formation of the letters.

Suspicion is like a pair of sunglasses—it makes all the world look dark.

A slanderer is a person who plays God.

Don't mind the complaints as long as your criticism is constructive.

Open-minded or empty-headed—it depends on whether you are defining yourself or someone else.

It is easy to shoot a skylark; it's not so easy to produce a song.

It is better to be blind than to see things wrongly.

The Christian who is too severe in his criticism of others usually is too lenient with himself.

If you take pleasure in criticism, it's time to hold your tongue.

Faults are the easiest things to find in others.

Never accuse others to excuse yourself.

Don't waste time criticizing conditions—improve them.

Adverse criticism from a wise man does more good than the enthusiastic praise of a fool.

A movie critic gets complimentary tickets so he can make uncomplimentary remarks.

The people who get the most kick out of life are those who kick the least.

It is easy to be critical. The real test is to come up with constructive alternatives.

The best way to criticize the other fellow's work is to do yours better.

Before passing judgment on a sermon, be sure to try it out in practice.

Nothing is easier than fault-finding; no talent, no self-denial, no brains, no character are required to set up in the grumbling business.

So long as you aspire, others will conspire; so long as you try, others will vie.

You'll have hostility to face in every place at every pace.

Most of the time people criticize in order to forget their own weakness.

An expert is a person who can tell you of your wrong—after you did it.

The best way to lose a friend is to tell him something for his own good.

Some computers are becoming so human they blame their mistakes on each other.

Critics are people who sit on the sidelines and utter snide lines.

If you rock the boat, you may be the one to get seasick.

Whether a man or a motor, something is wrong if either is knocking.

Only rarely is it worth what it costs to tell a man what you think of him.

There are few things more difficult than the art of making advice agreeable.

It's difficult to take advice from some people—they need it so much themselves.

Don't hesitate to give advice—it passes time and nobody will follow it anyway.

D

✦Death

In every abortion, something living is killed; this is a biological fact, not a moral judgment.

Death cannot sever what the cross unites.

For the Christian, death is the last shadow before heaven's dawn.

Three things never convenient—death, taxes, and childbirth.

Those who are prepared to die are the most prepared to live.

Death is the last chapter of time but the first chapter of eternity.

You cannot decide when or where you will die, but you can decide how you will live.

Everyone should fear death until he has something that will live on after his death.

What we weave in time we will wear in eternity.

Bumper sticker on hearse: Have a happy forever.

Sign on a tombstone: I expected this but not just yet.

Worldly pleasures turn sour in the heat of eternity.

The little things that we do for Jesus now will be the great things in eternity.

A little engine trouble during an airplane flight can reach more folks than a good preacher in a pulpit.

Every man must do two things alone; he must do his own believing and his own dying.

Death is not extinguishing the light; it is putting out the lamp because dawn has come.

If you live wrong, you can't die right.

Death guarantees the sinner's penalty and the saint's promotion.

A will is a dead giveaway.

Death for the Christian is not bane but blessing, not tragedy but triumph.

Only when we die to all about us do we live to God above us.

For the Christian, death is not *gloom* but *glory*.

Immortality is the glorious capstone of Christianity.

Every loss leaves a space that can be filled by God's presence.

◆Decision

A reaction follows somebody's action, or lack of it.

Of all creation, only man can say yes or no to God.

Every person faces this choice—Christ or condemnation.

To deny one's guilt and reject Christ is the worst kind of insanity.

Every man carries with him the world in which he must live.

No power on earth or under earth can make a man do wrong without his consent.

It is not a question as to who is right but what is right.

It is never too early to decide for Christ, but the time will come when it will be too late.

He who provides for this life but takes no care for eternity is wise for a moment but a fool forever.

It is better to do good than just talk about it.

It seems that more people today have a greater desire to live long than they do to live well.

The difference between a stumbling block and a stepping-stone is what you make of it.

An executive is a guy who can take as long as he wants to make a snap decision.

A wise man changes his mind; a fool, never.

A man should give a lot of thought to a sudden decision.

A successful journey does not depend on which way the wind blows but on the set of the sail.

◆Dedication

Nobody cares? They don't have to as long as you do.

There is a perfect freedom for people who do the work they want to do and live by that work.

God often uses small matches to light great torches.

Do the right thing—you will please some people and astonish the rest.

The best angle to approach a problem is the try-angle.

When something goes wrong, it is more important to decide who is going to fix it than who is to blame.

You lose a lot of battles in the process of winning the war.

Becoming number one is easier than remaining number one.

If you think that one person cannot make a difference in the world, consider what one cigar can do in a crowded restaurant.

With God's grace, you can do everything you ought to do.

It takes a long time to feather a nest when you are on a wild goose chase.

It is better to die for *something* than to live for *nothing*.

Doing things by halves may be worthless because it may be the other half that counts.

Morale is when your hands and feet keep on working when your head says it can't be done.

Commitment to Christ should go hand in hand with commitment to his Church.

Depression can come from lack of commitment.

God gives his best to those who leave the choice with him.

Promises made to God when sick require a better memory than some people possess.

Until you are sacrificial, you are artificial.

Spirituality can be compared to a ride in a plane—the higher we rise, the smaller things on earth become.

God's best is known by surrender, not struggle.

Prayer is letting the Master Mechanic do the repairs.

When a person gives God second place, soon he has no place at all.

If you want your influence to last, put Christ first.

He who abandons himself *to* God will never be abandoned *by* God.

We die by living to ourselves—we live by dying to ourselves.

Christ is not valued at all unless he is valued above all.

It is not the talented people who serve the Lord best but the dedicated ones.

No sacrifice we make is too great for the One who sacrificed his all.

To be rich in God is better than to be rich in goods.

If you want your dedication to Jesus to last, put him first.

Think seldom of your enemies, often of your friends, and constantly of Christ.

Before reaching the uppermost, we must keep Christ uppermost in our minds.

It takes unfair treatment to test the Christian's consecration.

Too many people expect God to work *through* them when they don't even let him work *in* them.

Lord, do in me what you need to do so you can do through me what you have to do.

There is no greater freedom than being a bond servant to Christ.

A Christian without commitment is like a promise made with your fingers crossed.

It is hard to be distracted by the world when we are attracted by Christ.

The Holy Spirit chooses the nobodies of the church and makes them somebodies.

The only fully satisfied person in the world is the fully consecrated person.

When the world is at its worst, Christians must be at their best.

When on vacation, don't make Christ your last resort.

If God has first place in your life, you won't have to worry about who has the other places.

The Lord's tomorrow of blessing is only waiting for our today of consecration.

Go with the crowd and get lost; go with the Savior and you will stand alone.

We can always live on less when we have more to live for.

The most powerful weapon on earth is the human soul on fire for God.

The Christian's greatest joy is found in letting God fully possess everything that is God's.

If you want to know how precious Christ can be, make him preeminent.

Making a great sacrifice nowadays means doing without things our parents never had.

God created the world out of nothing; as long as we are nothing he can do something with us.

God has included you in his plans; have you included him in your plans?

We keep ourselves only by giving ourselves to God.

The head may seek God, but it is the heart that finds him.

It doesn't take much of a man to be a Christian—it takes all of him.

You must keep in mind not *what* you are, but *whose* you are.

In the economy of God we have to give in order to have riches and die in order to live.

A useful life can't be entirely peaceful and carefree.

Some things are ruined when broken, but the heart is at its best when broken.

There would be less falling from the Lord if there were more calling upon the Lord.

Even if I knew tomorrow would go to pieces, I would still plant my apple seed.

No one can make you feel inferior without your consent.

God judges us not by what we give but by what we withhold.

He who walks close to God leaves no room for anything to come between.

No life is hopeless unless Christ is ruled out.

If God is kept outside, there is something wrong inside.

He who serves two masters has to lie to one.

It's human to stand with the crowd; it's divine to stand alone.

Have you ever noticed that although God demands a whole heart, he will accept a broken one if he gets all the pieces.

Attachment to Christ is the real secret of detachment from the world.

A fanatic is someone who would be called a "dedicated idealist" if he were on your side.

No gift is a substitute for yourself.

For top performance we must refuel daily from the Word.

If Christ resides in your heart, let him preside in your home.

If we are not as spiritual as we could be, we're not as spiritual as we should be.

A church member who believes nothing, says nothing, does nothing, and gives nothing is worth nothing.

Let us not pray to be sheltered from dangers but to be fearless when facing them.

Commitment could be your self-fulfilling prophecy.

When one truly first gives himself to the Lord, all other giving is easy.

If you make the commitment, God opens the way.

God isn't looking for ability—he looks for usability.

Commitment is the key that unlocks doors to great opportunities.

Some give their mite; some give with all their might; and some don't give who might.

Don't drive your stakes too deep—we're leaving in the morning.

True freedom is found in bondage to Christ.

To pray about something and not make yourself available is hypocrisy.

Allow Christ to make your life a mission—not an intermission.

Anything that matters more to you than God is an idol.

Putting God first brings satisfaction that lasts.

Many a person has convictions for which he wants someone else to supply the courage.

When we yield ourselves to the Spirit's control, we do not lose our self-control.

The smaller we are the more room God will have in our lives.

The hardest thing to give is to give in.

The three greatest needs of every man: to be dead in Christ, to be dead to sin, and to be dead to what people think.

You cannot pour deep spirituality into a shallow life.

✦Denial (*see also* Backsliding)

God remembers what we forget, and we remember, unfortunately, what God forgets.

You deny Christ when you fail to deny yourself.

It is far better to know our own weaknesses and failing than to point out those of others.

It is not by accident that the symbol of Christianity is the cross rather than a bed of ease.

Giving to God is not losing—it's winning.

When we die with Christ on the cross, he comes to live in us by his Spirit.

It is better to suffer for the cause of Christ than for the cause of Christ to suffer.

A cross around the neck is no substitute for a cross on your back.

There are no short cuts to the heavenly kingdom. It is not the *way across,* but the *way of the cross,* that leads home.

It is when we forget ourselves that we do things that are remembered.

Self-denial is the finest lesson in the school of grace.

In going the second mile, we find no traffic jams.

We are ruined, not by what we *really* want, but by what we *think* we want.

In this world it is not what we take up but what we give up that makes us rich.

Christ offers a crown only to those who take up his cross.

✦Determination (*see also* Courage)

Industry can do anything that genius can do and many things that it cannot.

It certainly pays to advertise—there are twenty-six mountains in Colorado that are higher than Pike's Peak.

You can't get anywhere unless you start.

Good gardening is largely a matter of taking pains—mostly in the small of the back.

There's no defeat except in no longer trying.

God doesn't ask you to *be* the best—only to *do* your best.

Learn to harness your handicaps.

There is more to be gained by being first than fast.

Not to be out-and-out for Christ is to be down-and-out.

King Saul thought Goliath was too big to fight—David thought he was too big to miss.

Have the courage to let go of the things not worth sticking to.

Aim for perfection—half right is always half wrong.

God is more ready to forgive the blotted page of endeavor than the blank page of giving up.

If you cannot be a runner-up, try not to be a runner down.

Courage isn't having the strength to go on—it's going on when you don't have the strength.

Quitters in the church are like motors—they sputter before they miss and miss before they quit.

The Golden Rule may be old, but it hasn't been used enough to look worn.

If you don't climb the mountain you can't see the view.

Every day something is being done that couldn't be done.

Be bold in what you stand for, but be careful what you fall for.

The hardest thing about climbing the ladder of success is getting through the crowd at the bottom.

Any dead fish can float downstream—it takes a live fish to swim against the current.

It's not the size of the dog in the fight but the size of the fight in the dog.

When the door is shut, we are bidden to knock.

He who doesn't hope to win has already lost.

Persistence will give you power to prevail over all problems.

When something can't be done, watch someone do it.

A quitter never wins—a winner never quits.

Most trouble is caused by too much bone in the head and not enough in the back.

If Columbus had turned back, no one would have blamed him. No one would have remembered him either.

Trying times are no time to quit trying.

The elevator to success is not running; you must climb the stairs.

Do the best you can—angels can do no more.

Great things are little things done with a desire to please God.

If you put heart into what you do, it will put heart into you.

Men seldom drift to their desired haven; they usually sail to it against most contrary winds.

A man without courage is like a knife without an edge.

If Caleb had asked Joshua for a valley instead of a mountain, who would be impressed?

The man who *falls* down gets up a lot quicker than the man who *lies* down.

Lincoln was not great because he lived in a log cabin but because he was able to get out of the cabin.

An ounce of determination is worth a ton of procrastination.

Curious people ask questions—determined people find the answer.

Often it takes as much courage to resist as it does to go ahead.

It takes determination to get to the top, but more to remain there.

Accept the circumstances, then seek to overcome them.

The shadows are behind you if you walk toward the light.

Today is not won by old victories nor lost by old defeats.

The best time to hold on is when you reach the place where the average person gives up.

The man who is not strong *against* anything is usually not strong *for* anything.

The only good luck any great man ever had was being born with ability and determination to overcome bad luck.

Success is biting off more than you can chew and chewing it.

It is not wrong when you are knocked down in life—but it is wrong when you fail to get up.

Some people have a giant brain but a midget's backbone.

A competitor is a guy who goes into a revolving door behind you and comes out ahead of you.

Discouragement is faith in the devil.

If the door to success is marked *pull* and still won't open, ignore the sign and push.

In most cases, *IQ* is less important to a person's education than *I will*.

The wise man doesn't expect to find life worth living; he makes it that way.

Don't be content by being average. Being average means you are as near to the bottom as you are to the top.

It takes courage to stand up and be counted, but it takes more courage to keep standing.

Morale is when your hands and feet keep on working when your head says it can't be done.

One of the greatest pleasures in life is doing what people say you can't.

The trouble with most of us in trying times is that we quit trying.

It takes courage to stand up and speak as well as to sit down and listen.

✦Diet

The best way to lose weight is to eat everything you don't like.

Many a person has dug his own grave with his fork.

Suppers have slain as many as the sword.

Dieting is the triumph of mind over platter.

The best way of losing weight—don't talk about it. Keep your mouth shut.

The reason some people are overweight is because there are times when they just go starch-craving mad.

Don't wail on the scale if you cheat when you eat.

The successful diet is based on eating more and more of less and less.

For most of us a diet is a brief period of starvation followed by immediate gain in weight.

A girdle is used to keep figures from telling the truth.

For compulsive snackers—a cookie jar with childproof caps.

Diets are for people who are thick and tired of it.

The minutes at the table will not make you fat but the seconds will.

It pays to count calories. You may not lose much weight, but you will improve your arithmetic.

A new Chinese diet—eat all you can, but use only one chopstick.

Strange that three square meals make round people.

Best advice to a dieter—no thyself.

Taste makes waist.

America has more to eat than any country in the world and more diets to keep us from eating it.

You never realize what a poor loser you are until you try dieting.

Overeating will make you thick on your stomach.

Counting calories has become for a lot of people just a weight of life.

What to do with your weight—pull it, but don't throw it around.

Self-control is needed these days in the supermarket.

The most fattening thing you can put into your food is your spoon.

One main reason for keeping one's diet—high school reunions.

Middle-age spread—too many nights around the table.

Health clubs make a fortune at our expanse.

If exercises remove fat, how come there are so many double chins?

The trouble with what melts in your mouth is the way it bulges in front of a mirror.

Overeating is the destiny that ends our shapes.

Overeating can easily give you a shape like a figure ate.

✦Discipleship

In the dictionary of true discipleship, you'll never find the word *retreat.*

If a Christian is careless in Bible reading, he will be careless in Christian living.

Let Christ first work in you; then he will work through you.

The cross is easier for the Christian who takes it up than for the one who drags it along.

True courage is like a kite—a contrary wind raises it higher.

Some people will do almost anything for their religion—they will argue, write, and even fight for it. They will do almost anything except live for it.

The largest room is room for improvement.

God will give you his best as you give him your best.

What you are is God's gift to you. What you make of yourself is your gift to God.

A man is rich in proportion to the number of things that he can afford to let alone.

If you *take* your problems to the Lord, that is natural. If you *give* your problems to the Lord, that is spiritual.

When you're all wrong and willing to admit it, you're all right.

Problems cause some to break while others use them to break records.

There is very little blessing or reward in serving the Lord conveniently.

The person who never changes his mind never improves his mistakes either.

The road to success is always under construction.

Salvation is free, but discipleship is costly.

People who live it up may some day have to live it down.

Many people aim to do right but are just poor shots.

To have God's smile will mean the frown of man.

It will cost you more to say no to God than to say yes.

When the going gets easy, you'd better check and see if you are going downhill.

Once it was a fashion to take a bath weekly and religion daily.

Learn from the mistakes of others—you'll never live long enough to make them all yourself.

The trouble with being a good sport is that you have to lose to prove it.

It's a sin to live a life short of what God intended your life to be.

The person who thinks he will live forever lives best.

Watch your step—everyone else does.

Not only believe the gospel—behave it!

Considering God's investment in us, what is he getting in return?

There is something wrong with the man who knows the right way to take and still wants time to think about it.

The wise Christian gears his goals to heaven's gains.

Jesus wants disciples and not admirers. An admirer is the cheap edition of a disciple.

God will give us all the direction we need for our lives if we will just listen to him.

Walking with Christ helps us enjoy our standing with Christ.

◆Discipline (see also Children; Education)

Correction does much, but encouragement does more.

Exercise your grace, or Satan will exercise your corruption.

There is more to be gained by being first than fast.

A switch in time saves crime.

If we want to be servants of others, we must be masters of ourselves.

Some people who don't know anything always want to tell you about it.

They who do not live up to their ideals soon find that they have lost them.

The roughest road oftentimes goes straight to the top of the hill.

The most miserable Christians are those who cannot reconcile their creed with their greed.

Whatever it may be—sports, pleasure, business, money or family—when put first, that is your God.

If God controls the inner man, the world cannot control the outer man.

It is never wise to slip the hands of discipline.

Those who master themselves are able to master all things and all people.

Morality, like art, consists in drawing a line somewhere.

One minute of folly could mean a life of time and regret.

Keep your head and heart going in the right direction and you'll not have to worry about your feet.

If the going is getting easier, you aren't climbing.

Don't smoke in bed—the ashes that fall on the floor may be your own.

Erasers are not only for mistakes, but for those willing to correct their mistakes.

Man doesn't plan to fail—he just fails to plan.

When alone guard your thoughts; in the family guard your temper; in company guard your words.

There may be a wrong way to do the right thing, but never a right way to do a wrong thing.

Many imperfections that we easily tolerate in ourselves are quite intolerable in others.

A positive conviction without accurate information is a dangerous thing.

The rest of your days depend on the rest of your nights.

If your willpower doesn't work, try your "won't" power.

People with horse sense know when to say nay.

The secret of achievement is not to let what you're doing get to you before you get to it.

Courage is what it takes to stand up and speak. Courage is also what it takes to sit down and remain silent.

If you kicked the one who causes you most of your troubles, you would not be able to sit down for six weeks.

A man who always says what he thinks is courageous—and without friends.

Three of the most difficult things in life are to keep a secret, to forget an injury, and to make good use of leisure time.

The business of living is not to get ahead of others but to get ahead of ourselves.

The surest way to encourage violence is to give in to it.

Prepare and prevent instead of repair and repent.

Freedom is not the right to do as you please but the liberty to do as we ought.

The first screw that comes loose in the head is the one that controls the tongue.

Self-respect is the thing for which you make any sacrifice because without it you would be nothing.

Some people could see better in the day if they didn't run around at night.

There are more self-marred people in the world than there are self-made.

Most people always aim to do right; they just fail to pull the trigger.

God is not looking for man to prove he is better than man; he wants him to be a better man.

Lessons that are bitter to learn usually are sweet to know.

No one has the right to do as he pleases unless he pleases to do right.

One advantage of traveling the straight and narrow road is that very few people are trying to pass you.

The best way to escape evil is to pursue good.

Never put your hand out farther than you can draw it back again.

A yawn is at least an honest opinion.

He that mindeth not his own business shall never be trusted with mine.

An undisciplined church member is a disgrace to Christ and a detriment to his church.

You are never defeated unless you defeat yourself.

The greatest conqueror is he who conquers himself.

To many people, the ideal occupation is the one that doesn't keep them occupied.

The heir as well as the hair can be trained properly through the use of a brush.

It is one thing to praise discipline and another to submit to it.

Freedom is a choice—it comes when we choose discipline.

The trouble with a lot of self-made men is they quit the job too early.

Remember that it is the daily grind that gives a person polish.

Most would like to change their circumstances, not themselves.

Water can quench your thirst, but too much water can drown.

It is one thing to praise discipline, but another thing to submit to it.

When there is pruning, the gardener is nearby.

Men, like rivers, become crooked because they follow the way of least resistance.

Go the extra mile, which is one stretch of highway where there are never any traffic jams.

If you have too many irons in the fire, some will cool.

Looking for a soft job is the job of a soft man.

If you want to make a point but not an enemy, don't make it too sharp.

One person with a conviction is equal in force to ninety-nine who only have opinions.

A person becomes wise by observing carefully what happens when he isn't.

We live in a nation where lawns are well kept but laws are not.

The man who goes through life looking for something soft can only find it under his hat.

It takes courage to change your mind about something when you know you ought to but would rather not.

No one becomes very good or very bad—suddenly.

An easy way to become poor is to pretend you are rich.

Before you let yourself go completely, be sure you can get yourself back.

Freedom without purpose leads headlong into chaos.

Good planning, carefully executed, is often mistaken by others as pure luck.

A person without a goal will get nowhere and won't know when he gets there.

Discipline yourself so others won't have to.

Many people are too busy making a living to make life worth living.

The earth is God's training camp for mankind, fitting him for the life to come.

Maybe it wasn't meant that way, but American ends with "I can."

✦Dishonesty

A nightclub is a place where they have what it takes to take what you have.

When someone pats you on the back, they may be trying to make you cough up something.

✦Doubt

It is easy to raise doubts about duties we do not want to perform.

When in doubt, always tell the truth.

A pessimist can hardly wait for the future so he can look back with regret.

Are you a thoughtful doubter—or a doubtful thinker?

A pessimist is a person who is seasick during the entire voyage of life.

Most of the shadows of life are caused by standing in our own sunshine.

A pessimist is a person who takes life's hard knocks with a grain of sulk.

A pessimist burns his bridges before he gets to them.

Unbelief is the door to hell.

A pessimist is someone who likes to listen to the patter of little defeats.

Doubt sees the obstacles—faith sees the way.

When you say, "I can't" you are saying, "God can't."

The pessimist is the one who is always looking through the wrong end of the telescope.

Believe your beliefs; doubt your doubts.

A pessimist is one who expects nothing on a silver platter except tarnish.

Two pessimists met at a party. Instead of shaking hands, they shook heads.

A pessimist is one who feels bad when he feels good for fear he'll feel worse when he feels better.

Some people believe in miracles but do not expect to see them happen today.

He who mistrusts most should be trusted least.

Some people pray for a bushel, then carry a pint cup.

I worry, I putter, I push and shove, hunting little molehills to make mountains of.

The pessimist sees only the mist.

✦Dreams

You cannot have good ideas until you have a lot of dreams.

The best dreams happen with your eyes wide open.

What's a genius? Someone who aims at something no one else can see and hits it.

Why grieve because all your dreams have not come true? Neither have all your nightmares.

A goal is a dream with a deadline.

✦Drinking (see also Temperance)

It's much better to sit tight than to drive that way.

Dignity is one thing that cannot be preserved in alcohol.

There is no situation so bad that a few alcoholic drinks won't make it worse.

Many things can be preserved in alcohol, but Christian character is not one of them.

Strong drink can weaken character.

Corkscrews have sunk more people than cork jackets ever saved.

The steady drinker soon becomes an unsteady drinker.

The tavern keeper is the only businessman ashamed of his customers.

When a man drinks to forget, he usually forgets to stop.

Liquor fools the man who fools with it.

The drunkard commits suicide on the installment plan.

The man who invented alcohol died thousands of years ago, but his spirit still lives.

It's all right to drink like a fish as long as you drink what a fish does.

He who drinks before he drives puts the quart before the hearse.

Drivers are safer when roads are dry, and the road is safer when the drivers are dry.

A drunkard's mouth dries up his pocket. All his money runs into the hole just below the nose.

Some people use statistics as a drunken man uses a lamppost—for support rather than for illumination.

People who live in glass houses shouldn't get stoned.

The man who drinks much thinks little.

Arresting a drunken driver is like destroying the web and leaving the spider alive.

Glasses change your personality, especially if you empty them too often.

Alcohol is something that often puts the "wreck" in recreation.

The person who thinks won't drink.

A good government cannot be preserved in alcohol.

Keeping blood free from alcohol is the best way to keep the highways free from blood.

Danger signs should be placed on all drivers who drive and drink.

A cocktail party is a place where alcohol removes the polish from furniture and people.

The hand that lifts the cup of cheers should not be used to shift gears.

The driver who has a few quick ones is bound to have a few close ones.

Only weak characters depend upon strong drink.

If a mad dog bites a person, we kill the dog. Drinking kills 25,000 yearly, yet we continue to permit alcohol to be sold.

✦Driving

Autos did away with horses; now the autos seem to try and do away with people.

The best thinkers on their feet are pedestrians.

Often the more horsepower in the car, the less horse sense in the driver.

The slower the mentality, the faster the driver.

It is better to be patient on the road than to be a patient in the hospital.

The worst wheel on the car makes the most noise.

The upkeep of a car doesn't worry one most—it's the possible turnover.

Two finishes for automobiles: lacquer and liquor.

A careful driver is one who just saw the driver ahead of him get a traffic ticket.

Freeway drinking is like a shower or bath—one wrong turn and you are in hot water.

It seems that our road manners become more crude as our gasoline becomes more refined.

If your wife wants to drive, don't stand in the way.

Some people learn the traffic rules by accident.

To speed is human—to get caught is a fine.

Pedestrians should be seen and not hurt.

The car was invented as a convenient place to sit out a traffic jam.

What happens to the people who fail their driving tests? They become parking lot attendants.

The way people drive, it's just an accident if you can get anywhere without an accident.

One way to make people slow down in their driving is to call it work.

It is safer to limit your speed than to speed your limit.

Drive carefully around the children—we value our tax deduction.

Whether it's on the road or in an argument, when you see red, stop.

Drive so that your driver's license will expire before you do.

It's better to step on the brake and be laughed at than to push the gas and be cried over.

A good driver isn't only able to obey the traffic rules but to dodge those who don't.

The driver who burns up the road often lands in the cooler.

What this country needs is a car that will go no faster than its driver can think.

Radar spelled backwards is radar—they get you going and coming.

You can tell Americans trust in God by the way they drive.

Law gives the pedestrian the right of way but makes no provision for flowers.

A motorist is a man who after seeing an accident drives carefully for several blocks.

One of the best automobile insurance policies is a Sunday afternoon nap.

For that tired, run-down feeling, try jaywalking.

If you have plans for tomorrow—drive safely today.

With all the vacation travel on the road, it's a good idea to drive with fender loving care.

One must be a speed reader these days if he expects to get the right exit off the freeway.

Patience is something you admire in the driver behind you and don't understand in the one ahead.

A steering committee: four persons trying to park a car.

A gas-saving device: ignition keys that don't fit.

Some motorists are in such a hurry to get into the next county that they go right on into the next world.

The car to watch is the car behind the car in front of you.

The cause of most traffic accidents is high HP and low IQ.

Men still die with their boots on—on the accelerator.

It is dangerous to drive in a fog, especially if it's mental.

Racing through traffic could result in limping through life.

Men no longer leave footprints on the sands of time—just tire tracks.

Always drive as if your family were in the other car.

Driving a car is like playing baseball; it's the number of times you make it home safely that counts.

Even some of the best-running cars have jerks in them.

The pioneers who blazed the trails now have descendants who burn up the roads.

Always drive as if the police were following you.

Drive carefully—it's not only cars that can be recalled by their maker.

Quite frequently, he who goes too fast gets there not only too late—but not at all.

More accidents are caused by pickled drivers than traffic jams.

Drive defensively—pass up higher gas pumps.

Many a tombstone is carved by chiseling in traffic.

Drive carefully in heavy traffic—the cars are being stacked against you.

A reckless driver is usually not wreckless for long.

When you drive, keep in mind the cost of replacing your car.

E

♦**Education** (*see also* Discipline; Parents)

Education requires a lot of books—wisdom requires a lot of time.

Natural ability without education has more often raised man to glory and virtue than education without natural ability.

A good teacher captures a student's attention so he can direct it toward God.

To teach is to learn twice.

School is a building that has four walls—with tomorrow inside.

In the dark ages, people belonged to the kings. When education spread, kings belonged to the people.

A little education properly applied is more important than much education not properly utilized.

Some folks may live and learn, but by the time they've learned it's usually too late to live.

While we may learn from the error of our ways, we would probably be happier with less education.

A child who knows how to pray, work, and think is already half-educated.

Some historians are deaf—they go on answering questions no one has asked them.

Education will survive when what some have learned will be forgotten.

Most students have the spark of genius—but a few seem to have ignition trouble.

An education is nothing more than going from an unconscious to a conscious awareness of one's ignorance.

Knowledge humbles great men, astonishes the common man, and puffs up the little man.

Knowledge is power only when it is turned on.

Intelligence is like a river—the deeper it is, the less noise it makes.

Knowledge is power, and so is dynamite. Both are dangerous unless handled wisely.

You can always tell a well-informed man—his ideas are the same as yours.

The highest knowledge is the knowledge of God.

Knowledge is power, but like power it must be hitched to something effective.

It isn't the things that people know that do the dirty work; it's the things "they know ain't so" that do the dirty work.

Ideas are like children—our own are very wonderful.

A person who "knows everything" has a lot to learn.

It's what you learn after you know all that counts.

He who can take advice is sometimes superior to he who can give it.

The reason some people say nothing worthwhile is there's nothing worthwhile inside.

Knowing that you don't know much is knowing more than most.

Half knowledge is worse than ignorance.

Definition of advice: those who need it don't heed it; those who heed it don't need it.

Machines are so nearly human that they can do things without using any intelligence.

The nice thing about dictating letters is that you can use a lot of words you don't know how to spell.

A college education never hurt anyone who was willing to learn something afterward.

The trouble with some people is that they are educated beyond their intelligence.

Knowledge is like money; the more a man gets, the more he craves.

If you think education is expensive, try ignorance.

Education covers a lot of ground, but it does not cultivate it.

Philosophy is the last refuge of thinkers.

A man who acquires knowledge and does not use it is like a farmer who plows his field but doesn't sow it.

One need not be smart to say things that are.

An ignorant person is the one who doesn't know something you learned yesterday.

Wouldn't it be nice to be as sure of anything as some people are of everything?

Education is not given for the purpose of earning a living; it is learning what to do with a living after you earn it.

Broad-minded: capable of seeing both points—the wrong one and his own.

Memory is what tells you that you know the guy but doesn't tell you his name.

The greatest aid to the education of adults is children.

Readers make good talkers.

The heart of education is the education of the heart.

He who will not learn from anyone but himself has a fool for a teacher.

Experience has been defined as "compulsory education."

Education is what you have left over when you subtract what you've forgotten from what you've learned.

Education is a chest of tools.

School days can be the happiest days of your life, provided the children are old enough to go.

He who ceases to learn cannot adequately teach.

If you divorce education from religion, you will produce a race of clever devils.

Education means developing the mind, not suffering the memory.

Only when you skate on thin ice is there greater safety in increased speed.

The school of hard knocks is the only way sense can be knocked into some people.

How much a man knows is of no importance; what matters is what he knows, and what he does with what he knows.

We all have the right to be wrong in our opinions but not in our facts.

There are more idle brains than idle hands.

The sign: "Proceed at your own risk" should be placed on all roads to higher education.

Reading makes a full man; writing an exact man.

Forget your mistakes, but remember what they taught you.

People who tell everything they know wouldn't be so bad if they'd stop there.

Too often man's intellect is measured by the size of his bank account.

You're never too old to learn—and what you learn is what makes you old.

He who knows how to read but doesn't read is no different than the man who can't read.

It's better to be straight than to be smart.

Fifty-one percent of being smart is knowing what you're dumb at.

It is better to make new mistakes than it is to repeat the old ones.

The best education is caught—not taught.

Nothing on earth has a harder road to travel than a new idea.

Education is the only thing people are willing to pay for and not get.

◆Enemies

The best medicine is to love your work and your enemies.

The most difficult test of the human heart is to hear of an enemy's success without becoming jealous.

Nothing makes us love our enemies as much as praying for them.

The only way to understand your enemies is to love them.

Be kind to your enemies—you made them.

Never waste a minute thinking about your enemies; pray for them.

Think seldom of your enemies, often of your friends, and constantly of Christ.

So long as your conscience isn't ashamed to acknowledge you as a friend, don't give a rap for your enemies.

People make enemies by complaining too much to their friends.

One evidence of the dynamic power of the Bible is its enduring character despite the attacks of its enemies.

The fire you kindle for your enemy often burns you more than him.

Enemies are made, not born.

◆Enthusiasm

Become a chronic enthusiast.

People grow old, not from playing, but because they quit playing.

God gave us a neck for a purpose—to stick it out sometimes.

A Christian will not amount to much unless there is enthusiasm in his Christianity.

Remember it is hard to steer a parked car.

The person with enthusiasm lives abundantly *in spite of* and not *because of* his situation.

Sooner or later the man with pull bows to the man with a push.

If you are satisfied just to get by, step aside for a man who isn't.

Some people's spirits grow gray before their hair.

The worst bankrupt in the world is the man who has lost his enthusiasm.

The biggest problem is not to add years to your life—but life to your years.

The fire of God in your heart will melt the lead in your feet.

When Mark Twain was asked the reason for his success he replied, "I was born excited."

The most contagious thing in the world is lack of enthusiasm, and the second most contagious is enthusiasm.

Nothing truly great was ever achieved without enthusiasm.

Even a live wire is not really live unless it has a good connection.

Truth accomplishes no victories without enthusiasm.

Enthusiasm is the spark that puts enjoyment into our lives.

If you get on fire for God, you will be too hot for Satan to handle.

Zeal without knowledge is a fire without control.

You cannot kindle a fire in another's heart until it is burning in your own.

None are so old as those who have outlived their enthusiasm.

Enthusiasm without knowledge is like running in the dark.

All you need to get ahead is luck and pluck—luck in finding someone to pluck.

A fanatic is a person who is highly enthusiastic about something in which you are not even remotely interested.

A fanatic is someone who would be called a "dedicated idealist" if he were on your side.

The world's work is done every day by people who could have stayed in bed, but didn't.

Believers in the early church were either expelled or repelled.

The man who cannot be angry at evil lacks enthusiasm for good.

Becoming number one is easier than remaining number one.

Enthusiasm is contagious—and so is the lack of it.

Inspiration plus perspiration combine to produce success.

No one ever stumbles over something while sitting down.

It is much easier to keep the fire burning than to rekindle it after it has gone out.

◆Example

There is never a man so poor or unknown that he does not have an audience.

If your neighbors had to depend on you to find out about salvation, how much would they know?

So live that when people get to know you, they will want to know Christ.

We cannot all be apostles; but we can all be living epistles.

Where we go and what we do advertises what we are.

You cannot become a saint by comparing yourself with a sinner.

Blessed are they who attend strictly to their own business.

Christians show what they are by what they do with what they have.

You cannot teach a man anything; you can only help him to find it within himself.

He who practices what he preaches may have to put in some overtime.

If people only knew about Jesus what they saw in you, how well would they know Him?

To lift up others, you must be higher than they are.

Don't pretend to be what you don't intend to be.

One proof of your love for God is your love for your neighbor.

Etiquette is a little better than what is absolutely necessary.

Let your testimony be written in large enough letters that the world can always read it.

Make sure that what you're living for is truly worth dying for.

People may die, but their ideas don't.

We often dislike a person not for what he is but for what we are.

You can do more good by being good than any other way.

People tend to make rules for others and exceptions for themselves.

If there is no sunshine in your religion, do not be surprised if nobody wants it.

Don't be a carbon copy of someone else; make your own impression.

Many of us spend half our time wishing for things we could have if we didn't spend half our time wishing.

Five minutes of demonstration is better than an hour of talk.

Man cannot be saved by perfect obedience because he cannot render it. He cannot be saved by imperfect obedience because God cannot accept it. The only solution to the sin question is Calvary.

If the teacher be corrupt, the world will be corrupt.

It is hard to sell a product you do not use and a religion you do not live.

Trim your lamp often so that it will give more light and less smoke.

You can't pray on your knees on Sunday and prey on your friends the rest of the week.

It is inconsistent to say you believe as you should when you behave as you shouldn't.

You cannot touch your neighbor's heart with anything less than your own.

To say little and perform much is the characteristic of a great mind.

No man is justified in doing evil on the ground of expedience.

The beauty of any day is reflected in your heart.

A person worth following is a follower of Christ.

To show others what Christ will do for them, show them what Christ has done for you.

If you would thoroughly know anything, teach it to another.

Everyone wants to be noticed; no one wants to be watched.

You can fake the gifts of the Spirit, but you cannot fake the fruit of the Spirit.

You win more friends with your ears than with your mouth.

Accept God's grace through faith, then prove his grace through works.

The world is more interested in what you *practice* than in what you *profess.*

Learning the golden rule is of no value until you practice it.

Whatever makes men good Christians makes them good citizens.

My life helps to paint my neighbor's picture of God.

The world is looking for good examples—not advice.

People take your example far more seriously than your advice.

He who is born of God is certain to resemble his Father.

The most valuable gift you can give to others is example.

If you don't live it, you don't have it.

What one does is the result of what one is.

Some people are a big bug at their job but a pest at home and the church.

It's a shame—but it's true—that a mirror doesn't make some folk see themselves as others see them.

The gods we serve paint themselves on our faces.

It isn't how high in life you go that counts but how you got there.

No one knows of your honesty and sincerity unless you give out some samples.

You hear a good many echoes in the world but mighty few real voices.

Some people spend money for things they don't need to impress people they don't like.

A pint of example is worth a thousand sermons.

What's wrong with the church? Look in the mirror.

Those who live in glass houses should take a hot bath. That blinds the windows with steam.

Anyone who talks by the yard and thinks by the inch should be moved by the foot.

Outward expression shows inner experience.

People are judged by the things they stand for and live for.

Don't feel useless—you can always be used as a bad example.

God has not called us to prove the gospel—he has called us to practice it.

If you don't daily walk the walk, then don't talk the talk.

The Christian's walk and talk must go together.

You may not be responsible for your name, but you are responsible for what men think when they call your name.

Where you go and what you do tell people what you are.

God wants spiritual fruit, not religious nuts.

We are mirrors to reflect the glory of God; a mirror never calls attention to itself unless there are flaws in it.

We spend half of our lives recovering from the effects of the other half.

When a man begins to realize the truth about himself, it lessens his desire to reform his neighbors.

God judges us by what we do—not by what others say.

I like to see a man proud of the place where he lives; and I like to see a man live so his place will be proud of him.

When we die, we leave behind us all we have and take with us all we are.

So live that even the funeral director will be sorry when you die.

Man would be more successful if he practiced the advice he gave to others.

He who demands mercy and shows none burns the bridges over which he himself must later pass.

When your work speaks for itself, don't interrupt.

If we could see ourselves as others see us, we wouldn't believe it.

Be an "Amen Christian" but don't shout it any louder than you live.

Your town will be a delightful town if you are a delightful person to live beside.

We know a bird by his song and a man by his talk.

So live that people will want your autograph and not your fingerprints.

The smallest deed is better than the largest intention.

You don't advertise your religion by wearing a label—you do it by living a life.

If you think the whole world is wrong, remember it is filled with people like you.

You never get a second chance to make a good first impression.

The actions of men are the best interpreter of thoughts.

The only people who really listen to both sides of the argument are the neighbors.

Don't pray and talk "cream" and live "skimmed milk."

What a fine world it would be if everyone should spend as much time practicing his religion as they do in quarreling about it.

You can never bury your influence.

People seldom improve when they have no other model but themselves to copy.

Live with men as if God saw you, talk with God as if men heard you.

You do not believe what you don't live.

A chip on the shoulder is the heaviest load you can carry.

Drifting people are like icebergs—wherever they go they lower the temperature.

If some people would be a little more careful where they step, those who follow would not stumble so much.

Of all things you wear, your expression is the most important.

People look at you six days a week to see what you mean on your seventh day.

If you want the world to heed, put your creed into your deed.

What this country needs is not new deals, fair deals, or even square deals, but *ideals.*

One's true religion is the life he lives, not the creed he possesses.

Anyone can preach—it's the living that counts.

He who brings evil to himself makes misery for others.

Others will follow your footsteps quicker than your advice.

It is what we are that gets across, not what we try to teach.

You preach a better sermon with your life than with your lips.

It doesn't matter how a person dies, but how he lives.

Every Christian should be a walking sermon.

Nothing is more confusing than the fellow who gives good advice and sets a bad example.

Your words may hide your thoughts, but your actions will reveal them.

Better to be rich in good than rich in goods.

I had rather be criticized than the criticizer; the hated than the hater; the wronged than the wrong.

Behavior is a mirror in which we show our image.

The most difficult advice in the world to follow is that which you give to others.

If you want your neighbor to know what the Lord will do for him, let him see what Christ has done for you.

The light of God's Son in your heart will put his sunshine in your face.

Example is not the main thing influencing others—it's the only thing.

If you are a Christian, people will judge the Lord by you.

A good example can overcome a lot of bad advice.

People may doubt what you say, but they will believe what you do.

If you were accused of being a Christian, would there be enough evidence to convict you?

Influence is something you think you have until you try to use it.

We do more good by being good than any other way.

God expects the stock in your warehouse to be as good as what you show in the window.

If you don't get something accomplished by giving good advice, then try by setting good example.

If you don't live it—don't teach it.

Godly talk does not always imply a godly walk.

When you were born, you cried and others rejoiced. So live that when you die, others will feel like crying and you will have reason to rejoice.

The fellow who's always kicking up his heels is going to leave some mighty strange footprints in the sands of time.

If we could see ourselves as others see us, we would probably have our eyes examined.

Some so-called "food for thought" is nothing more than baloney.

Regardless of how small, every bush casts a shadow.

To be trusted is a greater compliment than to be loved.

It is what we are that gets across, not what we try to teach.

What have you done today that nobody but a Christian would do?

There isn't any use trying to shine unless you take time to fill your lamp.

Christians please God when their walk measures up to their talk.

If you can give but one gift, make it a gift of good example.

If you were another person, would you like to be a friend of yours?

Love is the Christian's ID card.

Would you want Christ to represent you above in the same way that you represent him below?

What people practice, not what they profess, proves what they claim.

If a man finds his politics and religion don't mix, there is something wrong with his politics.

The creed you really believe is spoken, not by your lips, but by your life.

Praise loudly—blame softly.

Don't tell me about your labor pains—show me the baby.

Without example others won't know what they can do or how far they can go.

A promise is one thing, but performance is quite another thing.

Your walk talks; but your talk doesn't talk like your walk walks.

The gentleness of Christ is the comeliest ornament that any Christian can wear.

So live that you would not be ashamed to sell the family parrot to the town gossip.

A Christian shows what he is by what he does with what he has.

You learn that which you practice most.

Changing the label does not alter the contents of the bottle.

It's good to be a Christian and know it; it is even better to be a Christian and show it.

✦Excuses

Convention: An excuse for doing the unconventional.

Never explain—your friends do not need it and your enemies will not believe you anyway.

An ounce of performance is worth a ton of excuses.

An excuse is first cousin to a lie.

Avoiding a few hypocrites in church may result in spending eternity with all of them hereafter.

Love will find a way—indifference will find an excuse.

Excuses get in the way of being a success.

If all the crutches were laid end to end, there still wouldn't be enough for the lame excuses.

No one can get fat on excuses, but everyone can get fed up on them.

Some stumble over their feet, then blame others for tripping them.

Most failures come from people who have the habit of making excuses.

Blaming your faults on your nature does not change the nature of your faults.

Never accuse others to excuse yourself.

A good race horse does not ask for a dry track.

A poor workman always finds fault with his tools.

We are all manufacturers—making good, making trouble, or making excuses.

The reason that dollar bills wear out so quickly is that people are always passing the buck.

The successful man is always able to find excuses for others but not for himself.

The hardest tumble a person can take is to fall over his own bluff.

Excuses usually satisfy only those who use them.

Lame excuses come from lame Christians.

It is often in the summer that the Christian gets snowed under.

Never give an excuse that you would not be willing to accept.

◆Experience

A new broom sweeps clean, but an old broom knows where the dirt is.

The simpler solution may not be the right one, but it's the one to consider first.

One thorn of experience is worth a whole wilderness of warning.

Every time you graduate from the school of experience someone thinks up a new course.

Experience enables you to recognize a mistake every time you repeat it.

Experience is the one thing you can't get on the easy payment plan.

Experience is knowing a lot of things you shouldn't do, so prepare and prevent rather than repair and repent.

When people fail to learn from sermons, they later learn from experience.

Past experience should be a guidepost, not a hitching post.

There's no fool like an old fool—you just can't beat experience.

Good judgment often comes from experience gained through poor judgment.

Some learn from experience—others never recover from it.

Let's swap problems since all people know how to solve other people's problems.

Experience is a good teacher, but a hard one. She gives the test first and the lesson afterward.

Experience is a wonderful thing. It enables you to recognize the mistake when you make it again.

Ignorance is innocence—stupidity comes with experience.

There is no free tuition in the school of experience.

Experience is yesterday's answer to today's problems.

Experience is an expensive teacher sometimes.

Experience is what enables you to make a different mistake the next time.

There is nothing like a little experience to upset theory.

Experience is the name everyone gives to his mistakes.

Those who cannot remember the past are condemned to repeat it.

Experience is compulsory education.

Experience is what you get while you are looking for something else.

Experience gained the hard way brings knowledge that remains.

The most valuable thing you can learn from experience is not to rely on it.

F

✦Failure

People who make a hash of things are generally struggling with yesterday's leftovers.

If we are beginning to encounter some hard bumps, be glad. At least we are out of the rut.

No bird soars too high as long as it uses its own wings.

Bad men excuse their faults—good men abandon them.

Past failures are guideposts for future success.

Few blame themselves until they have exhausted all other possibilities.

Be willing to admit your faults, showing it is all right to admit mistakes.

Investigate mistakes only when you are calm.

Failure is merely an opportunity to start over again, wiser than before.

We can never profit from our mistakes as long as we blame others for them.

The greatest of all faults is to be conscious of none.

A mistake just proves somebody stopped long enough to do something.

The man who has no goal does not fear failure.

There is one thing to be thankful for—only you and God have all the facts about yourself.

Some people make such preparations for a rainy day that they aren't enjoying today's sunshine.

It is more honorable to acknowledge our faults than to boast of our merits.

Failure comes to those who indifferently allow themselves to become failure-conscious.

The three hardest words to say are, "I was mistaken."

Some of the best lessons we ever learned, we learned from our mistakes and failures.

He who determines to love only those who are faultless will soon find himself alone.

Justifying a fault doubles it.

Life's greatest failure—trying to please everyone.

A man can fail many times, but he isn't a failure until he begins to blame others for his failures.

A man doesn't become a failure until he is satisfied with being one.

In every soul is deposited the germ of a great future.

Failure can become a weight or it can give you wings.

Life's greatest failure is failing to be true to the best you know.

It is doubtful whether one can be good without being good for something.

Setbacks stiffen your backbone if it is made of the right stuff.

Don't apologize for failure—mend it.

If you never make a mistake, you may live and die without anyone ever noticing you.

An upright man can never be a downright failure.

You are only a failure when you do less than your best.

Failure is one thing that can be achieved without effort.

Many people fail in life because the wishbone is where the backbone should be.

To err is human, but when the eraser wears out before the pencil, you are overdoing it.

Some well-to-do young men prove to be n'er-do-wells.

Failure is the result of least persistence.

People never fail in anything—they just give up.

Vexation at fault is generally more of a fault than the fault itself.

If you can learn from your mistakes, then should you not make more mistakes?

By failing to prepare, you are preparing to fail.

You must have long-range goals to keep you from being frustrated by short-range failures.

Even the perfect people buy pencils with erasers.

Many fail by trying to get as much as possible for doing as little as possible.

There is no failure until you fail to keep trying.

The cost of failure is greater than the price of success.

People who fail to understand their past mistakes may be condemned to make them over again.

Don't worry when you stumble. Remember that a worm is about the only thing that can't fall down.

It's human to err—but it's stupid to continue.

Some are farsighted in seeing others' mistakes but too shortsighted to see their own mistakes.

Failure doesn't mean you'll never succeed—it will just take longer.

Failure is merely the opportunity to start over again, wiser than before.

We can never profit from our mistakes as long as we blame others for them.

To do nothing for fear of making a mistake could be the greatest mistake of all.

It's better to sleep on what you plan to do than to lie awake because of what you've done.

Success makes failures out of too many people.

While we learn from our mistakes, we would probably be more happy with less education.

When a known plan makes your plan unworkable, you are working on a bad plan.

Achieving a goal is never final, and failure to do so is never fatal.

The worst failure is failure to try.

Don't let yesterday's failure bankrupt tomorrow's efforts.

If you blame others for your failures, do you credit others for your successes?

The expert is one who avoids the small errors as he goes to a bigger one.

The ambition of many is to be weighed and found wanting.

Hurry is the mother of mistake.

If I were wrong, I'd be the last person to admit it.

The cost of failure is greater than the cost of success.

It's not whether you win or lose, but how you place the blame.

An obstacle is something you see when you take your eyes off the goal.

If you don't learn from your mistakes, there's no sense in making them.

Open up—show others that it's all right to make and admit mistakes.

A mistake is evidence that someone tried to do something.

Admit your mistakes—don't brag about them.

Failures are divided into two classes—those who thought they never did, and those who did and never thought.

◆Faith

Faith without works is like a car without gas.

Man says, "Seeing is believing." God says, "Believing is seeing."

Our work is to cast care: God's work is to take care.

What God promises, God will provide.

The optimist is the fellow who hopes to make enough money next month to pay last month's bills.

Faith is the person stepping out into the unknown, obeying God's commands.

Faith keeps the man who keeps the faith.

Faith looks beyond the darkness of earth to the brightness of heaven.

If you're having trouble coping, try hoping in God.

Those who don't trust themselves will never trust others.

The only way to create faith is to trust people.

When there is nothing for sure, everything is possible.

We do not need to possess a faith; we need a faith that possesses us.

Faith is like a muscle, and prayer is the exercise that helps it grow.

The feeblest knock of faith opens heaven's door.

The Christian who claims the promises of God should obey the commands of God.

Faith is the daring of the soul to go farther than it can see.

Faith in Jesus is the believer's passport to heaven.

A faith that's not all it's cracked up to be is headed for a crack-up.

Future prospects bring present joys.

To trust is to triumph.

Faith is remembering I am indispensable to God when I feel I only clutter up the landscape.

To let go is to surrender; to let God is belief.

Feelings are no substitute for facts and faith.

Every great achievement was once impossible.

Have old memories but young hopes.

Hope is most powerful when backed up by actions.

Faith is to believe what we do not see—the reward of faith is to see what we believe.

Faith is remembering I am God's priceless treasure when I feel utterly worthless.

When I try I fail; when I trust I succeed.

Faith is the simple confidence that God is and that he will do what he has promised.

Faith is not believing that God can—it's knowing that he will.

The eagle that soars in the upper air does not worry itself as to how it is to cross rivers.

Impossible is a hopeful word, for it's a direct invitation to let God in.

Faith is more than waiting upon God—it's expecting an answer.

Faith is a holy decision married to unswerving determination.

If God sees the sparrow fall, paints the lily short and tall, gives the sky its azure hue, surely then he cares for you.

He who doesn't fear God should fear everything else.

The business of faith is to believe things that are out of sight.

Pray for faith that will not shrink when it is washed in the waters of affliction.

Some people feel their faith is strong enough to take them to heaven, but it does not take them to church.

You don't trust God until you trust him for the impossible.

We are not saved by faith *and* works but by faith *that* works.

Only those who see the invisible can do the impossible.

In the night of despair men discover the light of new hope.

It's a slim margin between keeping your chin up and sticking your neck out.

Faith is developed more by action than argument.

It is sickly faith that is shaken because some frail human goes wrong.

Faith is telling a mountain to move and being shocked if it doesn't.

Pray in faith—if a friend gave you a check, would you wait until you cashed it to thank him?

When you cease to use faith, you lose it.

He pleases God best who trusts him most.

Even the turtle would get nowhere if he didn't stick out his neck.

Christian faith is assuring, insuring, and enduring.

Faith is spiritual life in action.

Faith never grows in a disobedient heart.

If you pray for rain, be sure to carry an umbrella.

Counting your chickens before they are hatched is optimism; selling them before they are hatched is enterprise.

Give us faith that will not worry, whine, or wrangle, but will watch, wait, and warble.

Faith makes the up-look good, the outlook bright, the in-look favorable, and the future glorious.

The world says, "Show me and I'll believe." Christ says, "Believe me and I'll show you."

Faith and fear cannot live together.

In the spiritual world believing is seeing.

The man who feels certain he will succeed is seldom mistaken.

Doubt asks, "Can God?" Faith says, "God can."

Doubt creates mountains; faith moves them.

Can't should never appear in the Christian's vocabulary.

The world will be more impressed by a demonstration of our faith than by a description.

Yesterday is past; tomorrow may never come; we have only today—but we have God with us today.

What God gives by promise we must accept by faith.

Feed your faith and your doubt will starve to death.

It is comforting to know that God, who guides us, sees tomorrow more clearly than we see yesterday.

Faith begins with an experiment and ends with an experience.

Don't be afraid to go out on a limb for God—that's where the fruit is.

He who is poor in faith will be bankrupt hereafter.

When fear knocks at the door, send faith to open it, and you'll find no one there.

Faith brings trust that conquers fear.

Keep your doubts to yourself, but share your faith with others.

If your faith fizzles before the finish, it was faulty from the first.

Some people have photographic minds—always negative.

Faith is like driving in the fog.

He who can wait shall see.

Faith is patience with a lamp in it.

When the outlook is bad, try the up-look.

Never put a question mark where God puts a period.

Confidence in others often compels their confidence in us.

Some people feel they need faith the size of a mountain to move a mustard seed.

Reach up as far as you can by faith, and trust God to do the rest.

Faith has the answer to ten thousand hows.

Confidence is the feeling you have before you know better.

If you would attain greatness, think no little thoughts.

Faith does not pray for bushels of blessings and then carry a pint measure to receive them.

Faith can never overdraw its account.

Faith never looks to circumstances, but trods onward with its steadfast gaze on Christ.

To be trusted is a greater compliment than to be loved.

The height of efficiency is reached in a calm and confident spirit.

Faith is like a toothbrush—every man should have one and use it regularly, but he shouldn't try to use someone else's.

Faith is not like gasoline, which runs out as you use it, but like a muscle, which grows stronger as you exercise it.

Life is full of shadows, but the sunshine makes them all.

To believe is to be strong—doubt cramps energy—belief is power.

Have old memories but young hopes.

First be a believer if you would be an achiever.

Optimist: a person who saves the seed catalog pictures to compare with the flowers and vegetables he actually grows.

Your outcome in life doesn't depend on your income but on how you overcome.

Only those who see the invisible can do the impossible.

Looking on the bright side of life will never cause eyestrain.

Pray not for faith to move mountains, rather pray for faith that will move you.

To the Israelites, Goliath was "too big to hit"; but to little David, he was "too big to miss."

Faith is the evidence—case closed.

Only those who care to lose sight of the shore can hope to discover new oceans.

God tries our faith that we may try his faithfulness.

Faith shines brightest in a childlike heart.

You can be a professor of the faith without being a possessor of the faith.

The man who has lost his confidence has nothing more to lose.

In the clouds of affliction, the eye of faith can always find God's rainbow.

Those who truly fear God need not fear death.

Full trust in the Lord puts anxiety to rest.

Faith in God is a perfect antidote for the fear of men and dread of circumstances.

Gardeners are people who think that whatever goes down must come up.

The Apostle Paul said, "I have kept the faith." But, he lost his head. Though he lost his head, he didn't lose his faith.

Some people need to have more faith in faith.

Faith is the profound *knowing* that comes before reality confirms it.

Give God all he asks and receive all his promises.

Faith is not belief without proof, but trust without reservation.

If you have the faith—God has the power.

Depending upon man, we get what man can do—depending on God, we get what God can do.

Part-time faith, like a part-time job, will not fully support you.

Belief comes not before following, not after following, but while following.

Faith is the gate between man's peril and God's power.

A ship in the harbor is safe; but that is not what ships are built for.

If David had slain a dwarf instead of a giant, who would remember?

Willpower is that admirable quality in ourselves that is detestable obstinacy in others.

If you want to walk on the water—get out of the boat.

Faith is the daring of the soul to go farther than it can see.

Faith will not always get for us what we want, but it will get what God wants us to have.

Faith keeps the sails of life filled with the breath of heaven.

Faith expects from God what is beyond all expectations.

The faith to move mountains is the reward of those who have moved little hills.

Many a fellow is praying for rain with his tub the wrong side up.

◆Faithfulness

Use what talents you possess. The woods would be very silent if no birds sang there except the nightingales.

Dependability has a much more satisfactory market than cleverness.

What one is in little things he is also in great.

Attendance is not for the building of records but for the building of Christians.

I would rather be a watchdog than an indifferent shepherd.

God does not ask how many talents one has; he asks for faithfulness.

One thing that is worse than a quitter is the man who is afraid to begin.

The consciousness of duty done gives us music at midnight.

We rate ability in men by what they finish, not by what they attempt.

Faithfulness in little things is a great thing.

It is better to be faithful than to be famous.

If one expects to answer "when the roll is called up yonder," he had better be present when the roll is called down here.

You may depend on the Lord, but can he depend on you?

The world crowns success; God crowns faithfulness.

If you consistently do your best, the worst cannot happen.

Man measures success by numbers; God measures success by faithfulness.

Your faithfulness is the yardstick of your faith.

The reward of a task well done is being called to a bigger task.

When faithfulness is most difficult, it is most rewarding.

Our problem is not inability but inconsistency.

Every spiritual investment bears eternal interest.

In God's book of remembrance, *faithful* and *famous* are one word.

◆Family (see also Children)

A small girl described her small brother as "my next to skin."

A bachelor is lucky—he can make a mistake and never know it.

Every successful rich man has a wife in back of him spending his money.

Grandparents are so simple that all grandchildren can control them.

Heredity is something people believe in if they have a bright child.

Thank God for fathers who not only gave us life but also taught us how to live.

Some people have the first part of their lives ruined by their parents and the second half by their children.

If your ancestors hung in trees, they probably hung by their necks rather than their tails.

When the devil brings up your past, bring up his future.

Your choice: family altar, or Satan will alter your family.

Never judge a man by his relatives. He did not choose them.

A grandmother is a baby-sitter who watches kids instead of TV.

Spend time, not money, on your children.

By the time a family pays for a home in the suburbs, it isn't.

The family that smokes together chokes together.

In-laws are often as bad as outlaws.

Don't brag about your ancestors—give your descendants something to brag about.

When your ship comes in, it will perhaps be loaded with your relatives.

Speaking of trade relations, almost everyone would like to.

The passing years makes youngsters ponder why Dad gets grayer and Mom gets blonder.

The way of the transgressor is hard—upon his family.

Family happiness is homemade.

◆Fear

Agility is the way you run when an angry dog is behind you.

Courage is fear that has said its prayers.

Fear God and you will have nothing else to fear.

For every man who stopped short of the goal because of a lack of power, ten ruin their chances by driving with their brakes on.

Fear makes man believe the worst.

If you are afraid of criticism, then you will never do anything.

There is one thing worse than a quitter, and that is the man who is afraid to begin.

There are no hopeless situations; there are only people who have grown hopeless about them.

Better to face danger once than to be always in fear.

Fear usually comes as the result of ignorance.

A good scare is worth more than advice.

There are 365 "fear nots" in the Bible—one for each day.

The only way to conquer fear is to keep doing the right thing you fear to do.

Courage is not the absence of fear; it is the mastery of it.

The way to take the fear *out* of living is to put faith *in* the Lord.

Obstacles are those frightful things we see when we take our eyes off our goal.

The fear of God can deliver us from the fear of men.

Caution is when you're afraid—cowardice when the other fellow's afraid.

✦Foresight

The proper time to do the proper thing is before you have to do it.

If you're properly prepared, you won't easily be surprised.

Live so when death comes the mourners outnumber the cheering section.

A thing done right means less trouble tomorrow.

It makes sense to know where a road is leading before traveling on it.

Don't be afraid to ask dumb questions—they're easier to handle than dumb mistakes.

Don't ever take a fence down until you know the reason why it was put up.

Don't try to grow an oak tree in a flowerpot.

If at first you don't succeed, try looking in the wastebasket for directions.

At the end of the day, think how many goofs you could have avoided had you planned things better.

We can choose our actions, but we do not determine the consequences.

◆Forgetting

Memory is what enables you to dial part of a telephone number correctly.

A filing cabinet is a place where things get lost alphabetically.

The things in life you can't forget are the ones you hadn't planned for.

There are so many good people that we should forget all the evil ones.

A retentive memory is often a good thing, but the ability to forget can be a token of greatness.

There was a man who discovered a cure for amnesia, but he forgot what it was.

Too often when we speak of repenting, we only mean forgetting.

The best way to get even is to forget.

Amnesia—blank account.

The best place for your trouble is in your pocket—the one with a hole.

It would be nice if we could forget our troubles like we forget our blessings.

A person is merely inviting future injuries if he tries to avenge past ones.

If you think you're lonely and neglected, just think of Whistler's father.

When the danger is past, we often forget the God who helped us.

◆Forgiveness

God does not forget the sinner; he forgets the sin.

An apology is a good way to have the last word.

Christ offers comfort for the grieving and cleansing for the guilty.

The first step to receiving eternal life is to admit that we don't deserve it.

Never bury a mad dog with his tail sticking out of the ground.

Everyone should have a large cemetery in which to bury the faults of their friends.

Forgiveness should be like burning the mortgage—it's gone and forgotten.

It is better to forgive too much than to condemn too much.

No one is ever stronger and stands higher than when he forgives.

It is easier to forgive an enemy than to forgive a friend.

Some forgive their enemies, but not until they are dead.

Education can polish men, but only the blood of Christ can cleanse them.

The only petition in the Lord's prayer that has a condition attached is the one on forgiveness.

The best way to get even is to forget.

Forgiveness means God buries our sins and does not mark the grave.

It is far better to forgive and forget than to resent and remember.

Love is asking to forgive what courtesy would have avoided.

Law keeps us limping in dark; grace keeps us walking in the light.

There are none so good that they can save themselves—none so bad that God cannot save them.

Getting revenge makes you even with your enemy, but forgiving him puts you above him.

Christian love bears and forbears—gives and forgives.

God forgives our sins, buries them in the sea of forgetfulness, and puts up a sign: "No fishing."

Getting even with a person means putting yourself on his level.

Quarrels would not last long if there were not faults on both sides.

You will never get ahead of anyone as long as you are trying to get even with them.

Forgiving makes a comfortable life—resentment is a sharp bedfellow.

Forgiveness has been called the virtue we profess to believe, fail to practice, and neglect to preach.

Everyone says forgiveness is a lovely idea, until they have something to forgive.

The bigness of any man is manifest in the number of little things he is able to overlook in others.

Never does the human soul become so strong as when it dares to forgive an injury.

◆Friendship

Don't worry about knowing people—just make yourself worth knowing.

Life benefits from serving others, for as it reaches out to help, it gathers something for itself—friendship.

A person who has a lot of friends either has a lot of money or is a good listener.

Associate with winners.

Friends are those rare people who ask how we are and then wait to hear the answer.

If you can buy a person's friendship, it is not worth it.

True friends have hearts that beat as one.

We will think and talk like the person we listen to the most.

Christian fellowship simply means an opening of Christian hearts.

If you have no enemies, you are apt to be in the same predicament in regard to friends.

You can bank on any friendship where interest is paid.

No one has so big a house that he does not need a good neighbor.

If you were another person, would you like to be a friend of yours?

Christ's friendship prevails when human friendship fails.

Short visits make long friends.

A good neighbor is one who neither looks down on you nor keeps up with you.

A friend is one who helps you bridge the gaps between loneliness and fellowship, frustration and confidence, despair and hope, setbacks and success.

Our greatest wealth is not measured in terms of riches but relationships.

A friend is never known till he is needed.

He is your friend who pushes you nearer to God.

Friendship is a responsibility—not an opportunity.

Friendship is the cement that holds the world together.

Friends are those who speak to you after others don't.

The reason a dog has so many friends is that he wags his tail and not his tongue.

Pick your friends, but not to pieces.

A friend is one who puts his finger on a fault without rubbing it in.

The difference between an enemy and a friend is that neither of them will help you when you're in trouble—except you don't expect an enemy to.

The way to have friends is to be willing to lose some arguments.

When a friend deals with a friend, let the bargain be well penned, that they may continue friends to the end.

If a friend makes a mistake, don't rub it in—rub it out.

If you *long* to be with Christians, you *belong* to Christ.

A hundred friends are not enough, but one enemy is too much.

Always hold your head up but be careful to keep your nose at a friendly level.

Never choose friends by their looks.

Friendship doubles our joy and divides our grief.

Don't tell your friends about your troubles: "How are you!" is a greeting—not a question.

You cannot see eye to eye with the person you look down upon.

You can meet friends everywhere, but you cannot meet enemies anywhere—you have to make them.

Being square creates a circle of friends.

It is just as difficult to get along in this world without a friend as it is to get along without food to eat.

Someone defined happiness as losing an argument to a friend and later finding out the friend was really wrong after all.

A friend is a person who can step on your toes without messing your shine.

The quickest way to wipe out a friend is to sponge on him.

A friend is someone to add up all your traits but to bring up only the good ones.

People are judged by the company they keep, and the company they keep away from.

Deal with others' faults as gently as if they were your own.

No matter how rich a man may be, there's nothing he can buy finer than a friend.

My enemies are my friends who don't know me.

Be friendly with the folks you know—if it weren't for them, you would be a total stranger.

If every Christian were as friendly as you are, would any visitor come back to your church?

An unwelcome guest is one of the best things going.

If you cannot think of any nice things to say about your friends, then you have the wrong friends.

A friend is someone who likes you even though he doesn't need you anymore.

Make friends before you need them.

If your friends misquote you, think how much worse it might be had they quoted you correctly.

To be without a friend is a serious form of poverty.

The best mirror is an old friend.

Make friends with your creditors, but never make creditors of your friends.

The best vitamin for developing friends is B1.

The best possession one may have is a true friend.

Friendship is the art of overlooking the shortcomings of others.

Make friendship a habit and you will always have friends.

Before borrowing money from a friend, decide which you need more.

The more arguments you win, the fewer friends you will have.

The art of being a good guest is knowing when to leave.

A friend is someone who knows all our faults but still loves us.

You will never have a friend if you must have one without faults.

An open enemy is better than a false friend.

Doing nothing for your friends results in having no friends to do for.

A person may live in a good neighborhood but be a poor neighbor.

Friends knock before they enter, not after they leave.

Regardless of what happens, some of your friends knew it would.

An old friend is better than two new ones.

Anyone can give advice, but a real friend will lend a helping hand.

You can make more friends by being interested in them than trying to have them be interested in you.

A man is not only known by the company he keeps, but by the enemies he makes.

A real friend is a person who when you've made a fool of yourself, lets you forget it.

A friend is a person who listens attentively while you say nothing.

Friends are made by many acts—and lost by only one.

In prosperity our friends know us; in adversity we know our friends.

You can buy friendship with friendship, but never with dollars.

True friends are like diamonds, precious but rare; false friends are like autumn leaves, found everywhere.

There is nothing like a long face to shorten one's list of friends.

If you're up to no good for a friend, your friend is no good for you.

To have money and friends is easy—to have friends and no money is an accomplishment.

A friend is someone who thinks you're a good egg even though you're slightly cracked.

The most miserable person on earth is the one who has money and no friends.

Life benefits from serving others, for as it reaches out to help, it gathers something for itself—friendship.

Those who suffer need more than sympathy; they need companionship.

There are three faithful friends—an old wife, an old dog, and ready money.

Solitude is very sad, but too much company is twice as bad.

Friendships earned before you need them are almost certain to be more lasting.

Perhaps we think more of our friends than our relatives because we selected them.

◆Future

We must ask ourselves, How much of eternity is in what we are doing?

Atheism has no future.

The heritage of the past is the seed that brings forth the harvest of the future.

Many who are well prepared for a rainy day are totally unprepared for eternity.

The greatest business of life is to prepare for the next life.

On a church bulletin board: Visit us on your way to eternity.

These are the good old days we shall be longing for a few years from now.

Don't get so busy preparing for a rainy day that you miss today's sunshine.

Plan for the future by taking a firm grip on the present.

The best preparation for the future is to live fully today.

Regardless of the past, you may have a spotless future.

The only way to get rid of the past is to get a good future out of it.

The future: that time when you'll wish that you would have done all the things that you aren't doing now.

The best thing about the future is that it comes only a day at a time.

One of the kindest things God ever did was to put a curtain over tomorrow.

The future does not change men; it unmasks them.

We need not worry about what the future holds for us if we know who holds the future.

Never be afraid to trust an unknown future to a known God.

Our eyes are in front of our head because it is more important to look ahead than to look back.

You can't plan for the future in the future—you have to start now!

A lot of nice, fat turkey gobblers would strut less if they could see into the future.

Like it or not, you will have to live somewhere forever; so you better learn how to live.

The future always holds something for the man who keeps his faith in it.

We need not fear the future as long as we hold to the hand of him who knows the future.

Take interest in the future—that is where you will spend the rest of your life.

There is no future in the past.

Live so that each day you will neither be afraid of tomorrow nor ashamed of yesterday.

The future belongs to those who prepare for it.

A man wonders what the future holds in store—a woman wonders what the stores have in the future.

The worst trouble with the future is that it seems to get here quicker than it used to.

You can't change the past, so don't ruin the present by worrying about the future.

Where there is no faith in the future, there is no power in the present.

Anytime the future looks gray, I have an attic full of yesterdays.

We cannot alter the past, but we can be alert for the future.

The trouble with our times is that the future is not what it used to be.

The future is purchased by the present.

The past is worth looking at if it is going to help you correct the future.

Nothing will put a beautiful farm in the middle of the city like twenty years from now.

Plan ahead—it was not raining when Noah built the ark.

Those who fear the future are likely to fumble the present.

He who takes care of the present will have a great future.

G

◆Gambling

The braver the bird, the fatter the cat.

Gambling is stealing by mutual consent.

A gambler is not getting something for nothing but giving much for nothing.

Discontentment is the penalty we pay for betting on race horses instead of cows.

A race track is the only place to find windows that clean people.

A man went to a horse race to make a "mental bet" and lost his mind.

The easiest way to improve your luck is to stop betting.

◆Generosity

It is better to give than to lend, and the cost is about the same.

Many of the debts we owe to God are payable to man.

Some people think they are generous because they give free advice.

The hand that gives, gathers.

Whatever we possess becomes of double value when we share it with others.

Christians show what they are by what they do with what they have.

The person who dies with a dollar in his pocket dies a dollar short.

You are not really giving to God until you enjoy it.

Avarice gathers itself poor—charity gives itself rich.

The longest chapter in the Bible is Numbers chapter 7—nearly two thousand words, all about giving.

Some say, "Give till it hurts." To some it hurts to give.

Christians don't own their wealth—they owe it.

Some pray high but give low.

Wanting less sometimes is a greater joy than having more.

Don't try to cheat the Lord and call it economy.

✦God

God's ear lies close to the believer's lips.

God's grace is immeasurable; his mercy inexhaustible; his peace inexpressible.

God can take the place of anything, but nothing can take the place of God.

The best way to face life's changes is to look at the unchanging God.

There are limits to man's love but not to God's.

There is much I do not know about God, but what I do know has changed my life.

God has two dwellings; one is heaven and the other is an open and thankful heart.

God's throne is mercy, not marble.

God without man is still God; man without God is nothing.

You can't claim God as your Father until you claim Christ as your Savior.

Some people see more of God in a walk around the block than others see in a trip around the world.

Nature is but a name for an effect whose cause is God.

The best way to face life's changes is to look to the unchanging God.

Nature is so inhuman—it never rushes.

A God of all mercy would be a God unjust.

When you spend time with God, you invest in eternity.

In an age of false superlatives, only God is truly great!

Hold to God's hand; he will do the holding if you do the trusting.

Loneliness is being unaware of the One who is with us everywhere.

To mistreat one of God's creatures is to offend God.

He who puts God first will be happy at last.

If you want to have a heart for God, you must let God have your heart.

Man shows he is more than an animal when he longs to be more like God.

To walk with God, we must make it a practice to talk with God.

Little things become great things when they are done to please God.

Talk it over with the great Physician—no appointment necessary.

We honor the righteous dead by serving the living God.

In God's pattern book of nature we can trace many valuable lessons.

If your life seems flat, accent it with the salt of God's grace.

To create, God had to only speak; to save, he had to suffer.

Some people desire to please God—as long as it doesn't offend the devil.

It is more important to know *the Rock of Ages* than to know the ages of the rocks.

Don't say "Our Father" on Sunday and spend the rest of the week like an orphan.

God isn't dead; I belong to his family; I talked to him this morning.

We serve God who is greater than any problems, bigger than any of our needs.

Man can't build a successful world without God; history has proved it.

God is a donor no one can outdo.

God can do without us, but we cannot do without him.

Don't forget that God is between you and your enemy.

Science helps man to know what God already knows.

You cannot be truly a son of God without resembling the Father.

Seek God's face—not his hands.

God shook the world with a babe—not a bomb.

Just because God is ignored doesn't mean that he doesn't exist.

Fear God and you'll have nothing else to fear.

He is wise who takes God for a teacher.

Every sunrise is God's greeting—the sunset his signature.

We may not always agree with God, but he is still the boss.

God writes with a pen that never blots, speaks with a tongue that never slips, and acts with a hand that never fails.

The closer you get to Christ, the closer you get to others.

Jesus is God spelling himself out in language that man can understand.

God delights to use minute means to perform mighty miracles.

How foolish to lean on the arm of flesh when we can be supported by the arm of omnipotence.

When you relate to God as a person, you develop a personal relationship with him.

All who are born of God should develop a likeness to their Father.

✦God's Provision

Far greater than man's first trip to the moon is Christ's second coming to earth.

Grace is *G*od's *R*iches *A*t *C*hrist's *E*xpense.

Lord, I don't know how you are going to solve my problems, but I know you have something in mind and I thank you for it.

A man ought to be afraid to run his own life the minute he knows there is a God.

Christ died to save us; he now lives to keep us.

Christ's sacrifice was exactly what God desired and we required.

The difficulties of life are intended to make us better, not bitter.

True freedom is not in choosing your own way but in yielding to God's way.

Tarry at a promise until God meets you there.

God performs what he promises and completes what he commands.

Be careful not to presume upon God's care.

The caterpillar calls it the end of the world; God calls it a butterfly.

To be filled with God, one must be emptied of self.

God owes us nothing but gives us everything.

Little things become great things when done in God's power.

We may face situations beyond our reserves but never beyond God's resources.

God invites us to burden him with what burdens us.

It's not the load that breaks you down; it's the fact that you carry it alone.

God never uses an answering machine; he takes each call personally.

God takes heed to our every need.

Nothing is too big for my God to accomplish, and nothing is too little for him to use in accomplishing it.

The ground at the cross is level—all may come.

God gives us vinegar with a teaspoon and honey with a soup ladle.

God always gives us what we ask—or something better.

You may be a number the computers can trace, but Christ knows your need, your name, and your face.

The triune God reveals himself to us not to confuse but to convict, to cleanse, and to comfort.

God has not promised to give us answers—just grace.

God's answers are always wiser than our prayers.

Man's limited potential underscores God's limitless power.

God gives strength in proportion to the strain.

When adversity is ready to strike, God is ready to strengthen.

What's behind us and what's ahead of us mean little when you stop to think what's within.

God never alters the robe of righteousness to fit the man but the man to fit the robe.

It is not the sense of his presence but the fact of his presence.

God's throne is mercy—not marble.

Many a life that seems marred by accident is only in process of being made by Providence.

Thinking we have some power of our own prevents our taking all power from Christ.

God's promises are always greater than our problems.

The finger that points the way is part of the hand that supplies the need.

Think less of the power of things over you and more of the power of Christ in you.

When you sit at the table of the Lord and taste his heavenly food, the devil's cooking doesn't taste good.

God doesn't take anything from his people without giving something better in return.

Those who bear the cross may also be sheltered by it.

There is no need to nervously pace the deck of the ship of life when the Great Pilot is at the wheel.

God will never let anything come to you that he and you cannot handle together.

God sends us the storms to prove that he is the only shelter.

He who knows the way of the Lord can find it in the dark.

Trust God in the light to find him in the dark.

God's wrath comes by measure; his mercy without measure.

God never sends a burden to weigh us down without offering his arm to lift us up.

The time God allows us is always enough for the work he allots us.

The more clearly we see the sovereignty of God, the less perplexed we are by the calamities of man.

God is with us in darkness just as surely as he is with us in the light.

God will take care of *what* you go through; you take care of *how* you go through it.

The God who knows our load limit graciously limits our load.

The divine shoulder is always under my load.

Divine sources are never exhausted.

God does not always change circumstances, but he may often change us.

Christ's *pardon* brings the soul to heaven; Christ's *presence* brings heaven to the soul.

God uses unique methods to perform mighty miracles.

Man's poverty is no strain on God's provision.

One may face situations beyond their reserves but never beyond God's resources.

The only limits to God's grace are the limits we put on it.

If God sends us on stony paths, he provides strong shoes.

Those God calls he qualifies—those he qualifies he uses.

Those God appoints he anoints.

God has no problems—he has only solutions.

God is in the business of turning all our losses into gains.

Clouds in our lives are sent many times to bring showers of blessing.

God's resources are always equal to his requirements.

You cannot break God's promises by leaning on them.

You have all the inner strength you will ever need to handle everything you will ever face.

God's friendship prevails when human friendship fails.

God will not allow any problem to come to you that cannot be a learning, a turning, or an earning experience.

God always gives us the right time and grace to do what he asks us to do.

A providence that provides for sparrows will certainly protect the saints.

God's promises are always greater than our needs.

God buries his workman, but carries on his work.

Christianity is not a way out—it's a way through.

God's promises are life preservers that keep the soul from sinking in the sea of trouble.

God provides resting places as well as working places.

Justice is the activity of God's holiness.

God gave us our memories so that we might have roses in December.

We cannot earn by our merit what Christ has secured for us by his grace.

If one allows God to guide, he will provide.

The Christian finds safety, not in the absence of danger but in the presence of God.

◆God's Will

God may conceal his purposes so that we will live on his promises.

Abraham did not know for sure where he was going, but he knew for sure with whom he was going.

Man shows that he is more than an animal when he longs to be more like God.

Doing the will of God leaves me no time for disputing about his plans.

Following Jesus implies doing business on Jesus' principles.

The Lord opens doors for each of us to become avenues of his love and grace on a daily basis.

Man's rules should never replace God's requirements.

Trusting God's providence means we stop trifling with his plans.

Many pray, not to find God's will, but to get his approval of their own.

The will of the majority may not be the will of God.

Only as we go God's way can we know God's will.

The secret of an unsuccessful life lies in an unsurrendered will.

A smooth sea never made a skillful sailor.

You cannot do God's will and satisfy everyone.

To ignore and miss God's will is to sin.

Rejecting God's way is simply asking for trouble.

The will of God will never lead to where the grace of God cannot keep you.

God can lead you around, but he will always lead you aright.

Outside of God's will there is no such thing as success; in his will there can be no failure.

If things don't seem to be coming your way, perhaps you are on the wrong road.

Nothing is or can be accidental with God.

It is better to ask the Lord to direct your paths than to correct your mistakes.

Christ came not to make life easy but to make men great.

When you go through trials, you are not being picked on; you are being picked out.

Don't expect God's approval of plans on which he has not been consulted.

The *stops* of a good man are ordered of the Lord as well as the *steps.*

You will be more happy doing *God's will* than doing *your will.*

Be sure—if God sends you on a stony path, he will provide you with strong shoes.

God's purpose is not to make us comfortable but conformable— conformable to Christ.

True freedom is not having our own way but yielding to God's way.

If God has called you, do not spend time looking over your shoulder to see who is following.

To know God's will is life's greatest treasure—to do God's will is life's greatest pleasure.

No trial would cause us to despair if we knew God's reason for allowing it.

Those who see God's hand in everything can best leave everything in God's hand.

God's delays are not God's denials.

God has a perfect plan for our lives, but it cannot be perfect until we accept it.

God's answers are wiser than our prayers.

When we know God's heart, we will never question his will.

Christians may become weary in God's work but never weary with his work.

God always gives us what we ask for—or something better.

The purposes of God are sometimes delayed but never abandoned.

Every time God closes a door, he always opens a window.

There are no such things as accidents, only incidents, in the perfect will of God.

Hope for the best, get ready for the worst, and then take what God chooses to send.

Remembering Christ's *wounds* should encourage us to do his *will*.

Nothing in life is accidental—those believing in accidents do not believe in God.

✦Goodness

Goodness is a special kind of truth and beauty. It is truth and beauty in human behavior.

Remembering God's goodness always puts a song in your heart.

The loveliest feature in human life is amiability; the most potent, wealth; the sublimest, mercy; the most luxurious, charity; the most stimulating, love; and the most desirable, self-respect.

◆Gossip

Blessed are the hard of hearing, for they shall miss much small talk.

A gossiper burns the scandal at both ends.

Nothing is dirt cheap anymore except gossip.

Gossip has neither legs or wings. It is composed entirely of tales, and most of them stings.

Some folks think the statement "It is more blessed to give than receive" has a reference to gossip.

Gossip is a case of tales and heads, both being losers.

There isn't much to see in a small town, but what you hear makes up for it.

Idle gossip keeps some people very busy.

Rumor is one thing that gets thicker as you spread it.

If people did not carry gossip, it would not go so far.

There is nothing busier than an idle rumor.

Not everyone respects gossip—some improve it.

Trying to squash a rumor is like trying to unring a bell.

Those who gossip should be hung by the tongue; those who listen to gossip should be hung by the ear.

A rumor is about as hard to unspread as butter.

Gossip has been described as halitosis of the mind.

To successfully combat gossip, ignore it.

Busy people have no time to be busybodies.

If what you say is something you wouldn't write down, don't say it.

A scandal is a little wind blown up by a couple of windbags.

A secret is something you tell one person at a time.

You can't have a gossiping tongue unless you have gossiping ears.

As one dog can start all the dogs to barking, so one person can start a whole group to gossiping.

Can you imagine anyone as unhappy as a person with a live secret and a dead telephone?

He who carries a tale makes a monkey of himself.

The guilty person is always the first to judge.

I don't like to spread gossip, but what else can I do with it?

A gossiper is the devil's postman.

Men never gossip—they merely investigate rumors.

Busy souls have no time to be busybodies.

Gossip should be spelled *gassip,* as it is flammable, combustible, and should be stopped.

A gossiper is like an old shoe—its tongue never stays in place.

Gossip is an art of saying nothing and leaving nothing unsaid.

A gossip is just a fool with a keen sense of rumor.

When a little bird has told you something, be sure that bird was not cuckoo.

More people are run down by gossip than by automobiles.

You can't believe everything you hear—but you can repeat it.

People who gossip are usually caught in their own mouth traps.

It is easier to float a rumor than to sink it.

Scandal is what one half of the world takes pleasure in telling and the other half believing.

Some people will believe anything that is whispered to them.

Running people down is bad business, whether you are a motorist or a gossiper.

Gossip: Something that goes in one ear and out the mouth.

The difference between gossip and news is whether you hear it or tell it.

Many people are wise until they open their mouth.

How can a rumor get around so quickly when it has no legs to stand on?

He who tells the faults of others to you will tell your faults to others at the first opportunity.

Three kinds of gossip: vest button—always popping off; vacuum type—always picking up dirt; liniment—always rubbing it in.

A tongue three inches long can kill a man six feet tall.

Gossip doesn't hurt anyone—unless it is about us.

A gossiper dumps his garbage on the listener.

The more interesting the gossip, the more likely it is to be untrue.

A gossip is someone who suffers from acute indiscretion.

Most of us figure gossip is like an old joke—there's always someone around who hasn't heard it yet.

A gossip is one who puts who and who together and gets whew!

Gossip could be called "ear pollution."

Whoever gossips *to* you will gossip *of* you.

A gossip is a person who will never tell a lie when the truth will do more damage.

When you ask someone to keep a secret, you are asking someone to do something you can't.

Gossip is like mud on the wall—you can wipe it off, but it leaves a spot.

Gossipers are like blotters—they absorb a lot of dirt, but usually get it backwards.

A fool's mouth is his destruction.

Gossip is hearing something you like about a person you don't.

Three can keep a secret if two are dead.

There are two kinds of gossipers—those who just pass the information along, and those who improve on it.

✦Government (see also Taxes)

It takes a certain kind of mind to be in politics—a small one.

Elections may be more successful if we choose the candidates according to what they won't stand for instead of what they will stand for.

A jury consists of twelve people chosen to decide who has the better lawyer.

Politicians are the same everywhere—they promise to build a bridge even where there is no river.

What this country needs is a man who can be right and president at the same time.

To make his speeches bear fruit, the smart politician will prune them a little.

A whale's tongue is found to contain eight percent of the oil in its system. Among politicians the proportion is even heavier.

One of the things we have to be thankful for is that we don't get as much government as we pay for.

Whatever makes good Christians makes them good citizens.

There is only one fact a politician needs to know: most people have very short memories.

Some members of Congress should have their mouths taped instead of their speeches.

When a politician makes the dirt fly, he's probably throwing it.

The Congress is a body of government that does not solve problems—it just investigates them.

The public business of their nation is the private business of every citizen.

Some of the best jokes are heard in just listening to the government and some of their decisions.

Remember that government of the people will be government for the people as long as there is government by the people.

Nothing is politically right that is morally wrong.

Bad officials are elected by good citizens who do not vote.

People were satisfied with their walk in life until politicians began to offer them a free ride.

A politician is an operator who takes money from the rich, votes from the poor, and then promises both sides protection from each other.

A lame duck—a politician whose goose has been cooked.

The more you listen to political speeches, the more you realize that ours is, indeed, a land of promise.

Old politicians never die—they just run once too often.

Welfare rolls are made up from our dough.

The government should be glad the public has what it takes.

Sign at recruiting station: We honor all draft cards.

What our country needs is not more liberty but fewer people who take liberties with our liberty.

America is not only a melting pot—sometimes it is a pressure cooker.

Political speeches are like the horns on a steer—a point here and there, with a lot of bull in between.

Politicians should be good in geometry—they know all the angles and talk in circles.

We need more watchdogs at the United States Treasury and fewer bloodhounds at the Internal Revenue Service.

Voters distrust politicians too much in general and too little in particular.

A politician is a man who approaches every problem with an open mouth.

Government rarely does something for you unless it does something to you.

Two things for successful political campaigns: hot issues and cold cash.

Many bureaucrats are like guns without triggers—they don't work and can't be fired.

Too many Americans believe it's easier to vote for something than to work for it.

A diplomat is anyone who thinks twice before saying nothing.

Judges are getting tougher with criminals—they're giving them longer suspended sentences.

It is said that politicians are more concerned with deals than ideals.

The main reason the government fights organized crime is because it resents the competition.

Some people take the money and run; politicians run and then take the money.

◆Grumbling (see also Contentment)

Most people don't mind suffering in silence as long as everyone else knows about it.

Don't grumble because you don't have what you want—be thankful you don't get what you deserve.

Grumbling requires no talent, no self-denial, no brains, no character.

Jealousy is nothing more than poison envy.

The sunlight of love will kill the germs of jealousy and hate.

There are too many cranks and not enough starters in the world.

You can't expect to be a lucky dog if you spend all your time growling.

Some people intend to be gratefully humble but instead turn out to be grumbly hateful.

If you feel "dog tired" at night, it is because you growled all day.

H

◆Habits

Some folks are always punctual in being late.

Little and often make much.

Habits are either the best of servants or the worst of masters.

We first make our habits, then our habits make us.

Bad habits, man's mortal enemies, must be slain or they will slay him.

The chains of habit are usually too small to be felt until they are too strong to be broken.

Habit is the deepest law of human nature.

Bad habits are like comfortable beds—easy to get into, but hard to get out of.

If you don't master your habits, they will master you.

One of the best freedoms is freedom from bad habits.

We build our lives each day with the bricks of habits we have.

It will pay those who cannot do as they please to please as they do.

One test of good manners is to be able to put up pleasantly with bad ones.

Bad habits take few holidays.

A bad habit is like good bread—better broken than kept.

It's easier to prevent bad habits than to break them.

Never make the mistake of thinking people will not always act like people.

✦Happiness *(see also* Contentment)

Happiness is when you see your husband's old girlfriend and she's fatter than you.

There are few dark days ahead for those who have learned to spread sunshine.

Happiness is like your shadow. Run after it and you will never catch it, but keep your face to the sun and it will follow you.

Some don't know what happiness is until it's gone.

Do something every day to make someone happy, even if it means leaving him alone.

The happiest people are those who discover that what they should be doing and what they are doing are the same things.

Three enemies that oppose happiness—worry, boredom, and self-centeredness.

Share laughter with others to help them understand that you and they have objectives in common.

The surest steps to happiness are the church steps.

A song in the heart will put a smile upon the face.

The light of God's Son in your heart will put his sunshine on your face.

You'll add to your joy when you count your blessings.

The Lord respects those who work, but he loves those who sing.

The most wasted day is the day when one has not laughed.

Joy is the best proof of having the presence of God.

Unhappiness always seeks to get—happiness always seeks to give.

A rejoicing Christian is one of God's best advertisements.

Laugh a lot, and when you are older, all your wrinkles will be in the right places.

A merry heart goes all day long, but a sad heart tires in a minute.

You have the rest of your life to be miserable, so enjoy today.

Remember—laughter is "internal jogging."

Some people find happiness by making the most of what they haven't got.

Happiness comes when we stop complaining about our troubles and begin to be thankful for the troubles we don't have.

The good we do today becomes the happiness of tomorrow.

Many people miss much happiness because they never stop to enjoy it while they have it.

One should not marry to find happiness but to share happiness.

You can attract sinners to Christ when you have his song in your heart.

In the eyes of the Christian, happiness is wanting what you get.

To be with Jesus forever is the sum of happiness.

It is easy to sing when we walk with the King.

Laughter can always be heard farther than weeping.

Happiness is usually the result of hard work.

Happiness can be thought, taught, and caught—but not bought.

Happiness multiplies as we divide it with others.

Sharing, whether good or bad, usually produces happiness.

Unhappiness is not knowing what we want and killing ourselves to get it.

The foolish man seeks happiness in tomorrow, but the wise man finds it today.

Life is always worthwhile to the person who can laugh, love, and lift.

A sense of humor is what makes you laugh at something that would make you angry if it happened to you.

Happiness is that peculiar sensation you encounter when you're just too busy to feel miserable.

If you are really concerned about what you wear, remember your facial expressions can be the most important.

The secret of happiness sometimes depends on what you don't do.

Wealth does not insure happiness, but then neither does poverty.

Joy is multiplied when you share it.

Joy comes from giving to Christ—not getting from him.

Happiness is not doing what you like—it's liking what you do.

A smile is a powerful weapon; you can break ice with it.

Happiness is a place between too little and too much.

Happiness in life seems to rest more heavily on interests than it does on assets.

The roots of happiness grow deepest in the soil of service.

Happiness is a perfume you cannot pour on others without getting a few drops on yourself.

Some Christians give the impression they were baptized in vinegar.

Some grin and bear it; others smile and change it.

Laughter is a mini-vacation.

Have you ever found any happiness in doing a mean thing?

Out of dismay and disappointment comes a lasting joy.

Happiness should be like childhood diseases—sooner or later, each of us should catch it.

Make one person happy each day—even if it's yourself.

Humor is to life what shock absorbers are to automobiles.

The good we do today becomes the happiness of tomorrow.

True happiness lies in satisfaction.

Usually people are as happy as they make up their minds to be.

Joy is not in things; it is in us.

The happiness of your life depends on the quality of your thoughts.

If you can laugh at your mistakes you will be much happier.

If you trust God in the dark, he'll change your midnight into music.

Happiness depends on happenings; joy depends on Jesus.

Too busy to be happy? Then you are too busy to enjoy life.

A smile will go a long way, but you must start it on its journey.

Joy is the by-product of obedience.

Joy is the flag that is flown from the castle of the heart when the King is in residence there.

One of the sure ways to happiness is to learn to enjoy all the things you think you dislike.

It takes seventy-three muscles to frown and only fourteen to smile. No wonder grouchy people are always tired.

Since you cannot have all you want, make your life happy by wanting what you have.

Three grand essentials to happiness are: something to do, something to love, something to hope for.

Laughter is a tranquilizer with no side effects.

The heights of happiness and holiness are precisely the same slopes.

An optimist laughs to forget; the pessimist forgets to laugh.

Some young people want life, liberty, and an automobile for the pursuit of happiness.

The truest expression of Christianity is not a sigh but a song.

The city of happiness is in the state of mind.

Laugh and the world laughs with you; complain and you live alone.

Cheerfulness oils the machinery of life.

Happiness depends mainly upon the improvement of small opportunities.

Happiness is not having and getting; it consists of giving and serving.

Share your joy—it takes two to be glad.

A man without a sense of humor is like a wagon without springs—he is jolted by every pebble in the road.

Some people bring happiness wherever they go; others whenever they do.

Laughter, if it comes from the heart, is a heavenly thing.

Keep your happiness in circulation.

He who laughs last probably intended to tell the story himself.

God often digs the wells of joy with the spade of sorrow.

He who laughs, lasts.

The trouble with happiness is that it can't buy money.

Make it your business to be happy and your business will be happy.

Some people find happiness by making the most of what they haven't got.

Happiness is not where you live but how you live.

The real secret to success is to be happy when you really aren't.

Real happiness is cheap enough, and yet we often pay dearly for its counterfeit.

✦Health

Remember when no medicine was any good unless it tasted terrible?

Never argue with a doctor; he has inside information.

Just when we learn to take things with a grain of salt, the doctor puts us on a salt-free diet.

A prune is a plum that did not take care of itself.

Virus is a Latin word used by doctors to mean, "Your guess is as good as mine."

If you look like your passport photo—you need the trip.

If you're tired of reading about the evils of smoking—give up either reading or smoking.

Tired jogger's prayer: "Give us this day our daily breath."

Miracle drugs are nothing new—Moses had two tablets that could cure the world's ills.

A sickly saint often resembles a healthy hypocrite.

You never know the worst when visiting the doctor until you get the bill.

Good humor is the health of the soul.

To be healthy one must have a happy mind.

Happiness and health go together. It's the surly bird that catches the germ.

The relative value and importance of health and wealth always depends on which you have lost.

Use, don't abuse, your vacation. Health is essential to success.

A bad cold can either be positive or negative—sometimes the eyes have it and sometimes the nose.

◆Heaven (see also Future)

Christ is the only way to heaven; all other paths are detours to doom.

Separation is the law of earth; reunion is the law of heaven.

The path to heaven is so narrow that many can go before and many can follow after, but only One can walk beside us.

The only thing on earth a man can absolutely gain is heaven.

Many buy cemetery lots in advance, but do nothing about preparing for a home in heaven.

Hold lightly to the things of earth, but cling tightly to heavenly things.

The gains of heaven will more than compensate for the losses of earth.

The door of heaven is open to everyone whose heart is open to God.

Earth is the land of the dying; heaven is the land of the living.

The road to heaven is never overcrowded.

The way to heaven—turn right at Calvary and keep going straight.

Interested in going to heaven? Get flight instructions from the Bible.

No man can be qualified for heaven until he first realizes that by nature he is qualified for hell.

It's not your *will* that keeps you out of heaven—it's your *won't*.

People who live a life of hell on earth cannot expect to enter heaven.

The cross is the only ladder tall enough to reach heaven.

If living means grace—to die means glory.

The way to heaven is too straight for the man who wants to walk crooked.

The man who wants to go to heaven should study the route that will get him there.

A man who walks with God always gets to his destination.

Have you ever noticed that the narrow road is not crowded but the broad way is?

The average person probably hasn't stored up enough treasure in heaven to make a down payment for a harp.

Praising yourself to the skies will not get you there.

It is better to creep along slowly on the right road than to march confidently along the wrong.

Men who sing at midnight are citizens of that city where there is no need of the sun or moon, since the Lord is the light.

It is hard to tune in on heaven's message if our lives are full of earthly static.

Heaven's delight will far outweigh earth's difficulties.

Christ who tells us of heaven with all its happiness also tells us of hell with all its horrors.

You will enjoy heaven more if you have a bit of it in your heart while on earth.

Heaven will mean the most to those who have put the most into it.

There is no place where earth's sorrows are more deeply felt than in heaven.

The greatest business in life is to prepare for the next life.

If a man could work his way into heaven, he would brag himself into hell.

The trials of earth are nothing compared to the triumphs of heaven.

Christians never meet for the last time.

Jesus was content to be born in a stable that we may have a mansion when we die.

There is one way to *stay* out of hell, but no way to *get* out of hell.

A sunset is heaven's gate ajar.

Where you go hereafter depends on what you go after here.

Lord, while you are busy preparing a place for me, prepare me, as well, for that place.

Those who live right won't get left.

It took days to reach the moon—in a moment we shall be translated to the "third heaven."

Let the word on the door of hell be written, "deserved," but on the door of heaven be written, "free gift."

If you are on your way to heaven, you will be busy finding others to take along.

✦Hell (*see also* Future)

Hell is truth seen too late.

Hell is prepared for those who prepare for it by rejecting Christ.

There are good parking places on the road to hell.

Every soul winner believes in hell.

Those trying to prove there is no hell usually have a reason for it.

If more hell was preached in the pulpit, there would be less hell in the community.

People may laugh themselves into hell but never laugh themselves out.

✦Holiness

Someone has figured that we have thirty-five thousand laws trying to enforce the Ten Commandments.

When there is no thirst for righteousness, the sermons seem dry.

A holy life is a voice—it speaks when the tongue is silent and is either a constant attraction or a perpetual reproof.

Holiness is not the way to Christ, but Christ is the way to holiness.

Sanctification requires consecration without reservation.

Purity in the heart produces power in the life.

Separate yourself from fellowship with the world, or the world will separate you from fellowship with God.

If you want to smell like a rose, stay out of the barnyard.

Unholy living follows unbelieving thinking.

The more we're attracted by Christ, the less we'll be attracted by the world.

The Christian is not ruined by living in the world but by the world living in him.

You cannot walk with God and run with the devil.

The world is whatever cools your affection for Christ.

Christians who move the world are those who do not let the world move them.

Godly talk does not always imply godly walk.

It is better to be alone than to be in bad company.

A retreat from the wrong direction is the only wise move in the right direction.

Keeping away from the mire is better than washing it off.

You are either leaving your mark on the world, or the world is leaving its mark on you.

He does not love what is good who does not hate what is evil.

Master that sin in your heart or it will master you.

Christianity is worth little if it doesn't change your life-style.

If your room is dark, it could be for one of two reasons—the sun isn't shining or the window is dirty.

You can wash the windows—you can't make the sun shine.

Religious practices may induce a form of piety, but never will they produce purity.

Attachment to Christ is the real secret of detachment from the world.

The world wants good mixers; God wants good separators.

War is the result of the polluted and perverted nature of man.

Our own dirt always seems cleaner.

A "holy week" is meaningless to an unholy life.

True holiness is doing God's will with a smile.

Worldly values are poor investments—they never pay what they promised.

If God approved of today's permissiveness he would have given us the "Ten Suggestions."

The man who pays an ounce of principle for a pound of worldly popularity gets badly cheated.

Christ does not take us out of the world; he takes the world out of us.

Worldliness is simply pursuing the activities of the present life with no thought of God.

The more of heaven there is in our lives, the less of earth we will covet.

There is no detour to holiness; Jesus came to the resurrection through the cross—not around it.

To be in step with the world means to be out of step with Christ.

Some church members have heaven *on* the tip of their tongue and the world *at* the tip of their tongue.

Righteousness doesn't consist of being a little less sinful than our neighbors.

Whitewashing the pump will not purify the water.

The flesh and the Spirit cannot cooperate.

Some people's hearts are so full of the world that there is no room for God.

A person is known not only by the company he keeps but by the company he avoids.

The beauty of holiness is companionship with God.

Holiness is not transferred, but unrighteousness is.

Purity in the heaven produces power in the life.

God would never save us by grace so we could live in disgrace.

Holiness is like riding a bicycle—either you keep moving or you fall down.

I would as soon listen to a gangster lecture on honesty as watch Hollywood portray the Bible.

Isn't it amazing—we call Sunday the Lord's day and then use it as our own.

Garments of righteousness never go out of style.

Love will endure if you keep it pure.

Keep out of your life all that will keep Christ out of your mind.

Loose living gets many people into tight places.

Lie down with the dogs and you will get up with fleas.

Pollution of the heart is man's greatest ecological problem.

It takes holy citizens to make a holy city.

Trash isn't made—it accumulates.

The early church had its greatest impact upon the world when it lived least like the world.

Holiness is living that pleases God.

There is nothing as tragic as combining high mentality with low morality.

Righteousness in your heart produces beauty in your character.

◆Holy Spirit

The Christian's heart is the Holy Spirit's home.

Have you felt God nudging you lately?

Unless we have *within* us that which is *above* us, we soon shall yield to the pressures *around* us.

If you have the Holy Spirit on the inside, you can stand any kind of battle on the outside.

Christ departed so that the Holy Spirit could be imparted.

The human spirit fails unless the Holy Spirit fills.

A pastor's prayer: "Do something for us today that isn't in the bulletin."

You cannot drink of the Holy Spirit on Sunday and the spirits of the world during the week.

The Holy Spirit can do more in a minute than we can do ourselves in a lifetime.

When the Holy Spirit works, there is always a want—I want more holiness, more grace, more of Jesus.

✦Home (see also Children; Family)

Home is the chief school of human virtues.

Home is the sweetest type of heaven.

King or peasant, the happiest place is still the home.

Our home should face the Father's house.

A house is not a home unless it contains food for the soul as well as for the body.

When a small girl was asked, "Where is your home?" she replied, "Where Mother is."

You don't realize how complicated the simple life really is until you and your family spend the weekend in a tent.

How your children see the world depends on what you show them.

Cleaning your house while the kids are still growing is like shoveling the sidewalks while it's still snowing.

A small house will hold as much happiness as a mansion.

If you want your children to turn out well, spend twice as much time with them and half as much money.

If you want to write something that will probably live forever, sign a mortgage.

A home is a house with a heart inside.

The man who has houses everywhere has a home nowhere.

The church can preach, the school can teach, but the home must convert sermons and lessons into the way of life.

To train up children at home, it is necessary for the parents and children to spend some time at home.

Children may tear up a house, but they never tear up the home.

Train up children in the home (by example), and when they are old, they will not forsake it.

The nation can be no stronger than its homes.

A happy home is more than a roof over your head—it's a foundation under your feet.

Home is more than four walls; home is where affection calls.

Many people appear to be a big bug at work but are just a pest at home.

Home should be a retreat to which a son or daughter can return in triumph or defeat, in victory or disgrace, and know they will be loved.

Be reasonable—don't expect your youngsters to listen to your advice and ignore your example.

Some young men who leave home to set the world on fire have to come home for matches.

Many houses need to be altered into homes.

Your home will be happier if you kiss more and cuss less.

Home is a place where the great are small and the small are great.

A husband who shops with his wife is a wait-watcher.

Don't treat your home like a pit stop on the raceway of life.

When love adorns the home, other things are secondary.

A family altar would alter many a family.

Every person should have three homes: a Christian home, a church home, and a home in heaven.

A good architect can make an old house look better by just discussing the cost of a new one.

A wife can get annoyed when company drops in unexpectedly and finds the house as it usually is.

The right temperature at home is maintained by warm hearts, not by hot heads.

A broken home is the world's greatest wreck.

The most important things in your home are people.

Yelling at children is not the way to make the home a howling success.

A house is built by hands, but a home is built by hearts.

✦Honesty

Complete honesty in little things is not a little thing at all.

If honesty isn't kind, it's the wrong kind.

There are no degrees of honesty; either you are honest or you are not.

Some people are honest only because they never had a good chance to steal anything.

An honest heart prepares one for a clear vision.

The employee who will steal *for* his boss will steal *from* his boss.

Common honesty should be more than common.

Every time dishonesty wins, it gets harder to convince our kids that honesty is the best policy.

There is no substitute for basic honesty and integrity in one's life.

A great handicap for some golfers is honesty.

Funny that some men should take up a life of crime when there are so many legal ways to be dishonest.

Parents who are untrue to their children will be dishonest to adults.

Some men are known by their deeds; others are known by their dishonesty.

Only those on the level can climb the highest peaks.

The badge of honesty is simplicity.

◆Hope

When you reach for the stars, you never get a handful of mud.

A gardener is someone who believes that what goes down must come up.

The greatest enemy of man is not disease—it's despair.

◆Humility (*see also* Modesty; Pride)

Burying your talents is a grave mistake.

Humble pie may taste awful, but it contains much nourishment.

Whatever you dislike in another person be sure to correct in yourself.

A worm is the only thing that can't stumble.

Freedom starts by kneeling at the cross.

Knowing God makes us humble; knowing ourselves keeps us humble.

Take your honors and rewards lightly.

Before God exalts a person, he humbles him.

To reach the mountain of fame, one must go through the valley of humility.

Those who would build high must remain low.

The branches that bear the most fruit hang the lowest.

The closer people get to God, the lower they will be in their own esteem.

God expects the whole heart, but he will accept a broken one.

A good violinist is able to play first violin and willing to play second fiddle.

No person will learn anything without first learning humility.

God uses Christians who stay cool in hot places, sweet in sour places, and little in big places.

Every time I feel how humble I am, I feel proud.

True humility is not looking down on yourself but looking up to Christ.

He who stands high in his own estimation is still a long way from the top.

False humility is true pride.

Other things may be the worse for breaking, yet a heart is never at its best till it be broken.

The bigger the man, the less he is aware of his size.

An inferiority complex could be a blessing if the right ones had it.

Humility is a strange thing—when you think you've gained it, you've lost it.

It is strange, but a big head is a sign of a small man.

If you cannot come to God *with* a broken heart, then come to him *for* a broken heart.

If you're a nobody, you don't have to worry about making a comeback.

If you are too big to be willing to do little things, you are probably too little to be trusted with big things.

A humble man never blows his "knows" in public.

A humble talent that is used is worth more than one of a genius that is idle.

Humility is that precious quality that makes us feel smaller as we grow greater.

Some people display a lot of talent when it comes to acting like a fool.

There is an *I* in every accident and a *U* in every excuse.

The smaller we are, the more room God has for us.

They who govern the most make the least noise.

The most difficult test of the human heart is to hear of a rival's failure without a feeling of triumph.

The man who humbly bows before God will walk upright before man.

Some Christians pray to be humble, then tell everyone how humble they have become.

Stay humble or stumble.

Faith gets most; love works most; but humility keeps most.

No man is so tall that he never needs to stretch nor so small that he never needs to stoop.

The more a man knows about himself, the less he speaks of it.

Humility is the acceptance of the place appointed by God, whether it be in the front or rear.

The bigger the man's head, the easier it is to fill his shoes.

Some people are so humble that they will fight to prove it.

The bigger the head, the smaller the heart.

Flattery is never complimentary.

It is amazing how much can be accomplished when we quit worrying who gets the credit.

A mountain shames a molehill until both are humbled by stars.

The trouble with some people is they don't admit their faults. I would, if I had any.

To grow tall spiritually, a man must first learn to kneel.

God wants great men to be small enough to be used.

He who stoops to help someone stands tall before God.

The fellow who has the right to boast doesn't have to.

Don't brag—it's not the whistle that pulls the train.

There is a great difference between being humble and being downcast.

If we were half as concerned as we pretend, we could accomplish twice as much.

Better to be the least in the kingdom of God than the greatest outside.

When a person becomes as humble as sheep, he soon finds the world is full of wolves.

Praise of self is good provided it comes from another's mouth.

Meekness is power under control.

Too many people are humble and proud of it.

Some people can't bend to be human until misfortune has taken the starch out of them.

No good idea ever came from swelled heads.

The man who bows the lowest in the presence of God stands the straightest in the presence of sin.

Humility is always dignity.

Until you do the little things carefully, you will never do the big things carefully.

The world hasn't yet been inherited by the meek, but it is sure being supported by a lot of them.

Most of us will never do great things, but we can do small things in a great way.

If there is one thing we should let others find out for themselves, it's how great we are.

Big people are those who make us feel bigger when we are with them.

Walk tall—but remember how to stoop.

Most can stand adversity, but if you want to test most people, give them power.

Everyone you meet is your superior in something.

We should ask God for humility but never thank him that we've attained it.

Having to swallow your own medicine makes the spoon seem extra large.

The higher the ape climbs the more he shows his tail.

◆Hypocrisy

People trying to be affable often are laughable.

An atheist is an unbeliever who prefers to raise his children in a Christian community.

The man who knows just what he would do if he were there is the man who never seems to get there.

We flatter those we scarcely know; we please the fleeting guest; yet oft we deal a thoughtless blow to those we love the best.

The inconsistent Christian is one of the devil's best workers.

A fair skin can cover a crooked mind.

The world doesn't doubt Christianity as much as it does some Christians.

Don't curse the devil openly and serve him secretly.

Better to be one-sided than two-faced.

People will follow your footsteps quicker than your advice.

You cannot lift others to a level higher than the one on which you live.

I

◆Ignorance

Never argue with a fool—people might not notice the difference.

Is the world being run by smart imbeciles or dumb geniuses?

Nothing is more dangerous than a big idea in a small mind.

Silence is the best and surest way to hide ignorance.

If ignorance is bliss, then why aren't there more happy people?

Being proud of learning is the greatest ignorance.

The worst ignorance man can experience is ignorance of God.

Nothing pleases an ignorant man so much as a chance to hand out information.

Ignorance is not the problem—it's not knowing we are ignorant that causes difficulty.

The recipe for perpetual ignorance is to be satisfied with your opinions and content with your knowledge.

Being ignorant is not so much a shame as being unwilling to learn.

Ignorance is the devil's college.

Everyone is ignorant—only on different subjects.

It is true that ignorance of the law is no excuse, but it may be better than no alibi at all.

It is said that a professor is not smarter than other people—he just has his ignorance better organized.

An ignorant person is one who doesn't know something you learned yesterday.

Always remember a man is not rewarded for having brains but for using them.

Discussion is an exchange of knowledge; argument is an exchange of ignorance.

◆Indifference *(see also* Laziness*)*

Moderate: a fellow who makes enemies left and right.

The last nation before damnation is stagnation.

A vacation from God can be a grave affair.

Misdeeds and missed deeds are sins of commission and omission.

The way some people act nowadays they must think that hell has been air-conditioned.

The person who stands neutral usually stands for nothing.

Even if you are on the right track, you will get run over if you just sit there.

There are many living who seem dead—there are many dead who continue to live.

The tragedy of man is that he dies inside while he is still alive.

No one cares who is pulling the cart until the horse is dead.

Love will find a way—indifference will find an excuse.

Some people take a stand for Christ and never move again.

Looking at the way some people live, they ought to obtain eternal fire insurance soon.

Our most recent poll showed that 90 percent of the people are not interested in the opinions of others.

Knowing without doing is like plowing without sowing.

Too many people follow the path of least assistance.

Some people think the opposite of love is hate, but it really is indifference.

The only person worse than a quitter is the person who didn't try.

After all is said and done, more is said than done.

While we deliberate on how to begin a thing, it grows too late to begin it.

Beware of the musty, dusty, and crusty Christian.

Easy street is a blind alley.

Some people spend a whole lifetime developing one part of their body—their wishbone.

Nothing is as tiresome as doing nothing.

Some ask what this nation stands for and the answer is easy—not much.

A man too busy to take care of his health is like a mechanic too busy to take care of his own tools.

You cannot expect to feel God's presence if you are too busy.

Hardening of men's hearts ages them quicker than hardening of the arteries.

So many people are so afraid of being taken in that they are always left out.

The toughest kind of climbing is getting out of a rut.

Definition of average—lowest of the best and the best of the lowest.

One who has light views of the Son will never have great thoughts of God.

The road to ruin is always in good repair.

We cannot avoid growing old, but we can avoid growing cold.

God's greatest problem with laborers in his vineyard is absenteeism.

We speak of the *average American* but maybe what's wrong with our nation is that we have too many who are average.

People seldom lose their religion by a blowout; it's usually a slow leak.

Too many Christians have the truth on ice instead of on fire.

By the time most people have made up their minds, opportunity has passed them.

The man who does as he pleases is seldom pleased with what he does.

No one is as busy as the man who has nothing to do.

Half of the people are trying to get something for nothing—the other half are trying to give nothing for something.

It is not possible for a person to be what he ought to be until he does what he ought to be doing.

When you are coasting, you are either losing speed or going downhill.

When a man doesn't care what people think of him, he has reached either the top or the bottom.

We cannot really be *for* something we don't understand.

People who wait until they feel like doing a job rarely do.

A little planning is a fine thing; too much planning may be an excuse for not getting anything done.

The road to failure is greased with the slime of indifference.

A wrongdoer is often one who has left something undone, not always one who has done something wrong.

It is the greatest of all mistakes to do nothing because you can do only a little.

People who never do any more than they are paid for never get paid for any more than they do.

To know what is right and not to do it is just as bad as actively doing wrong.

As long as you tolerate even the slightest sin and inconsistency in your life, the devil has a toehold.

The less one has to do, the less time one finds to do it.

The devil is never too busy to rock the cradle of a sleeping saint.

God is never satisfied with people who are satisfied with themselves.

Laziness travels so slowly that poverty soon overtakes it.

A lot of people have the right aim in life; they just fail to pull the trigger.

Some people are flexible—they can put either foot in their mouth.

The seven last words of the church: "We never did it that way before."

Dollars are not put in the bank by depositing your rear quarters in an easy chair.

The biggest cemetery in the country is where unused talents are buried.

They too are evil who see an evil act and do nothing.

Some people lose their liberty by taking too many liberties.

There are many "lily Christians." They toil not, neither do they spin.

Our faith and friendship are not shattered by one big act, but by many small neglects.

There are too many semi-Christians.

It is neglect of timely repair that makes rebuilding necessary.

Waiting for a brain wave is the surest way of missing the tide.

We invite defeat when we remember what we should forget.

The more you leave to chance, the less chance you have for success.

You put a great deal of pressure on your dignity when you stand on it.

Ask the fisherman—loose floaters soon drift away.

It doesn't do much good to put your best foot forward if you are dragging the other one.

Be careful of apathy—like pessimism, it's catching.

The greatest of all evils is indifference toward evil.

Getting rid of the rust is a spiritual must.

The most dangerous day in any man's life is the day he decides he knows enough.

What people call their fate is often the result of their own foolishness.

The man who fiddles around seldom gets to lead the orchestra.

◆Ironies of Life

If you build a large business, you're a sinister influence; if you don't, you're a failure.

We blame bad luck on others but take credit for good luck for ourselves.

Luck is what enabled others to get where they are—talent is what enabled us to get where we are.

If God had really intended men to fly he'd make it easier to get to the airport.

The "metallic age"—gold in your teeth, silver in your hair, and lead in your pants.

A desk is a wastebasket with drawers.

Both sugar and vinegar are preservatives, so it seems to boil down to whether you want to be pickled or in a jam.

Rapp's Law of Inanimate Reproduction: If you take something apart and put it back together enough times, eventually you will have two of them.

If the milk business ever becomes a public utility, we suppose that will make a cow a holding company.

It's a sin to play golf on Sunday, the way some play it.

A dentist is a person who puts two instruments and a hand in your mouth and then asks you a question.

The only way to stay awake during the after-dinner speech is to make it.

Campers usually end up with tents nerves.

It's true, people who snore always seem to fall asleep first.

The straight and narrow path would not be so narrow if more people would walk it.

Most of the time the shortest distance between two points is under construction.

A repairman is one who can smile when everything goes wrong.

A perfectionist is one who takes great pains—and gives them to other people.

The slow thinker lives longest—but not if he tries to cross the street.

Jelly is a food usually found on bread, children, and piano keys.

If people should visit the moon, they wouldn't have an earthly thing to do.

Now that man has reached the moon, maybe we can make another try getting the pigeons down from our public buildings.

Pollution is getting so bad, magicians complain there's no more thin air to make people disappear into.

Picnics are occasions on which people have their outings and insects their innings.

The early fish gets hooked for the same thing the early bird gets credit for.

The last accurate weather report was when God told Noah it was going to rain.

Whoever said swimming is good for the figure should take a good look at the whale.

Why do shipments go by car and cargo by ship?

Weather forecasters are becoming more accurate, but they are still several hours behind arthritis.

A celebrity is someone who works hard to become well known and then wears dark glasses to avoid being recognized.

A flea circus may be a good act, but it takes termites to bring down the house.

If you are all sugar, the world will eat you. If you are all vinegar, the world will spit you out.

Our nation's foreign relations at times become very poor relations.

A foot is a device for finding furniture in the dark.

It's a short road to some people's wit's end.

A minor operation is one performed on someone else.

Nothing wrong ever happens at the right time.

The only exercise some people get is jumping to conclusions, sidestepping responsibility, and pushing their luck.

Our days are like identical suitcases—all the same size, but some people pack more in them than others.

Many a live wire would be dead if it weren't for his connections.

An atheist is a man who has no visible means of support.

Everybody is a little neurotic these days; you can't be normal if you aren't.

War does not, and cannot, prove which side is right; only which side is stronger.

An argument is the longest distance between two points of view.

To make a long story short, there's nothing like having the boss walk in.

Human nature is such that the distant wars, earthquakes, and other calamities seem less catastrophic than the first scratch on your new car.

One sure way of becoming a prophet is to keep on saying things are going to get bad.

Everyone can do something better than anyone else—reading his own handwriting, for instance.

Suspenders are just about the oldest form of social security.

Statistics can be used to support anything—especially statisticians.

No two people are alike, and both are glad of it.

Why can't we realize that independence is one of our benefits?

If your life seems flat, accent it with the salt of God's grace.

A sign over a welding shop: We mend everything except a broken heart and the break of day.

J

✦Jealousy

Envy shoots at others and wounds herself.

If you want to travel light, take off all jealousies, selfishness, and fears.

✦Jesus

Being ready for Christ's return shows we are either disinterested or delighted.

If Christ is the Way, we waste time traveling any other.

Try Jesus before you reject him.

Christ has replaced the dark door of death with the shining gate of life.

Jesus is God spelling himself out in language that man can understand.

The birth of Christ brought God to man, but it took the cross of Christ to bring man to God.

Jesus can change the foulest sinner into the finest saint.

Jesus: not a law-giver, a life-giver.

To face Christ as judge is to know him as a friend.

We may love Jesus too little, but we can never love him too much.

The humble Carpenter of Nazareth was also the mighty Architect of the Universe.

No day is dark when the Son is present.

Christ was born here below that we might be born from above.

The Son of God became the Son of Man that he might change the sons of men into sons of God.

If the world doesn't hate you, you are not like Jesus.

The Bread of Life never becomes stale.

The Light of the World knows no power failures.

Christ's incarnation brought the infinite God within reach of finite men.

God's communication to man has come through the Christ of the cross.

In the bank of righteousness, the sinner has no account; his only hope is Christ's account.

When Christ is the center of your focus, all else will come into proper perspective.

Jesus invested his life in you; have you shown any interest?

The Bread of Life needs no butter.

It's tragic to know Psalm 23 but not know the Shepherd.

When you meet a person who has all things, why not introduce him to Jesus?

Jesus began and ended his ministry the same way—alone.

We may travel the sea of life without Christ; but what about the landing?

Man's best friend, Jesus, has conquered man's worst enemy, death.

Jesus Christ forgave voluntarily; he died vicariously; he arose visibly; and he lives victoriously.

We are never alone when we are alone with Jesus.

K

✦Kindness

A good rule for going through life is to keep the heart a little softer than the head.

A lot of people mean well, but their meanness is greater than their wellness.

Compassion offers whatever is necessary to heal the hurts of others.

The closer Christians get to Christ, the closer they get to one another.

The way we treat our neighbor is the way we treat God.

Train your heart to give sympathy and your hand to give help.

Cultivating kindness is a most important part of your life.

Never waste a minute thinking about your enemies; pray for them.

Compassion invests whatever is necessary to heal the hurts of others.

Gentle words fall lightly, but they have great weight.

One of the strongest of all virtues is kindness.

There is no law against being polite; even when you aren't the candidate for some office.

When you are good to others, you are best to yourself.

A man cannot touch his neighbor's heart with anything less than his own.

A beautiful heart seems to transform the homeliest face.

Charity gives itself rich; covetousness hoards itself poor.

Kindness is like snow—it beautifies everything it covers.

Count that day lost in which you have not tried to do something for someone else.

Kindness has converted more sinners than either zeal, eloquence, or learning.

Remember the kindness of others; forget your own.

Nothing is as strong as gentleness; nothing is as gentle as real strength.

Keep your head up, but be careful to keep your nose on a friendly level.

Don't expect to enjoy life if you keep your milk of human kindness bottled up.

A little oil of courtesy will save a lot of friction.

Politeness is good nature regulated by good sense.

We cannot heal the wound we do not feel.

To handle yourself, use your head; to handle others, use your heart.

Courtesy is the quality of heart that overlooks the broken garden gate and calls attention to the flowers beyond the gate.

Do unto others as if you were others.

If you lovingly remember others, they will never forget you.

Real charity doesn't care if it's tax deductible or not.

Kindness is the language the deaf can hear and the blind can see.

Men are great only when they are kind.

A broken heart can be mended into a more beautiful pattern if the stitches are made with kindness and love.

The sunshine of love will soften the hardest sinner's heart.

Kindness is the insignia of a loving heart.

No one is too big to be kind and courteous, but many people are too little.

The milk of human kindness furnishes the cream of society.

It's nice to be important—but it's more important to be nice.

Never be afraid to be gracious. Look what a little polish can do for scuffed shoes.

Pity sees man's problems; compassion helps man with his problems.

There is no sympathy so deep and strong as that which springs out of common suffering.

Sympathy is two hearts tugging at one load.

Kindness pays most when you don't do it for pay.

Funny thing about kindness: the more it's used the more you have of it.

He who is supremely strong can afford to be supremely gentle.

Always try to be a little kinder than necessary.

A great man shows his greatness by the way he treats little men.

A kind word can cool a hot head.

Kind words never wear out the tongue.

True charity is the desire to be useful to others without the thought of recompense.

Speak kindly today; when tomorrow comes you will be in better practice.

Men with clenched fists cannot shake hands.

A good heart does no ill; a better heart thinks none.

Goodness is greatest, even though you may never be heard of outside your backyard.

They say courtesy is contagious. If so, we need to start an epidemic.

Be kind today because there may be no tomorrow.

If all people would speak as kindly of the living as they do of the dead, all gossip would cease.

Kindness is the oil that takes the friction out of life.

One of the greatest victories you can gain over a man is to beat him at politeness.

A kind deed often does more than a large gift.

You will never get ahead of the person you are seeking to get even with.

The only people you should get even with are those who have helped you.

Nothing costs so little and goes so far as Christian courtesy.

Leave your grouch outside.

The right temperature at home is maintained by warm hearts, not hot heads.

Sympathy—your pain in my heart.

You will be happier if you give a piece of your heart instead of a piece of your mind to those who oppose you.

Always measure people's character around the heart.

To speak kindly does not hurt the tongue.

If you are too busy to be kind, you are too busy.

Every moment is the right one to be kind.

Wherever there is a human being, there is an opportunity for kindness.

You can't antagonize and persuade at the same time.

Think of what others ought to be like, then start being that yourself.

Goodwill is achieved by many actions; it can be lost by one.

Always try to be a little kinder than necessary.

Kind words are short to speak, but their echoes are endless.

Hospitality is the art of making people want to stay without interfering with their departure.

Real love is helping someone who can never return the favor.

Kind words are music to a broken heart.

No one ever invented a good substitute for a good nature.

Generous gestures yield the most when that isn't their purpose.

Sowing kindness is life's best investment.

People who are unkind are the wrong kind.

Courtesy makes everyone feel good.

If you don't want to be forgotten, write your name in kindness, love, and mercy on the hearts of others.

Grace is everything for nothing for those who don't deserve anything.

We are not made rich by what is in our pockets but by what is in our hearts.

He who pities others remembers himself.

The best way to remember people is in prayer.

How beautiful a day can be when kindness touches it.

Smooth words create an atmosphere of gentleness that heals roughness and bitterness.

Tears shed for self are tears of weakness, but tears shed for others are a sign of strength.

Kindness is the golden chain by which society is bound together.

Blunt people can get to the point quickly.

A kind word picks up a man when trouble weighs him down.

You cannot do a kindness too soon because you never know how soon it will be too late.

He who wishes to secure the good of others has already secured his own.

Learn to say kind things; no one resents them.

A kind word is never lost; it keeps going from person to person until it returns unto you.

Kindness may go a long way lots of times when it should stay right at home.

L

◆Laziness (*see also* Indifference; Work)

If you have been going in circles, perhaps you have been cutting corners.

Nothing cures insomnia more than the realization that it is time to get up.

The turnover is highly important, whether it's business or when the alarm clock goes off in the morning.

By the time you reach your station in life, the train has left.

The American people spend more for chewing gum than for books—it's easier to chew than to read.

Fill a place—not just space.

A humble talent that is used is worth more than one of a genius that is idle.

Some people will spend half an hour sharpening a knife just so they can whittle a stick.

Some people who boast about how broad-minded they are may just be too lazy to find out which side they're on.

A hen is the only thing that can lay around and produce.

If you insist on standing still, stand aside; others may be going somewhere.

Sleeping saints serve Satan.

Many people are on the gospel train, but too many are in the sleeper.

Rip Van Winkle is the only man to become famous while he slept.

The hardest work one can do is to do nothing.

Easy is the enemy of ambition.

Laziness is a quality that prevents people from getting tired.

A lot of people who complain about being up to their ears in work are just lying down on the job.

There are no idle rich. They're all busy dodging people who want some of it.

The person who thinks the world owes him a living may be too lazy to work for it.

Too many people not only think the world owes them a living, but expect the government to collect it for them.

The reason there is much room at the top is the crowd at the bottom is waiting for the elevator to take them up.

Indifference and laziness are the devil's chief tools against Christians.

A lazy person tempts the devil to tempt him.

When an idler sees a completed job, he is sure he could have done it better.

The world is full of people making a good living but not good lives.

The most serious idleness of all is being busy with things that do not matter.

The Christian cannot afford the luxury of loafing.

Luck is a lazy man's estimate of a worker's success.

Most all sins come from laziness.

You cannot leave footprints in the sands of time while sitting down.

We may be on the right track, but if we just sit there, we may get run over.

Sloth, like rust, consumes faster than labor wears.

To do nothing is tiresome because you cannot stop and take a rest.

God calls men when they are busy; Satan when they are idle.

Bread is the staff of life, but there is no reason why our life should be a continual loaf.

One of the saddest sights in life is the man who can only do nothing when he finds himself with nothing to do.

People seldom want to walk over you until you lie down.

God promises no loaves to the loafer.

The lazy person speaks much about yesterday and tomorrow.

Some people are like blisters—they never show up until the work is done.

The most serious idleness of all is being busy with things that do not matter.

Nothing conceals your laurels so much as resting upon them.

The road to success is marked with many tempting parking places.

It takes an honest man to tell whether he's tired or just lazy.

To many people, the ideal occupation is the one that doesn't keep them occupied.

Some things must be put off many, many times before they finally slip our minds.

The lazy man does not know what it is to enjoy rest.

One thing for sure—you'll never stumble on anything while sitting down.

◆Leadership

Authority does not make you a leader; it gives you the opportunity to be one.

Leadership depends on the ability to make people want to follow voluntarily.

Concentrating attention on one thing at a time is still the best way to get things done.

A good leader not only knows where he is going, but he can persuade other people to go along with him.

Learn self-control before attempting to control others.

Good supervision is the art of getting average people to do superior work.

You cannot lead anyone farther than you have gone yourself.

The problem of being a leader is to tell if the people are following or chasing you.

A conference room is a place where everybody talks, nobody listens, and everyone disagrees afterwards.

A good boss is a guy who takes a little more than his share of the blame and a little less than his share of the credit.

One is not qualified to give orders until he is capable of receiving orders.

Master concentration and you can master anything.

Action is the only true test of ability.

Be your own efficiency expert by doing your job the best way it can be done.

Good leaders never set themselves above their followers—except in carrying out responsibilities.

An executive is one who hires others to do what he is hired to do.

The difference between promised ideas and productive results is a good manager.

A good leader inspires others with confidence in him—a great leader inspires them with confidence in themselves.

A boss is a person who is always early when you're late and late when you are early.

People have a way of becoming what you encourage them to be—not what you nag them to be.

The best investment you can make as a leader is hard work.

You cannot teach something you don't know. After all, you cannot come back from where you haven't been.

Note to the bosses: A pleasant word will get more results than extra pay.

Authority can never take the place of leadership.

Effective teachers find a way; others find excuses.

It is easier to follow the leader than to lead the followers.

You have won others when you cause them to share the goals, problems, and rewards.

Make people feel they are working with you—not for you—and you will get far more out of them.

Two kinds of men who never succeed: one cannot do what he is told; the other cannot do anything unless he is told.

Be an individualist—one who follows another is always behind.

Sunday school teachers, to be prepared, must be pre-prayered.

A leader is not someone who leads unless he has followed.

◆Life

Life is a series of accomplishments and failures that begin with learning to walk.

If you want life's best, see to it that life gets your best.

The most rewarding end of life is to know the life that never ends.

Life is like a mirror—if we frown at it, it frowns back at us; if we smile, it returns the greeting.

The greatest use of life is to spend it for something that outlasts it.

More important than the length of life is how we spend each day.

Your life will have been misspent if you get to the end of the road without Christ.

Life is a canvas—you fill in the picture.

Life is like a garment constantly being altered but never fitting perfectly.

About the time you learn to make the most of life, the most of it is gone.

Life is either what you make of it, or what it makes of you.

We live on momentum—if you stop you are finished.

Live today as you will wish you had lived when you stand before God.

Could life be an emergency sandwiched in between time and eternity?

In the great supermarket of life, may the wheels on your grocery cart all move in the same direction.

You can't run your life on empty.

Life takes on new interest when we invest in the lives of others.

The real tragedy of life is not in being limited to one talent, but in the failure to use the one talent.

Half of our troubles are due to the fact that we live on the assumption that this is the only life and only world.

Life is hard by the yard—by the inch it's a cinch.

Life may be short, but it gives most people time to outlive their good intentions.

Life is like a mirror—we get the best results when we smile at it.

Life makes some people better and others bitter.

Life is what happens while you're making other plans.

A long life might not be a good life, but a good life is a long life regardless of the number of years.

Life is like a game of tennis; the one who serves seldom loses.

Life is not measured by accumulations but by outlay.

Life is like a well—the deeper you go in God, the more living you will find.

Life becomes more difficult to hold together with the credibility gap, the generation gap, and the billfold gap.

Life is tragic for the person who has plenty to live on, but nothing to live for.

The abundant life is often smothered by the abundant things of this life.

Life is full of endings, but every ending is a new beginning.

Life can only be understood by looking backward, but it must be lived by looking forward.

What part does God play in your life—spare tire or the steering wheel?

The more sand that has escaped from the hourglass of our life, the clearer we should see through it.

A life given to God is a life well spent; a life not given to God is a life wasted.

One way to live longer is to cut out all the things that make you want to live longer.

To some, life is a breeze and for others it's just one head wind after the other.

Many a man lives a rich full life because he knows how to turn his failures into assets.

Life is like a camel—it never backs up.

Life, however short, is made still shorter by a waste of time.

The world is just a bridge; pass over—don't fear what lies beyond.

Life is like a cafeteria—there are no waiters to bring success to you. You must help yourself.

A person who leads a double life often goes through it in half the time.

The great use of life is to spend it for something that outlasts it.

The business of living is not to get ahead of others but to get ahead of ourselves.

Your life is like a coin: you can spend it any way you wish, but you can spend it only once.

Since life is short, we ought to make the experience as varied and broad as we possibly can.

Life is filled with shadows, but it is sunshine that makes them all.

Life is like a bank—you get out what you put into it with interest.

Don't worry what you could do if you lived your life over; get busy with what's left.

Our lives are never more secure than when they are abandoned to God.

Don't be satisfied with a saved soul and a wasted life.

If you are not doing something with your life, it really doesn't matter how long it is.

Life is very interesting if you make mistakes.

Your outlook on life will be brighter from behind a smile.

Your life is God's gift to you; what you do with it is your gift to God.

To have an upright life, lean on Jesus.

Use your life carefully—there are no reruns.

Life is too short as it is to waste time uselessly.

The best physicians are: Dr. Diet, Dr. Quiet, and Dr. Merryman.

Life is either a daring adventure or it is nothing.

This is prime time! Life is in session *now*. And there will be no rerun.

Life is not the candle or the wick—it's the burning.

Life, for most of us, is getting used to the things we hadn't expected.

Among the hard things about the business of life is minding your own.

The most important things in life are not things.

✦Listening

You can win more friends with your ears than with your mouth.

Some people are broadcasting when they should be listening.

Be a good listener, but be careful who you listen to.

A good listener is not only popular, but after a while he knows a few things.

If you think twice before you speak, you may never get into the conversation.

It takes great listening as well as great preaching to make a good sermon.

A great deal of what we see depends upon what we are listening to.

The first step to wisdom is silence—the second is listening.

Lend a man your ears and you will immediately open a pathway to his heart.

God speaks to those who have time to listen.

There needs to be more fear that we will not hear the Lord than that he will not hear us.

When people seek counseling, they don't really want advice as much as for you to listen.

✦Loneliness

Loneliness is being unaware of the One who is with us everywhere.

Many Christians suffer from loneliness because they are sitting instead of serving.

A friend is one who helps you bridge the gaps between loneliness and fellowship, frustration and confidence, despair and hope, setbacks and success.

Loneliness and solitude are quite different. One is defeat—the other victory.

Loneliness is sensing the spirit of the one you love pulling away from you.

Some people are lonely because they build walls and not bridges.

◆Love

No one knows the age of the human race, but it is surely old enough to know how to love better.

Love is woman's eternal spring and man's eternal fall.

To some people, love is only the last word in a telegram.

Love is like a fabric that never fades when washed in the water of adversity and grief.

Love does not keep a ledger of the sins and failures of others.

Love is not based on a person's intelligence or state in life but rather on the size of the heart.

True love is willing to help people even if it hurts them.

True love is what you've been through with somebody.

Love is made visible by work.

Some people have enough religion to make them hate but not enough to make them love.

Love is giving someone your undivided attention.

Love is the fountain from which all goodness flows.

He who truly loves the Lord will love his brother.

Love will endure when you keep it pure.

God loves his children, not because of who they are, but because of who he is.

Love may be blind, but it certainly finds its way around.

Real love is helping someone for Jesus' sake who can never return the favor.

The measure of our love is the measure of our sacrifice.

The biggest drawback to budding love is that it leads to blooming expense.

Love is more than a sentimental feeling—it's putting another's welfare ahead of your own.

Compassion is the capacity to put love into action.

Love is asked to forgive what courtesy would have avoided.

Not to hate a neighbor is good, but to love him is better.

A bit of love is the only bit that will bridle the tongue.

It is impossible for two persons to hate each other and both of them to love God.

God measures how much we love him by how much we love others.

Charity is the virtue of the heart—not of the hands.

Respect is what we owe; love is what we give.

The measure of love is what one is willing to give up for it.

Duty makes us do things well, but love makes us do them beautifully.

The power of loving is strongest in those who suffered most.

Faults are thick where love is thin.

When you are out of love, you are out of Jesus.

No person really lives until he learns to love.

Some folks we click with. Some folks we cross with. Love is manifested when we love those we cross with.

Love is the only service that power can't command or money buy.

Love never asks, "What can I get?" It asks, "What can I give?"

The only way to understand your enemies is to love them.

Those who deserve love least need it most.

Love that doesn't understand the language of sacrifice is not love.

The mystery of love is that the more you give, the more remains in your heart.

No gift is a substitute for yourself.

A good diamond will cut into anything, especially a man's bank account.

After all, you've got to say something for a religion that produces a man that loves.

Many things can give me gifts of wisdom, but only love can make me wise.

Time heals grief; and love prevents scar tissue.

The ultimate miracle of love is this—that love is given to us to give to one another.

Christian love goes the second mile, the third, and the fourth if necessary.

When God measures a man, he puts the tape around the heart—not the head.

A love that will not bear all, care for all, share all, is not love at all.

It is grievous to be poor in purse, but poor in love is greatly worse.

Love looks through a telescope—envy looks through a microscope.

Love at first sight is often cured by a second look.

People don't care how much we know until they know how much we care.

Love quickens all senses except, perhaps, common sense.

Love is what makes two people sit in the middle of a bench when there's plenty of room at both ends.

Tears flow freely from the fountain of a love-filled heart.

Love born at Calvary bears and forbears, gives and forgives.

Love is a fabric that never fades, no matter how often it is washed in the water of adversity and grief.

Where love reigns, God reigns.

Humans are made to run on love, and they do not function well on anything else.

Love does not consist of gazing at each other. but of looking together in the same direction.

Love is an ocean of emotion surrounded by expanses of expenses.

◆Lying

Those who cook up stories usually find themselves in hot water.

A white lie soon gets tanned from exposure.

Some people stretch the truth; others mutilate it.

A lie is like a banana peel thrown on a sidewalk—you later slip up on it.

A good memory is needed once you have lied.

It isn't right to lie even about the devil.

No one has enough money to be a successful liar.

A whispered lie is just as bad as one published.

A lie may take care of the present, but it has no future.

The trouble with telling little white lies is that they pick up so much dirt while traveling.

Those who think it is permissible to tell white lies soon grow color blind.

Little white lies always lead to a case of the blues.

An excuse is a skin of reason stretched over a lie.

Sin has many tools, but a lie is a handle that fits them all.

People who do a lot of kneeling do not do much lying.

Never chase a lie; if you let it alone, it will run itself to death.

"They say" is often proved to be a great liar.

Sometimes how well you sleep depends on how little you lie.

M

✦Manners

That person has good manners who can put up with someone who has bad manners.

One of the greatest victories you can gain over a man is to beat him at politeness.

✦Marriage (see also Family)

Why do brides buy their wedding gowns and grooms rent their wedding suits?

A happy wife sometimes has the best husband but more often makes the best of the husband she has.

God is the only third party in marriage that can make it work.

Many women don't care if a man has money as long as his credit is good.

Marriage is an expensive way for a girl to get free rent.

Marriage would work out better if the couple operated on a thrifty-thrifty basis.

Some women spend more time in selecting their wedding gown than they do in selecting a husband.

There's one word for a man who marries a rich woman—*smart*.

Some marry for beauty—others for booty.

Honeymoons are apt to set like the other moon.

Choose a wife rather by your ear than by your eye.

It is a sorry house where the hen crows and the cock is silent.

Some say singleness is bliss and marriage is a blister.

The sea of matrimony is filled with hardships.

It takes two to make a marriage—a single girl and an anxious mother.

Never be yoked to one who refuses to be yoked to Christ.

Plenty of music will keep the husband home, provided it isn't chin music.

Some husbands lay down the law and then accept their wife's amendments.

Some men are born meek; the others get married.

When a girl marries a man to mend his ways, she is apt to find that he isn't worth a darn.

Love at first sight never happens before breakfast.

Marriage can be the bloom or blight of happiness.

Keep your eyes wide open before marriage and half shut afterward.

Never speak loudly to each other unless the house is on fire.

A good marriage is like a casserole—only those responsible for it really know what goes into it.

A guaranteed way to keep your wife happy—let her think she's having her own way, then let her have it.

Nothing makes a marriage rust like distrust.

If you think it's possible to love your wife too much, you probably haven't loved her enough.

Love is blind—marriage is the eye-opener.

A well-informed man is one whose wife has just told him what she thinks of him.

In the area of love, an engagement is an urge on the verge to merge.

Many a flare-up between a man and his wife has been caused by an old flame.

When a wife runs her fingers through her husband's hair, he should be careful—she may be after his scalp.

Marriage is either a holy wedlock or an unholy deadlock.

There would be fewer divorces if the husband tried as hard to keep his wife as he did to get her.

Success in marriage is more than finding the right person; it is the matter of being the right person.

Some women work so hard to make good husbands that they never manage to make good wives.

Don't go around with someone else's wife unless you plan to go several rounds with her husband.

Man to marriage counselor: "She went from hard-to-get to hard-to-handle to hard-to-take."

Courtship is that time during which the female decides whether or not she can do any better.

Henpecked husbands soon learn that he who hesitates is bossed.

The test of a marriage comes after the billing and cooing—when there are too many bills and not enough coos.

The marriage broke up because of illness in the family—they got sick of each other.

Of all remedies, a good wife is the best.

A groom is one who has underestimated the power of a woman.

A happy marriage is the union of two forgivers.

In the word *wedding,* the *we* comes before the *I.*

She's two-thirds married—she's willing and so is her mother.

A honeymoon is a thrill of a wife's time.

Single people die earlier; marriage is a slow death.

Before criticizing your wife's faults, remember that they may have prevented her from getting a better husband.

I always have the last word with my wife, even if I have to go into another room to say it.

The wife who nags much may have a husband who horses around.

Some men marry poor girls to settle down; others marry rich ones to settle up.

If you do housework for fifty dollars a week, that's domestic service—if you do it for nothing, that's matrimony.

Some husbands are real comforters while others are just wet blankets.

Courtship makes a man spoon, but it's matrimony that makes him fork over.

Marriage is like two people riding a horse—one must ride behind.

A wedding ring is the smallest handcuff in the world.

A bridegroom is a guy who has lost his liberty in the pursuit of happiness.

A woman likes a strong, silent man because she thinks he is listening.

Every man needs a wife because there are some things that go wrong he can't blame on the government.

The attorney's young bride bought a sewing machine. She thought she might help her husband to make loopholes.

A husband is a man who expects his wife to be perfect and to understand why he isn't.

The wife who henpecks her husband is likely to find him listening to some other chick.

Divorce is the hash made from domestic scraps.

Because many couples "harp at each other," does this mean their marriage was made in heaven?

Why do parents cry at their daughter's wedding? The expense.

If you marry a child of the devil, you will have trouble with your father-in-law.

The honeymoon is over when the groom looks into the paper instead of into the bride's eyes.

A marriage is a success when they live happily ever after.

Ambitious wife: The power behind the drone.

The ship of matrimony will move more smoothly if the wife stays away from the sails.

Marriage is like a violin. After the beautiful music is over, the strings are still attached.

Wedding: a ceremony at which a man loses complete control of himself.

A man needs a woman to take care of him so she can make him strong enough for her to lean on.

Behind every successful man stands a devoted wife and a surprised mother-in-law.

Sometimes you can't tell if a man is trying so hard to be a success to please his wife or to spite his mother-in-law.

When a man opens the door of his car for his wife, you can be sure that either the car or the wife is new.

Don't marry for money—you can borrow it cheaper.

Marriage is great—no family should be without it.

The trouble with marriage is that a fellow can't support a wife and the government on one income.

An optimist is a single man contemplating marriage; a pessimist is a married person contemplating it.

Sometimes absence makes the heart wander.

A young man prayed, "Lord give me a wife that loves Thee—for then I know she will love me."

Some women marry for money, then divorce for love.

When Adam's son asked why they didn't live in the Garden of Eden, he answered, "Your mother ate us out of house and home."

One thing about early marriages is they shorten the generation gap.

In some marriages most troubles are relative.

The sea of matrimony can become rough if the young lady is tied to the wrong buoy.

Most matrimonial problems are caused by the marriage of two people who are in love with themselves.

Marriages can be made in heaven, but man is responsible for the maintenance work.

Some girls are like baseball players—always trying to turn a single into a double.

Marriage is mutual partnership if both parties know when to be mute.

Marriages are made in heaven, but so are thunder and lightning.

A wise monkey will not monkey with another monkey's monkey.

A wise lover values not so much the gift of the lover as the love of the giver.

A good wife is God's smile from heaven.

Wedlock should be a padlock.

A successful marriage is the result of falling in love often—with the same person.

A good salesman is the fellow who can convince his wife she looks fat in a fur coat.

Husband and wife agreement—the wife stops driving from the backseat and the husband quits cooking from the dining table.

Love is the glue that cements friendships; jealousy keeps it from sticking.

Something every couple should save for their old age—their marriage.

Too many marry for better or for worse, but not for good.

Marriage is the most expensive way to get your laundry done.

Judging from some of the specimens they pick for husbands, no wonder brides blush.

Many husbands are second-story men—their wives seldom believe the first one.

Marriage is educational—there's no surer way of learning about your faults.

Advice to girls—never play ball with a man unless he furnishes the diamond.

Marriage is like an army—everybody complains, but look at the guys who reenlist.

When a man marries a woman, they become one—the trouble starts when they try to decide which one.

A wife knows how to keep a husband guessing—by saying something and saying nothing.

Husband to wife, "Stick to your washing, ironing, cooking, and scrubbing. No wife of mine is going to work."

It is an unhappy nation in which marriage certificates are issued like bus transfers.

A successful marriage is built on trust—and an occasional compliment.

A bachelor never quite gets over the idea that he is a thing of beauty and a boy forever.

Many of those who embark upon the sea of matrimony know little about navigation.

Marriages are like diets—they can be ruined by having a little dish on the side.

The thing that married men will never understand is why all bachelors aren't rich.

The bonds of matrimony are good investments only when the interest is kept up.

Men never realize how short a month is until they pay the alimony.

Many girls marry men just like their fathers; then people wonder why their mothers cry at the wedding.

A man should give his wife a hand around the house, but most wives are not satisfied with the applause.

Marriage is an investment that pays dividends, if you pay interest.

If more husbands would be self-starters, their wives wouldn't have to be cranks.

A happy marriage is when a couple is as deeply in love as they are in debt.

On anniversaries the wise husband will always forget the past—but not the present.

To have a successful marriage—whenever you are wrong, admit it; when you are right, keep your mouth shut.

My husband's retirement cured his ulcer but gave me one.

Troubles in marriage often start when a man is so busy earning his salt that he forgets his sugar.

If a man has enough horse sense to treat his wife like a thoroughbred, she'll never grow into an old nag.

A honeymoon is the vacation a man takes before going to work for a new boss.

It is a woman's business to get married as soon as possible and a man's to keep unmarried as long as he can.

A career girl is one who would rather bring home the bacon than fry it.

The marriage knot should be tied tight enough to prevent easy loosening but not tight enough to feel like a noose.

In the final analysis what a sensible woman looks for in a man is fiscal fitness.

No matter how lovesick you may be, don't take the first pill that comes along.

Strange, but it seems to be true: charm is a woman's strength, while strength is a man's charm.

They never knew what true happiness was until they were married—then it was too late.

The honeymoon is over when he takes her off a pedestal and puts her on a budget.

If you want to kill your wife with curiosity, simply clip a brief item before you hand her the day's newspaper.

All girls should learn how to fix household appliances. Most of them will probably get married.

They were married in a garage—she's (he's) been trying to back out ever since.

Every chap with money to burn will meet his match.

The world's greatest bargain—a happy marriage.

Having a maid today does not mean status—it means a full-time working wife.

Love is a game two can play and both can win.

The moon affects the tide—also the untied.

Many marriages crack up when the installment collector cracks down.

◆Maturity

A well-adjusted person is one who can play bridge or golf as if they were games.

There are no shortcuts on the way to spiritual maturity.

When a man has a pet peeve, it is remarkable how often he pets it.

When growth stops, decay begins.

Growth is more important than status; growth is fit for eternity, status built for time.

When trouble comes, a man's true quality is revealed.

The mature man wants to live and have a cause—the immature man wants to die for a cause.

Some people are consistent—they remain immature all their lives.

Adults should not only produce children in marriage but the children should produce adults.

Adulthood is learning to have not only the right to be right, but the right to be wrong.

Any fool can find fault, but it takes maturity to find good in all people.

You are only young once, but you can stay immature all your life.

If we're not perfect, let us at least be progressing.

Big people are those who make us feel bigger when we are with them.

The more we grow up the less we will blow up.

Don't be like the wheelbarrow—it has to be pushed all the time and is easily upset.

The longer you nurse a grudge, the longer it takes to get better.

Mature people take disappointments in stride.

The conversion of a soul is the miracle of a moment—the growth of a saint is the work of a lifetime.

Where you cannot invent, you can always improve.

Mature believers should use their strength to undergird, not to overpower.

He who guides himself has a fool for a follower.

The true Christian is one who is right-side up in an upside-down world.

The human race has improved everything except the human race.

Be willing to die for your convictions but not for your preferences.

If you're properly prepared, you won't easily be surprised.

A lot of people believe in law and order as long as they can lay down the law and give the orders.

In days of sunshine so live that in the days of rain you will still be happy.

Even if half of our wishes came true, then we would have twice as many troubles.

When you speak to others for their own good, it's advice—when they speak to you for your own good, it's interference.

People with much to do are rarely in trouble. It is the vacant, tumble-down minds that cause unhappiness to themselves and to others.

Many a person has convictions for which he wants someone else to supply the courage.

Watch a goat from the front, a horse from behind, and a man from every side.

Accepting good advice increases your ability.

If all the cars in America were lined up in a row, someone would pull out and try to pass them.

Courage is what it takes to stand up and speak. Courage is also what it takes to sit down and listen.

The moon could never do its work if it paid attention to all the dogs that barked at it.

It is never too late to mend because the older we become, the more repairs we need.

The longer you dwell on your misfortunes, the greater is their power to harm you.

Some adolescents are like salad—pretty green, full of vinegar, and all mixed up.

Most people don't know what they want, but it is something different than what they have.

The trouble with being a good sport is that you have to lose to prove it.

Can you take it? Hammering hardens steel but crumbles putty.

Energy spent in getting even is better spent getting ahead.

Many great ideas have been lost because the folks who had them couldn't stand to be laughed at.

It seems that heads, hearts, and hands would settle the world's differences much better than "arms."

It's funny how we never get too old to learn some new way to be stupid.

The most difficult test of the human heart is to hear of an enemy's success without becoming jealous.

There are some Christians with beards on their faces who are babies.

Don't depend on the rabbit's foot for good luck—it didn't bring him good luck.

Authority makes some people grow—others just sweat.

Think of what others ought to be like; then start being like that yourself.

We are moving forward at twice the speed of sound and half the speed of sense.

Only fools and dead men don't change their minds. Fools won't—dead men can't.

If men grew physically at the rate they grow spiritually, many of them would spend their lives in a playpen.

A good test of maturity is the amount of danger you feel when you meet up with a new idea.

✦Mediocrity

The man who says he is just as good as half the folks in the church seldom specifies which half.

Remember that "average" is simply the best of the poorest and the poorest of the best.

When you are just average, you are just as near the bottom as you are the top.

Beware of living casually instead of contagiously.

The middle class: People who are not poor enough to accept charity and not rich enough to donate anything.

♦Men

Anyone who believes that men are the equal of women has never seen a man try to wrap a Christmas present.

A wolf is a guy who whistles while he lurks.

A fox is a wolf who sends flowers.

Rest assured that God knows that the best of men are but men at their best.

The measure of a man: he is the size of the thing it takes to get his goat.

Behind every successful man in the world is a woman who couldn't be more surprised.

Behind every successful man is a proud wife and a surprised mother-in-law.

A love of heaven makes a man heavenly.

The seven ages of man: spills, drills, thrills, bills, ills, pills, and wills.

Big men became big by doing what they didn't want to when they didn't want to do it.

Men, not things, get into God's way.

You can depend upon fat men—they'll never stoop to anything low.

Satan covets a tired man and uses him; God rests a tired man and inspires him.

A bachelor is a rolling stone that gathers no boss.

Man is an able creature, but he has made over thirty-five thousand laws and hasn't yet improved on the Ten Commandments.

One machine can do the work of fifty ordinary men, but no machine can do the work of one extraordinary man.

You can always tell an informed man—his ideas are the same as yours.

Men are the only people on earth who think they have more sense than women.

Any man who cares for only one thing, whatever it is, is dangerous.

All gentlemen are men, but not all men are gentlemen.

It isn't fair—girl's best friend is a diamond—man's best friend is a dog.

To measure a man, note the height of his ideals, the depth of his convictions, the breadth of his sympathies, and the length of his sacrifices.

We do not need methods or more money; we need better men.

There is only one way to be a gentleman—there are hundreds of ways not to be.

Lipstick on the collar can be more dangerous than lipstick on the lip.

A good business man is a gambler without gambling instinct.

If a man wants his dreams to come true, he must wake up.

If a man takes his hat off in an elevator, it means he either has good manners or hair.

The difference between most men is little enough—but that little makes the difference.

The world steps aside for the man who knows where he is going.

Only those who have questions about their manhood must prove that they are men.

This country has turned out some great men, and there are quite a few others not so great that it ought to turn out.

In the good ole days a bad man would go around with notches in his gun handle instead of his fenders.

No man ever told a woman she talked too much when she was telling him how wonderful he is.

◆Missions (see also Witnessing)

Your love has a broken wing if it cannot fly across the sea.

You will never win the world to Christ with your spare cash.

If God calls you to the mission field, your prayers and money are poor substitutes.

If you fail to support missions, you are voting to bring missionaries home and to cease missionary work.

If the Bible is a missionary book, the people of the Book are charged with being a missionary people.

God's salvation takes into account the *lost*, the *last*, and the *least*.

A church without missions is a church without a mission.

There's one thing you cannot do about missions: get rid of your responsibility.

It costs less to send missionaries to foreign countries than it does to send soldiers—one goes to save, the other to destroy.

God is the head of the missionary movement—the devil heads the opposition.

A church that is not reaching out is passing out.

Evangelism, like charity, begins at home.

If it had not been for missions, where would you be today?

There is no *home* or *foreign* in God's vocabulary.

Would you believe in the necessity of missions if you traded places with the heathen?

Every Christian is a missionary—if only in the supermarket.

The best remedy for a sick church is to put it on a missionary diet.

The disciples of Christ did not proclaim the gospel because it was their duty—they did it because they could do nothing else.

A church that is not a missionary church will soon be a missing church.

The principal way to lay up treasure in the bank of heaven is through missionary interest.

A missionary is God's man, in God's place, doing God's work, in God's time, in God's way.

A church with *one* heart and *one* mind will make for a *won* world.

Every heart without Christ is a mission field—every heart with Christ is a missionary.

A missionary is a person who never gets used to the thud of Christless feet on their way to eternity.

Instead of the Shepherd looking for the one lost sheep, he must spend his time looking for the ninety-nine.

We would give more support for the missionaries if we traded places with them.

He who has a little heart for the lost will have a little heart for the Savior.

The return of the Lord Jesus should be the strongest incentive to soul winning, sacrificial giving, and missionary outreach.

God has only one Son and he was a missionary.

God's voice is always loud enough so that repentant sinners can hear the message of salvation.

Some people do not believe in missions because their religion is not worth sharing.

World service means the whole church at work around the world.

The cross is a symbol of God's heartbreak over a world that has gone astray.

The gospel is not something only to go to church to hear—but to go from church to tell.

The light that shines farthest for Christ away from home will shine the brightest at home.

Christ alone can save the world—but he cannot save the world alone; he needs your help.

◆Misunderstanding

So many mistake sex for love, money for brains, and a transistor radio for civilization.

Some people read enough to stay misinformed.

It is better to be despised for the right than to be praised for the wrong.

Just because you are slippery doesn't mean you are polished.

A reformer is someone who wants his conscience to be your guide.

A positive conviction without accurate information is dangerous.

Considering the fact that there are two sides to every question, it's amazing that so many people choose the wrong side.

A well-beaten path is not necessarily the right way.

To be great is often to be misunderstood.

◆Modesty (see also Humility; Pride)

Where modesty is absent virtue has no means of protection.

The closer we get to God, the more modest we shall become.

Modesty is the triumph of mind over flatter.

The modest person is one who doesn't blow all he knows.

The hardest secret for a man to keep is his opinion to himself.

Modesty is for those who have no talent.

◆Money (see also Generosity)

Sign in the store window: Use our easy credit plan—100 percent down, nothing to pay each month.

A fine cage won't feed the bird.

We live in a jet-age. Many want to change this to a get-age.

A thing is worth what it can do for you, not what you can pay for it.

God looks at the heart, not the hand—the giver, not the gift.

When you buy real estate, you soon learn nothing is dirt cheap.

No one is rich enough to do without a neighbor.

There are bigger things in life than money—bills.

The bitterness of poor quality lingers long after the sweetness of a cheap price is forgotten.

To be rich in God is better than to be rich in goods.

How much better to be honestly poor than questionably rich.

One could live on next to nothing if the neighbors would live on less.

Extravagance is a curse, and the extravagant human being is accursed.

Hardly anything is as upsetting as picking up a lunch check for someone who is too rich to carry money.

I'm far from being poor. I'm even farther from being rich.

One thing you can still get for a penny—your incorrect weight.

Prosperity keeps many people in debt.

Money is relative—the more money, the more relatives.

More money in your purse means greater obligation to God and man.

If we belong to Christ, it's logical that everything we have belongs to him.

Giving is a thermometer of our love.

When holdings are worthless, giving is worth more.

The secret of financial success is to spend what you have left after saving, instead of saving what is left after spending.

When giving to God, we are just taking our hands off what belongs to him.

Economy is often defined as a reduction in some other fellow's salary.

It is said that if all the world's economists were placed end to end, they wouldn't reach a conclusion.

Material riches have no intrinsic value in the perspective of eternity.

How pleasant life would be if people with money used it the way the people who don't have any say they would spend it if they did.

The real measure of our wealth is what will be ours in eternity.

Though a man without money is poor, a man with nothing but money is poorer.

A living wage, it has been said, is a little more than you are making now.

April is the month when the green returns to the lawn, the lilac, and the IRS.

Some people never seem to do anything on time except buy.

The difference between you and other folks is that their money looks bigger and their trouble looks smaller.

Money is a universal provider for most everything but happiness and a universal passport to most any place but heaven.

It's inflation when you have to be pretty well off just to be poor.

The saddest words of tongue or pen are "The car installment's due again."

Most of us spend our time like it wasn't worth anything—and our money like it was.

Twenty-five years ago $15,000 bought a lot of house. Today it buys a lot.

Credit is what keeps you from knowing how far past broke you are.

Despite inflation, a penny for some people's thoughts is still a fair price.

They say you can't take it with you, and I'm sure that's true. But my problem is to make it last until I'm ready to go.

Debt is the slavery of the free.

Do not be sorry if your purse is half empty—be glad it is half full.

Some Christians suffer from cirrhosis of the giver.

Blessed are those who can give without remembering and take without forgetting.

Those who think money grows on trees are the ones who have a hard time getting out of the woods.

George Washington never told a lie—how come his picture is on a bill not worth a dollar?

Don't try to cheat the Lord and call it economizing.

A Christian is one who does not have to consult his bank book to see how wealthy he really is.

No one is poor who by prayer can open the storehouse of God.

Your use of money shows what you think of God.

We would all be happy to pay as we go—if only we could finish paying for where we've been.

Making money last is no easier than making it first.

Total commitment could turn your "collection" into an "offering."

Too many apply the principles of "saving grace" to their pocketbooks rather than their souls.

One way to keep your head above water is to avoid expensive dives.

The cost of living has gone up, but most people think it's worth the price.

One thing everyone understands about money matters is that it does.

Credit cards tend to make us a debt-propelled people.

Some folks have a craving for saving—others an urge to splurge.

If you want to improve your memory, loan money to others.

What you don't owe won't hurt you.

The best things in life may be free, but things money can buy aren't bad either.

No one's credit is as good as his money.

Life would be far more pleasant if you could make money first—then make it last.

Try to live within your income—it's easier than living without one.

Running into debt isn't nearly as bad as running into your creditors.

Some people are always in debt because they keep spending what their friends think they make.

You cannot take your money to heaven, but you can invest it for eternity.

Poverty is a state of mind often induced by a neighbor's new car.

The nice thing about a gift of money is that it's so easy to exchange.

Probably the real reason the dog remains man's best friend is that neither borrows money from the other.

You are only poor when you want more than you have.

It used to be if you were "sound as a dollar" you were considered in perfect health—today, it means you are in bad shape.

A good way to save money: buy $2,000 worth of traveler's checks for a vacation; then don't go.

One good thing about living in the past—it's cheaper.

Misers aren't much fun to live with, but they do make wonderful ancestors.

The person who can squeeze a dollar is usually the one who can stretch it.

Strange we call money dough—everyone knows dough sticks to your fingers.

We're living in a land of plenty—everything we want costs plenty.

Some people give God a tenth—a tenth of what they ought to give.

Establish an emergency fund and you'll be surprised how quickly an emergency develops.

We are rich only through what we give, and poor only through what we keep.

The darkest hour in any man's life is when he sits down to plan how to get money without earning it.

The place to "pass the buck" is in the offering.

If you cannot give, God understands—if you can give and won't, God knows.

The poorest man is he whose only wealth is money.

People who used to live from payday to payday used to be called shiftless; now they are called good managers.

If you want to feel rich, just count all the things you have that money can't buy.

Money—you can't take it with you, but it is good to know there is a place where you can go without it.

Money is something that things run into and people run out of.

Just when you think you can make both ends meet, someone moves the ends.

If your outgo is greater than your income, your upkeep will soon be your downfall.

With many people, money comes first, yet they can't seem to make it last.

Money can't buy happiness—unless you spend it on somebody else.

If money talks, why didn't it cry for help a long time ago?

Money may talk, but today's dollar doesn't have enough cents to say very much.

The definition of a living wage depends upon whether you are getting it or giving it.

If a fool and his money are soon parted, how come they got together in the first place?

Funny how the U.S. makes money—while the rest of us earn it.

You should file your income tax, not chisel it.

No patient should leave the hospital until he's strong enough to face the cashier.

Inflation is when the buck doesn't stop anywhere.

Money talks but it never debates.

Everyone pays for their mistakes—Congress does it with our money.

It isn't money that makes people work harder but appreciation.

A batch of credit cards fattens a wallet before it thins it.

A sign for taxpayers—the buck starts here.

In the war against inflation, there are no hawks or doves—just pigeons.

Beware of the chap who reminds you that you can't take it with you—he's trying to take it with him.

Definition of proof of purchase—an empty wallet.

Some people put "zero" in the church offering and complain that the church is too cold.

The real measure of our wealth is how much we'd be worth if we lost all our money.

In the old days, big spenders spent their own money—not other people's.

Money may not buy happiness, but it surely helps one look for it in more interesting places.

The best labor-saving device is an inheritance.

Inflation is when after you get money to buy something, it isn't enough.

It's costing Americans twice as much to live beyond their means as it did ten years ago.

Some people are certainly going to have a lot of nickels in heaven judging by their offerings.

The trouble is that our earning capacity doesn't match our yearning capacity.

A nickel goes a long way now; you can carry it around for days without finding a thing to buy.

The "upper crust" is just a bunch of crumbs stuck together with their own dough.

One reason you can't take it with you is that it goes before you do.

The dime isn't entirely worthless; it makes a fairly good screwdriver when you need it.

People used to say, "It's not the cost—it's the upkeep." Today it's always both.

Prosperity provides enough credit to live beyond your means.

No amount of cash is ever petty.

Why do bills always arrive on time when everything else the postal service delivers comes late?

To paraphrase an old axiom—what you owe won't hurt you.

Do you remember way back when church collection plates got most of the money that service stations get Sunday?

It used to be a fool and his money were soon parted, but now it happens to everybody.

No man is a success in life if he goes through life earning nothing but money.

Anybody who thinks that money grows on trees is bound sooner or later to get caught out on a limb.

Money will buy a fine dog, but only love will make him wag his tail.

Two ways to get rich—spend less than you make and make more than you spend.

Poverty of purpose is worse than poverty of purse.

Credit enables anybody to start at the bottom and go into the hole.

Two things ruin a church—loose living and tight giving.

He who has a fixed income is in a bad fix.

You cannot take your money with you, but you can send it ahead.

There are many who will give the Lord credit but never give him cash.

If the "love of money is the root of all evil," then pleasure is one of the limbs.

The person who gambles with his money will gamble with his soul.

The poorest man in the world is the man who has nothing but money.

I must be successful—I owe everyone money.

Wealth is not his who has it but his who enjoys it.

The man who saves money nowadays isn't a miser—he's a wizard.

A pig bought on credit is forever grunting.

Counterfeit money is homemade bread.

God has enough money in the pockets of Christians to do everything he expects the church to do.

Giving is grace—not giving is a disgrace.

When prosperity comes, do not use all of it.

Credit, like dope, when used to excess leads to the gutter.

When you give till it hurts, it makes you feel good.

The rich may not live longer, but it certainly seems like it to their poor relatives.

The worst place to live is beyond one's income.

Inflation is paying more and getting less.

Some people pay tithes to the waitress but tip God.

A poor man cannot afford to be lazy.

Many people spend their health for wealth, then try to spend their wealth for health.

We make a living by getting, but we make lives by giving.

If all the economists were laid end to end, they'd still point in all directions.

Money is tender when you have it and tough when you haven't.

The high price of meat today keeps many families in a perpetual stew.

The way you handle God's money tests your maturity as a Christian.

A man doesn't own his wealth—he owes it.

Economics is the art of satisfying infinite wants with limited resources.

It's a small world; why does it cost so much to run it?

Money will not buy happiness, but it makes misery more comfortable.

Whether a boy ends up with a nest egg or a goose egg depends upon the chick he marries.

It's easy to tell when you got a bargain—it doesn't fit.

Give to God what's right—not what's left.

We should give according to our income, lest God make our income according to our giving.

Today—a dollar earned is a nickel saved.

Buying what you do not need is an easy road to needing what you cannot buy.

A recession is a period when sales go down and staff meetings go up.

If you think nobody cares you are alive, just miss a couple car or mortgage payments.

Beware: money can create hardening of the attitudes.

Just when you've gotten everything in the house automated, electricity is so expensive you can't afford it.

The best place to spend your vacation is somewhere near your budget.

Early to bed, early to rise—till you make enough money to do otherwise.

A fool and his money are soon spotted.

With everything else going up these days, it's a wonder the Lord hasn't increased tithing to 15 percent.

It only takes a little "jack" to lift a car, but plenty of "jack" to keep it up.

Waste of wealth is sometimes retrieved; waste of health seldom; waste of time never.

Definition of prosperity: that period from Friday's paycheck to Saturday's shopping.

The trouble with some people who give till it hurts is that they are so sensitive to pain.

Most people don't start economizing until they run out of money.

If people were to give according to their means, they would not act mean when asked to give.

The reason the dollar does not do as much today is that people don't do as much for the dollar as they used to.

The manner of giving shows the character of the giver more than the gift itself.

People do not become rich by what they earn, but by what they save.

Money used to talk, then it whispered, now it just sneaks off.

Many men lay down their life trying to lay up money.

A vacation can put you in the pink, but it may leave you in the red.

Hard work is the yeast that raises the dough.

Some people are not only pleasure bent—they are pleasure broke.

True wealth is the satisfaction of talent used in Christian service.

If you want to keep out of debt, you must earn more than you yearn.

Early settlers started this country, but it's those who settle the first of the month who keep it going.

The two things most open to mistakes are the pocketbook and the tongue.

By the time you have saved for a nest egg, inflation turns it into chicken feed.

Maybe one reason budgets don't work is that we only work five days a week but we spend money all seven.

Inflation has been defined as a process that allows one to live in a more expensive neighborhood without ever moving.

Some people think they are worth a lot of money because they have it.

Fools can make money—it takes a wise man to know how to spend it.

Car sickness is the feeling you get every month when the payment falls due.

Bill collectors always come at the wrong time—when I'm home.

Justice often leans to the side of the purse hand.

The reason people put so many pennies in the offering is there is no smaller coin.

Benjamin Franklin may have discovered electricity, but it was the man who invented the meter who made all the money.

The kind of wealth most of us need isn't dollars as much as sense.

Money talks. If it's the dollar, it's small talk.

A luxury is something you don't need but you can't do without.

A tither's problem is seldom money.

If you spend lavishly on your own pleasure but complain that you have no money for the Lord, check to see who is your master.

The only thing that doesn't become smaller when you contract it is debt.

He who serves God for money will serve the devil for bigger wages.

A tenth for God is more rewarding than a fifth for Satan.

People get into debt trying to keep up with those who already are.

Money has little value to its possessors unless it also has value to others.

What this country needs is a dollar that will not be as much elastic as it is adhesive.

A dollar will not go as far as it used to, but it will go faster.

Today is ready cash—spend it.

Something you can get for nothing is usually worth it.

Some people lay down their life trying to lay up money.

A real estate sign read, "For sale: Oleo Acres—one of the less expensive spreads."

A luxury becomes a necessity whenever you are able to make the down payment on it.

The average married couple has already spent next year's salary and hasn't paid this year's bills.

We're better off financially if we always act our wage.

A vacation is nothing but a sunburn at premium prices.

Keeping too much in your pocketbook may drive the Lord from your heart.

Money isn't everything—sometimes it isn't enough.

The most sensitive nerve in the body seems to be the one that runs to the pocketbook.

God does not look at the face of your check but at the balance on the stub.

Strange how big a dollar looks when you give it to the church but how little when it goes for groceries.

There is an advantage in being poor—the doctor will cure you faster.

Banks call them "personal" loans because if you miss a payment they get personal about it.

Money ain't everything—but it sure comes in handy when you lose your credit cards.

If you are stingy with a small income, it's likely you'll not be generous with a large one.

Riches are a blessing only to those who make them a blessing to others.

Some people give their mite, others give with all their might, and some don't give who might.

Inflation is being broke with a lot of money in your pocket.

Inflation is the price we pay for those government benefits we thought were free.

People who live beyond their means should be given a lot of credit.

He made money the old-fashioned way—he inherited it.

How much money does it take for a rich person to be happy? Just a little more.

Depression is a time when you can't spend money you don't have.

It's good to have things that money can buy, but better to have things money can't buy.

Money can't buy everything—including what it used to.

Man makes counterfeit money—sometimes money makes counterfeit men.

The hand that gives is the hand that receives.

The only place you can find financial security is inside your income.

When we give our finances to God, we are not really giving to God; we are just releasing what already belongs to him.

The safest way to double your money is to fold it over and put it in your pocket.

Remember when you looked forward to receiving the salary you can't live on today?

If you set the pattern for giving—would your church receive a token or a tithe?

Some people don't think they are having a good time unless they are doing what they cannot afford.

What we give determines our wealth, not what we get.

Beware of the Christian with the open mouth and closed pocketbook.

When a man becomes rich, either God gains a partner or the man loses a soul.

Do your givin' while you are livin'—then you're knowin' where it's goin'.

Give until it feels good.

Most couples need two incomes these days; one for the principal and one for the interest.

◆Morality

Things that once were a disgrace now bring a movie, book, or TV contract.

Wrong is wrong, even if everyone is doing it. Right is right, even though no one else does it.

✦Mother

Mothers are handicapped; they have but two hands.

A mother is not a person to lean on, but a person to make leaning unnecessary.

Mother is a bank where we deposit all our hurts and worries.

The successful mother sets her children free and becomes more free herself in the process.

A godly mother will point her children to God by the force of her example as much as by the power of her words.

An ounce of mother is often worth more than a ton of clergy.

Motherhood is the salvation of womanhood.

Helpful hint for the new mother—just fill up at one end and empty at the other.

Abraham Lincoln said, "The greatest lessons I ever learned were at my mother's knees."

A community or nation can be no stronger than its mothers.

Mother's Day is when everybody waits on mother and she pretends she doesn't mind the extra work.

It's easy to spot an overprotective mother; she's the one who controls her kids better than you control yours.

History shows almost all the greatest workers for God had godly mothers.

There is no modern pain medicine as effective as a mother's kiss.

Mothers write on the hearts of their children what the world's rough hand cannot erase.

Sign in restaurant: pies like mother used to make before she took up bridge and cigarettes.

If evolution works, how come mothers still have only two hands?

Thank God for nagging mothers—they do their work until God can take over.

The chain of a mother's prayers can link her child to God.

N

◆Nostalgia

Living in the past has its advantage—it's cheaper.

Nostalgia is like a grammar lesson; you find the present tense and the past perfect.

Nostalgia consists of longing for the place you wouldn't move back to.

Nostalgia is trying to recapture the feel of the good old daze.

O

◆Obedience

Although God created man without man's help, he will not save man without his consent or obedience.

One step forward in obedience is worth years of study about it.

There is no harmony in the heart without the joyful notes of obedience.

The most fitting response to undeserved blessing is unreserved obedience.

He is wise who learns to obey where others go astray.

Obedience sheds light on the hidden things of God.

It is ours to obey his commands, not to direct his counsels.

It is not facing the music that hurts—sometimes it is listening to it.

Your obedience to God today determines what you'll be for God tomorrow.

True spirituality is not judged by what we do but by our obedience to him.

Delayed obedience is disobedience.

The Christian who claims the promises of God should obey the commands of God.

A small step of obedience is a giant step to blessing.

Before we can speak God's message, we must listen—the open ears always come before the open mouth.

Obeying God is the best prescription for spiritual health.

The cost of obedience is nothing compared with the cost of disobedience.

God's laws last longer than those who break them.

Obedience to God removes pretense from our prayers.

✦Old Age

Vacation is one time when older people find out they are not as young as they feel.

To avoid old age, keep overdrinking, overeating, and overachieving.

In gardening, it's a race between your back and your enthusiasm—to see which will give out first.

Middle age is when you start out with your spirits up and end up with a rubdown.

Middle age is when you're not inclined to exercise anything but caution.

You cannot take credit for beauty at sixteen, but if you are beautiful when sixty, it will be your soul's doing.

Don't worry about getting old. It is better to be "over the hill" than under it.

Wrinkles are receipts for living.

When I was younger I could remember anything, whether it had happened or not.

If you can't run with the dogs, stay off the porch.

The world gets better every day—and then gets worse toward the evening.

The first step to senility is to believe you have all the answers.

Middle age is when you look into the mirror and wish you hadn't.

The way I see it, you're only young once—and it takes years of middle age to get over it.

We cannot avoid growing old, but we can avoid growing cold.

Most folks like the old days better—they were younger then.

Middle age is when the products you bought with a lifetime guarantee begin to wear out.

The persons most difficult to convince that they're at retirement age are children at bedtime.

You've reached middle age when pulling your weight is a real drag.

You know you're getting old when your back goes out more often than you do.

Retirement is when you stop making a living and start making a life.

No one grows old by living—only by losing interest in living.

An excellent way to grow old is to stay young.

Old age is ready to undertake tasks that youth shirked because it would take too long.

You've reached middle age when you feel great when you're only fair.

Middle age is that time of life when after one night out you need two nights in.

Middle age is when you can remember how comfortably you lived on what Uncle Sam now deducts from your paycheck.

The worst thing about growing old is listening to your children's advice.

Nothing makes a woman feel older than meeting a bald-headed man who was two grades back of her in school.

You are getting old if it takes you longer to rest than it did to get tired.

Retirement is when you putter around the yard and mutter around the house.

People are funny—everyone wants to live a long life, but no one wants to get old.

Middle age is too young for Medicare and too old for men to care.

You are an old-timer if you can remember when the sky was the limit.

Middle age starts the day you become more interested in how long your car will last than how fast it will go.

Growing old is nothing more than a bad habit that a busy man has no time to form.

Living in the past has one thing in its favor—it's cheaper.

Most of us as we grow older, get sadder and wider.

Middle age is when you know all the answers, but no one asks the questions.

I'm at that age where I have nothing to do with natural foods; I need all the preservatives I can get.

I feel I am growing old for want of somebody to tell me that I am looking as young as ever.

Some men, when they get too old to set a bad example, start giving good advice.

An old-timer is one who remembers when people wore blue jeans to work.

Middle age is the time of life when work begins to be a lot less fun and fun begins to be a lot more work.

The good old days are those days that I could master. The pace was slower and I was faster.

There are three things that indicate old age—the first is a failing memory . . . and I don't remember the other two.

By the time a man is old enough to watch his step, he is too old to go anywhere.

Middle age is when the narrow waist and the broad mind begin to change places.

Some people say that as you get old you have to give up things. Perhaps, you get old because you give up too many things.

One old-timer says he's in favor of progress, just as long as nobody changes anything.

If you're over the hill, why not enjoy the view?

You can tell you're getting older when everything hurts, and what doesn't hurt doesn't work.

Middle age is that difficult time between adolescence and retirement when you have to take care of yourself.

Having fun is like buying life insurance—the older you get, the more it costs.

You've reached middle age when weight lifting consists of just standing up.

Retirement is that marvelous time of life when the sun rises and you don't.

Remember the good ole days when "swingers" were people who relaxed on the front porch?

When saving for old age, be sure to put away a few pleasant thoughts.

An old-timer is someone who remembers when charity was a virtue, not an organization.

By the time a person gets into greener pastures, he usually can't climb the fence.

Middle age is that period when looking backward makes one sad and looking forward makes one miserable.

No one is rich enough to buy back his past.

Old age is not coasting—it's climbing.

The young sow wild oats—the old grow sage.

You've reached middle age when a lot of living under your belt begins to show there.

When you are young you want to change the world—when you are old you want to change the young.

You can tell how healthy a man is by what he takes two at a time—steps or pills.

A sure sign of old age is when you feel your "corns" more than your "oats."

Old age is when you get out of the shower and you're glad the mirror is fogged up.

Middle age is that time of life when a woman won't tell her age and a man won't act his.

You are getting old when the candles cost more than the cake.

Wrinkles should merely indicate where the smiles have been.

Retirement is a matter of attitude—I'm retreaded, not retired.

Too many of us keep from going forward by looking back to the good old days.

It is doubtful if any person really enjoys reaching threescore and ten if he has never learned to keep score by God's rules.

A person is old only when he shuts his mind and stops learning.

Middle age—too many nights around the table.

Age doesn't matter unless you are cheese.

Forty is the old age of youth—fifty is the youth of old age.

The paradox of age—the young want to be old, and the old want to be young.

God gave us memories so we could have roses in December.

Middle age is when what used to give you heart throb now gives you heartburn.

Old age is like everything else. To be a success, you've got to start young.

An old man continues to be young in two things—love of money and love of life.

◆Old in Your Profession

Old housewives never die—they just wash away.

Old janitors never die—they just kick the bucket.

Old FBI Agents never die—they just get fed up.

Old cardiologists never die—they just become disheartened.

Old golfers never die—they just lose their drive.

Old baseball players never die—they just strike out.

Old football players never die—they just fumble away.

Old hockey players never die—they just lose their puck.

Old tailors never die—they are just divested.

Old detectives never die—they are just dissolved.

Old orchestra leaders never die—they just become disbanded.

Old musicians never die—they just become disconcerted.

Old chiropractors never die—they just become disjointed.

Old politicians never die—they just become devoted.

Old clerks never die—they just become defiled.

Old Elks never die—they just become dislodged.

Old dentists never die—they just lose their pull.

Old math teachers never die—they just subtract.

Old magazine editors never die—they just expire.

Old school principals never die—they just lose their faculties.

Old skiers never die—they just go downhill.

Old mountain climbers never die—they just peak out.

Old gluttons never die—they just waist away.

Old teachers never die—they just lose their class.

Old funeral directors never die—they just go underground.

Old bus drivers never die—they just transfer.

Old truckers never die—they just lose their drive.

Old bowlers never die—they just end up in the gutter.

Old singers never die—they just lose their tune.

Old doctors never die—they just lose their patients.

Old garbage collectors never die—they just fail to pick up.

Old locksmiths never die—they just lose their keys.

Old insurance salesmen never die—they just lose their premiums.

Old bankers never die—they just lose their balance.

Old telephone operators never die—they just hang up.

Old welders never die—they just blaze away.

Old electricians never die—they just lose their shock.

Old accountants never die—they just lose their figures.

Old mailmen never die—they just lose their zip.

Old bank tellers never die—they just yield to maturity.

Old dictators never die—they just fly the coup.

Old parade leaders never die—they just float away.

Old chairpersons never die—they just go through the motions.

Old travel agents never die—they just never return.

Old bakers never die—they just fail to rise.

Old pilots never die—they just fly away.

Old jewelers never die—they just lose the time.

Old photographers never die—they just never develop.

Old carpenters never die—they just lose their pound.

Old taxi drivers never die—they just lose their drive.

Old TV repairmen never die—they just lose their picture.

Old joggers never die—they just run down.

Old boxers never die—they just lose their punch.

Old painters never die—they just lose their color.

Old florists never die—they just wither away.

Old lawyers never die—they just lose their will.

Old nurses never die—they just lose their pulse.

✦Opportunity

Every man carries with him the world in which he must live.

Opportunity typically favors those who have paid the price of years of preparation.

God's best gifts are not things but opportunities.

The danger is that we don't aim too high and we miss it, but that we aim too low and reach it.

What we call adversity God calls opportunity.

Everyone faces the choice: Christ or condemnation.

All who don't hearken to the "come" of salvation will one day hear the "depart" of damnation.

When embracing opportunity, give it a big hug.

Do that good deed now; you never know how soon it will be too late.

Small opportunities are often the beginning of great achievements.

Opportunity knocks only once, but temptation stays at the door for years.

A rejected opportunity to give is a lost opportunity to receive.

Obstacles are opportunities in disguise—let opportunity do all the knocking.

A gloomy day only makes a human rainbow all the more noticeable.

When you kill a little time, you may be murdering opportunity.

No opportunity is ever lost; the other person takes those you miss.

Today is a once-in-a-lifetime opportunity that comes everyday.

Real opportunity for success lies within the person—not the job.

Opportunity may knock only once, but temptation leans on the doorbell.

Great opportunities come to those who make the most of small ones.

By the time most people have made up their mind, opportunity has passed them by.

A wise man makes more opportunities than he finds.

When opportunities knock, you have to get up and answer the door.

No one knows what he can do until he tries.

All the flowers of all the tomorrows are in the seed of today.

You can never find a lost opportunity.

One door may be shut, but there are many others still open.

Instead of crying over spilled milk, go and milk another cow.

Yesterday is a canceled check; tomorrow is a promissory note; today is the only cash you have—spend it wisely.

Wherever there is human need, there is opportunity to do a kind deed.

An opportunist is one who goes ahead and does what you had always been planning to do.

Opportunity is often dressed up in work clothes.

Weak men wait for opportunities—strong men make them.

Education is the key to the door of opportunity.

When opportunity knocks, about all some people do is complain about the noise.

Luck is when preparation meets opportunity.

Keeping your eye too closely on the future may obscure present opportunities.

Opportunities, like parking places, are plentiful for those who get there first.

There is no security on earth, only opportunity.

Those who look for opportunities to hate miss many opportunities to love.

Three things come not back in this life: the spoken word, the sped arrow, the neglected opportunity.

Opportunities look bigger going than coming.

First deserve, and then desire.

Don't wait for an opportunity to come; it's already here.

✦Optimism

There is no such thing as bad weather—there are just different kinds of good weather.

It's just as easy to look for the good things in life as the bad.

An optimist looks at an oyster and expects to find a pearl—the pessimist looks at the oyster and expects ptomaine poisoning.

The worst pest in the world is a pessimist.

Goals are like stars: they may not be reached, but they can always be a guide.

In the long run the pessimist may be proven right, but the optimist has a better time on the trip.

When a pessimist thinks he's taking a chance, the optimist feels he is grasping a great opportunity.

A pessimist is one who feels bad when he feels good for fear he will feel worse when he feels better.

Looking on the bright side of life will never develop eyestrain.

If you never undertake more than you can possibly do, you will never do more than you can possibly do.

When he smells the flowers, a pessimist looks around for the funeral.

Two men looked out prison bars; one saw mud, the other saw the stars.

An optimist is one who makes the best of it when he gets the worst of it.

People don't get weak eyes from looking at the bright side of life.

Optimism is having three teenage boys and one car.

A pessimist has no starter; an optimist has no brakes.

No matter what happens there is someone who knew it would.

Every day holds the possibility of miracles.

An optimist says his glass is half full; a pessimist says the glass is half empty.

Optimism is waiting for a ship to come in when you haven't sent one out.

An optimist is a person who is always looking for new definitions of the word *optimist*.

P

✦Parents

A father is generally happier to have his child look like him than act like him. It ought to be the other way around.

Most fathers try to bring up their sons to be as good a man as they meant to be.

It's hard to train a child in a way the parents don't go themselves.

Parents wonder why the streams are bitter when they themselves have poisoned the fountain.

Train up a child in the way he should go; then go that way thyself.

Just about the time you think your problems are all behind you, you get to be a grandparent.

The father who does not teach his son his duties is equally guilty with the son who neglects them.

Our children are the only possessions we can take to heaven.

A child's life is really determined by just how hard his mother and father work at being parents.

If my parents were so awful, how come I am so wonderful?

Heredity is something you believe in when your child's report card is all *A*'s.

The most important thing a father can do for his children is to love their mother.

Some are so anxious to give their children what they didn't have that they have neglected to give them what they had.

Parents who are afraid to put their foot down usually have children who step on their toes.

Some people can trace their ancestry back three hundred years, but they cannot tell where their children were last night.

Some parents are not on "spanking terms" with their children.

If fathers took their sons fishing when they were young, they wouldn't have to go hunting for them when they are older.

A young girl's view of parents: "The trouble with parents is they are so old when we get them, it's hard to change their habits."

Live so that your son, when people tell him that he reminds them of you, will stick out his chest—not his tongue.

People who handle other people's money are required to account for every cent. Are children less valuable?

Grandparent—one of those things that is "so simple a child can operate."

Very frequently rich parents are poor parents.

The trouble with being a parent is that by the time we're experienced we're unemployed.

Parents can tell but never teach, until they practice what they preach.

It is a tragedy of our time that many become parents before they cease being children.

Parents should always remember that some day their children will follow their example instead of their advice.

The accent's on youth, but the stress is on parents.

When dad says he wants me to have everything he didn't have when he was a kid, he means an *A* on my report card.

◆Pastors and Preaching

The world has lost many good businessmen by having them become preachers.

Jonah learned more in the fish than some learn in seminary.

The pastor is called to be a shepherd, not a sheepdog.

Some preachers have a wealth of thought; others have a thought of wealth.

There is no pulpit so vacant as the one without the message of the blood of Christ.

There is a lot of preaching done that the devil likes to hear.

The preacher who does not evangelize will fossilize.

Some ministers are dying by degrees.

Always aim at the heart when preaching—never at the head.

He who feeds others' hearts must speak from his heart.

The most spiritual preacher is a natural preacher.

All ministers should remember when they preach that God is one of their hearers.

Don't use a gallon of words to express a spoonful of thought.

If you would win the world, melt it down—don't hammer it down.

If people sleep during the sermon, the pastor needs to wake up.

It takes more grace to preach to one than to the multitude.

Get so full of your message that when you speak there is no room for self.

It is easier to preach ten sermons than it is to live one.

A true preacher is more pleased when people tell him how wonderful the Lord is instead of telling him how great his sermon was.

It is the duty of the pastor not only to comfort the distressed but to distress the comfortable.

When speaking, do not target your speech to the bystanders but to those for whom your speech is meant.

The great preacher makes a simple subject easy to understand instead of complicating it.

The sermon that you would enjoy the most is not likely to be the one that will do you the most good.

The sinner in the pew will not be cleansed by soap in the pulpit.

If the pastor is good, he deserves a four-week vacation—if he is not, the congregation deserves it.

When there is no thirst for righteousness, the sermons seem dry.

Many pastors know what to say, but not when to quit saying it.

Difficulties, to the Christian, are only miracles that have not yet happened.

A caring preacher will build his church, and a caring church will build its preacher.

Biscuits and sermons are improved by shortening.

Great preaching requires great listening.

The after-dinner speaker: a gust of honor.

Unless the sermon makes the listener dissatisfied with either himself or the preacher, then it is classified as a poor sermon.

If you don't strike oil in the first thirty minutes, stop boring.

A sermon need not be everlasting to have eternal value.

Many pastors preach from a text—too far from it.

Much preaching is answering questions people are not asking.

Long preaching—some ministers don't know when to put the caboose on the train.

Preach the Bible, it will scare the hell out of people.

More preaching about hell in the pulpit will mean less hell in the community.

Biblical preaching will make some glad and others mad.

Popular preaching—one pastor remarked, "When I preach, people stand in line—to get out."

Successful preaching is not only *what* you say but *how* you say it.

If the preacher has something worthwhile to say, people will *listen* and *remember.*

Long-winded preacher, keep in mind that few souls are saved after twelve noon on Sunday.

Many ministers aim at nothing and hit it every time.

Prison preaching: A seminary graduate preached his first sermon in prison and said to the men, "I am happy to see all of you here."

Prison preaching: A minister read his text as he started to preach in prison, "How shall we escape . . . "

Poor preacher: A minister complaining to an auto mechanic that his bill was too high said, "I'm a poor preacher." The mechanic said, "I know, I've heard you preach."

There was a "drive-in confessional"—it was called "toot and tell."

One young minister thought high cholesterol was a church holy day.

A pastor was shy about meeting a young lady. He opened the songbook to "I Need Thee Every Hour" and handed it to her. She turned to "God Will Take Care of You" and handed it back to him.

A pastor was speaking of the prophets one by one. After seventy minutes, he said, "We now come to Isaiah—what should we do with him?" An impatient person said, "He can have my seat; I'm going home."

A pastor was known to have a Bible verse for everything that happened. One Sunday as he was preaching a bug flew into his mouth. He gulped and said, "He was a stranger and I took him in."

The pastor had a Band-Aid on his chin. While shaving, he had thought of his sermon and cut himself. After the sermon, a member said, "Why didn't you think of shaving and cut your sermon?"

Minister's library burns—all two books burned; one he had not colored.

Preaching moves men—prayer moves God.

Prayer by the people in the pew will give the pastor power in the pulpit.

The reason for poor preaching is poor praying in the pew.

It's good to follow the pastor when the pastor follows the Master.

Sermons should be built around the Scripture, not the Scripture around the sermon.

A sermon that pricks your conscience has good points.

A sermon is not an argument—a sermon is a piece of bread.

After the pastor preaches the Word of God, the people should take up the work of God.

✦Patience

Perhaps the most important trip you will ever make is going the second mile.

Today is not won by old victories nor lost by old defeats.

You lose a lot of battles in the process of winning the war.

Patience is waiting without worrying.

I would rather *be* hurt than *do* hurt.

The difficult things take a long time—the impossible take a little longer.

Investigate mistakes only when you are calm.

The wonderful thing about patience is that it goes a long way, and yet the more we use it, the more we have.

Christ's forbearance and long-suffering transformed Peter. It changes us, too.

Do not ask to have your life's load lightened, but to have courage to endure.

Do not ask for fulfillment in your life but for patience to accept frustration.

The truest test of moral courage is the ability to ignore the insult.

Instead of putting others in their place, trying putting yourself in their place occasionally.

A watched pot never boils—the secret of patience is to divert your attention to something else.

A man without patience is like a car without brakes.

All things come to him who waits. Sometimes, though, it's just the leftovers from the fellow who got there first.

If the Lord loves a cheerful giver, he also loves a thankful loser.

He will not have a barren mind who knows how to bear in mind.

When we pray for rain, we must be willing to put up with some mud.

It takes courage when you are in the minority—but tolerance when you're in the majority.

Patience is often simply not being able to decide what to do.

It's the little things that annoy us; we can sit on a mountain but not on a tack.

It's better to help others to get on than to tell them when to get off.

Patience is the ability to keep your shirt on when you are hot under the collar.

Patience is the companion of wisdom. A day ahead is better than ten years behind.

The end never justifies the meanness.

If you are able to pat a fellow on his head when you feel like bashing it in, you are a patient person.

There are times when God asks nothing of his children except silence, patience, and tears.

This world would be a fine place if people were always as patient as they are when they are waiting for a fish to bite.

It's easier to have patience with others when we remember God's patience toward us.

Hurry will get you one place ahead of time—the cemetery.

Patience is not always a virtue—especially when you are in quicksand.

Patience is a great virtue—but work while you wait.

Those who wait on the Lord will run without the weight of sin.

The secret of patience is to do something else in the meantime.

If you love rainbows, you must be willing to put up with some rain.

Patience is a virtue that carries a lot of wait.

A weakness many have is they want others to be better than they are willing to be themselves.

Tolerance is sometimes the uncomfortable feeling that the other fellow may be right after all.

Better to be patient on the road than a patient in the hospital.

With patience, a well can be dug with a needle.

The best way to stop stepping on other people's toes is to put yourself in their shoes.

When problems come your way, get ready to sing and rejoice—God is about to do something great in and through you.

It is best to look for the good in others because that's the best way to find the good in yourself.

One test of good manners is to be able to put up pleasantly with the bad ones.

You cannot antagonize and persuade at the same time.

Patience is a tree whose root is bitter, but its fruit is very sweet.

Patience strengthens the spirit, sweetens the temper, subdues the pride, and bridles the tongue.

◆Patriotism

Our country, right or wrong. When right, to be kept right; when wrong, to be put right.

If our country is worth dying for in time of war, let us resolve that it is truly worth living for in time of peace.

He loves his country best who strives to make it best.

America is a great country—if you can't make it in the rat race, they give you free cheese.

◆Peace

Christ as Savior brings peace *with* God; Christ as Lord brings the peace *of* God.

The surest way to encourage violence is to give in to it.

The person who keeps clean, square, and cool within will never collapse when the world without falls in on him.

Peace of mind depends upon strength of mind.

What you eat doesn't give you ulcers—it's what's eating you.

What we need is a peace conference with the Prince of Peace.

It seems that heads, hearts, and hands would settle the world's differences much better than arms.

You cannot have the peace of God until you know the God of peace.

How strange that men fight for peace and work for leisure.

When the Christian stays his mind upon Christ, he develops a wonderful "calm-plex."

In this confused world, some people have peace while others go to pieces.

The practice of peace is the practice of Christianity.

Peace rules the day when Christ rules the mind.

A person cannot be a peacemaker until first he finds peace for himself.

In the care of God means to be in the peace of God.

Only the living water can quench the driving thirst of the soul.

No God, no peace; know God, know peace.

◆Praise

The best way to boost the morale at the office is to tell the boss when someone is doing a good job.

Man weighs the deeds, but God weighs the intentions.

People have a way of becoming what you encourage them to be—not what you nag them to be.

Nobody has ever been bored by someone paying them a compliment.

Morning praise can make your days.

Praise, like sunlight, helps all things to grow.

Nothing will improve a person's hearing more than praise.

We can never praise Jesus too much.

God gives blessings to us so we can give glory to him.

It's amazing how much can be accomplished when we quit worrying about who gets the credit.

A pat on the back accomplishes much more than a slap in the face.

The trouble is most of us would rather be ruined by praise than saved by criticism.

Be sure to concentrate on your blessings—not your distresses.

Don't expect applause—earn it.

A heart of praise and love shows others just what Jesus can do in the lives of men.

Praise is the soil in which joy thrives.

God's work of creating is done; our work of praising has just begun.

A tongue of praise has no time to gossip.

When we cease to wonder, we cease to worship.

If you find yourself wearing a spirit of heaviness, put on a garment of praise.

◆Prayer

Arguments never settle things, but prayer changes things.

Nothing makes us love our enemies as much as praying for them.

A small boy asked his parents, "I'm going to pray now—do you need anything?"

An important part of praying is a willingness to be a part of the answer.

If we pray in times of victory, we will not need to plead in times of defeat.

Many prayers end up in the dead-letter office because they lack sufficient direction.

The best way to influence people for God is to intercede with God for people.

When it seems hardest to pray, we should pray the hardest.

You can turn any care into prayer anywhere.

Too much of prayer is asking instead of thanking.

Bending our knees in prayer keeps us from breaking under the load of care.

Prayer is not a way of getting what we want, but the way to become what God wants us to be.

Spiritual growth soars up when we have prayed up, made up, and said up.

Prayerless pews make powerless pulpits.

Prayer is the breath of the soul; without it you will turn blue.

Prayer is like a computer—you can only get out of it what you put into it.

Pray is one four-letter word you can use anywhere.

Nothing is discussed more and practiced less than prayer.

Prayer must come not from the roof of the mouth, but from the root of the heart.

Prayer will either make a man stop sinning, or sin will make him stop praying.

People who do not believe in prayer will make an exception when tragedy strikes.

Prayer is not a device for getting our wills done through heaven, but a desire that God's will may be done on earth through us.

No one is poor who can by prayer open the storehouse of God.

Prayer is measured by its depth, not its length.

Prayer is a golden river at whose brink some die of thirst while others kneel and drink.

Overheard in a prayer meeting: "Lord, I talk too much."

God not only prompts the asking—he also provides the answer.

The melody of prayer is best played with the notes of praise, adoration, confession, and thanksgiving.

We lie to God in prayer if we don't rely on God after prayer.

Prayer must mean something to us if it is to mean anything to God.

Prayer is the place where burdens change shoulders.

Prayer is not a last extremity—it's a first necessity.

If a care is too small to be made into a prayer, it is too small to be made into a burden.

If there is no appointed time for prayer, soon there will be no time at all for prayer.

Prayer is asking for rain, and faith is carrying the umbrella.

No man who is selfish, cynical, and superficial on his feet is ever a saint on his knees.

You can expect God to intervene when you have taken time to intercede.

There is no time lost in waiting if you are waiting on the Lord.

Keep a secret and it is yours; tell it to God and it's prayer; tell it to people and it's gossip.

The prayer that yields the richest rewards of grace is the prayer we pray for our enemies.

I reach new heights when I get down on my knees to pray.

God is easier to talk to than most people.

Strange that you can sell drugs in school and show X-rated movies in health classes, but you are forbidden to pray.

A praying man will never be a useless man.

Prayer is not a substitute for working, thinking, watching, suffering, and giving.

Prayer is the one weapon the enemy cannot duplicate or counterfeit.

A church stays on its feet when its members get on their knees.

He who *waits* on the Lord will not be crushed by the *weights* of adversity.

Never take on more work than you have time to pray about.

When it comes to prayer, don't hang up—hang on.

Prayer is the pause that empowers.

When life knocks you to your knees, you are then in the best position to pray.

Productive prayer requires earnestness, not eloquence.

God does more than hear words—he reads hearts.

Don't expect a million-dollar answer to a five-cent prayer.

The tragedy of our day is not unanswered prayer but unoffered prayer.

Prayer is the mortar that holds our house together.

Trouble will drive you to prayer, but prayer will drive away the trouble.

More is said about prayer and less done about it than any other subject in the Bible.

Prayer is a time of exposure of the soul to God.

Anything worth worrying about is worth praying about.

While prayer ascends, God's mercy descends.

Fifty percent of sick persons need prayer more than pills, aspirations more than aspirins, meditation more than medicine.

God does not measure our prayers—he weighs them.

Let your prayer be without words rather than your words being without prayer.

Strength in prayer is better than length in prayer.

Nothing lies outside the reach of prayer except that which is out of the will of God.

Change your prayers sometimes—wake up in the morning and say, "God, what can I do for you today?"

Instead of praying for God to change things, situations, and people, pray, "Lord, change me."

If your troubles are deep-seated and long-standing, try kneeling.

The kindness of Christ is best developed in the darkness of prayer.

Courage is fear that has prayed through.

Adversity should never get the Christian down—except on his knees.

A short prayer will reach heaven if you don't live far away.

If you cannot sleep at night, don't count sheep—talk to the Shepherd.

God hears the heart without words but never words without heart.

Satan laughs at our toil, mocks at our wisdom, but trembles when we pray.

Prayer doesn't need proof—it needs practice.

The world seeks victory by trying to get back on its feet—the Christian by getting down on his knees.

We do our best praying when the I, me, and mine have worked their way out of our way.

Things begun in prayer usually end in power.

If you work for God, form a committee; if you work with God, form a prayer group.

The Christian can see more on his knees than the educated can see on his tiptoes.

Let prayer be our portion. Let prayer be our pastime, our passion. Let prayer be our practice.

Prayer: Lord, when we are wrong, make us willing to change—and when we are right, make us easy to live with.

Sooner or later we will need some foreign aid—the kind we get from prayer.

Some people could well pray in the morning, "Now I lay me down to sleep" for all the spiritual effort they make during the day.

Keep praying, but be thankful that God's answers are wiser than our prayers.

He who walks upright must learn to kneel daily.

Prayer is not overcoming God's reluctance but taking hold of God's willingness.

Never face a day until you have prayed.

The devil is never very far away when you are too busy to pray.

God will supply that for which we have knee'd.

You cannot pray for peace with your hands clenched into fists.

He who cannot pray when the sun shines will not know how to pray when the clouds come.

The angel brought Peter out of prison, but it was prayer that brought the angel.

Short prayers have the largest range and the surest arms.

Some tears are liquid prayers.

Living a life of prayer is worth more than writing a book on it.

Don't pray for an easy life; pray to be stronger men.

You'll never find a busy signal on the prayer line to heaven.

Don't wait to be driven to your knees by the realization you have nowhere to go.

Preaching moves men, prayer moves God.

A saint is a person whose life makes it easier to believe in God.

Peace of mind depends upon strength of mind.

Some people talk more about their problems than praying for them.

Some people pray one way then live another.

The devil would rather you wear out your shoes going to church than your trousers praying.

Life is fragile—handle with prayer.

Prayer: Lord don't let anything come my way that we cannot handle.

Prayer need not be long when faith is strong.

The prayers of a man on his feet are just as important as those he says on his knees.

No one can live wrong and pray right—no one can pray right and live wrong.

To walk with God, we must make it a practice to talk with God.

The man who does all his praying on his knees does not pray enough.

True prayer is a way of life, not just a case of emergency.

Tarry at a promise until God meets you there.

If prayer does not drive sin out of your life, sin will drive prayer out.

Prayer is the child's helpless cry to the Father's attentive ear.

Long prayers in public could indicate short prayers in private.

Prayer and praise are like the wings of a bird—both must work together.

Too many want God to change things and people when they pray, but they are not willing to let God change them.

Powerful praying is not a pretty phrase; but persistent prevailing.

True prayer does not begin when we kneel, nor does it cease when we rise.

He who moves God must be first moved by God.

By praying, learn to pray.

Most people have too little prayer and too much propaganda.

Pray, yes, but when you get off your knees, don't sit down—hustle.

Prayer will loosen many a knot that my own hands cannot untie.

God has a solution planned before we even know we have a problem.

A person who takes time for prayer will find time for all the other things needing his attention.

Morning prayers lead to evening praise.

The best way to bring people to God is to bring them to God in prayer.

It may be difficult to wait on the Lord, but it's worse to wish you had.

Strange that in prayer we often ask for a change in circumstance rather than in our character.

Stay on your knees before God and on your feet before men.

True prayer is a way of life, not just an emergency detour.

How rare it is to find a person quiet enough to hear God speak.

Christians need to pray two prayers: "Lord, give me light," and, "Give me grace to walk in the light."

God tells us to burden him with whatever burdens us.

When you pray and aim at nothing, you are sure to hit it.

Frequent prayers lessen daily cares.

God rules the world by the prayer of his saints.

Through prayer, finite man taps the power of the infinite God.

◆Prejudice

Accurate knowledge is the basis of correct opinion; the want of it makes the opinions of many people of little value.

A lot of people will be unhappy in heaven when they discover that it is not the exclusive property of one denomination.

The longest leap in the world is to jump to a conclusion.

Prejudice is being down on something you are not up on.

Fanatics don't change their minds and won't change the subject.

Have convictions, but be sure your convictions are not prejudices.

Some convictions are nothing more than prejudices.

Prejudice is the child of ignorance.

Prejudice is a loose idea held tightly.

It takes a lot of cheek to uphold a narrow mind.

The difference between a conviction and a prejudice is that you can explain a conviction without getting angry.

Prejudice is having the answers without knowing all the facts.

Only a new love can destroy an old prejudice.

A closed mind is like a locked, shuttered house—it is secure and quiet, but also dark and gloomy.

A one-track mind rarely has anything worthwhile to offer in the way of views.

◆Pride (see also Humility; Modesty)

A golfer has one advantage over the fisherman—he doesn't have to show anything to prove it.

He who has too much brass seldom has the necessary polish.

The reason some computers run into trouble is that some of the punch cards think that they are holier than the rest.

The most conceited man in the world? He called Dial-a-Prayer to see if there were any messages.

You can't glorify self and Christ at the same time.

Don't brag—it isn't the whistle that pulls the train.

Bragging may not bring happiness, but no man having caught a large fish goes home through the alley.

The greatest barrier between some Christians and God's omnipotent power is their own supposed strength.

A snob is an inferior person with a superiority complex.

Flattery is the ability to tell another person what he wants to hear.

If you serve only for the approval of men, you will lose the approval of God.

Most self-made people stop working too soon.

The best remedy for conceit is to sit down and make a list of all the things you don't know.

The man who has the right to boast doesn't have to.

Flattery is all right as long as you don't believe the one giving the flattery.

The greatest of all passions—seeking self-approval.

Status is a poor substitute for stature—a man should be able to get ahead without getting a swelled head.

People who place too much importance on their standing are generally too big for their shoes.

You don't have to be much of a musician to toot your own horn.

An egotist is a man who thinks that if he had not been born, people would have asked why not.

When the "I" becomes dominant, the "spiritual eye" sees the entire world in a distortion.

If tempted to sound off, remember a drum makes noise though it is empty.

Not even an egotist is all bad; at least he doesn't go around talking about other people.

We seem to think the kingdom of God will not come unless we personally bring it about.

Nothing makes you listen more carefully to your neighbor's conversation than to hear your name mentioned.

Talk to a man about himself and he will listen for hours.

Pride is the only poison that is good for you when swallowed.

The strength that comes from confidence can be quickly lost to conceit.

Too much uplift nowadays is confined to noses.

Our work is to cast care; God's work is to take care.

How to dislocate your shoulder—pat yourself on the back.

A man is usually as young as he feels; but he is seldom as important as he feels.

Pride, stubbornness, and exploitation of others form an incendiary trio.

Swallow your pride—it contains no calories.

The people most preoccupied with titles and status are usually the least deserving of them.

If there's one thing we should let others find out for themselves, it's how great we are.

Wouldn't it be nice to be as sure of anything as some people are of everything?

People who run down others are taking a roundabout way of praising themselves.

The trouble with the self-made man is that he worships the creator.

The egotist is always someone who is me-deep in conversation.

Some folks try to push themselves forward by patting themselves on the back.

People who sing their own praises do so without accompaniment.

Pride is the only disease that makes everyone sick except the one who has it.

The mental cases most difficult to cure are those people who are crazy about themselves.

Conceit is the devil's gift to little men.

Something that's hard to keep under your hat is a big head.

Some people have their backs to the wall because they've been putting up too much a front.

A perfectionist is one who takes great pains—and gives them to other people.

The man who toots his horn the loudest is the one who is in the fog.

The easiest way to crush your laurels is to rest on them.

Flattery is the art of telling another person exactly what he thinks of himself.

A form of advertising that's a liability instead of an asset is a person blowing his own horn.

Conceit is what makes a little squirt think he is a fountain of knowledge.

Flattery looks like friendship the way a wolf looks like a dog.

Egotism has been described as just a case of mistaken nonentity.

When you are completely satisfied, remember what happens to the fat turkey.

Many a man satisfied with himself is awfully disappointing to other people.

Just when the world begins to admire a man, he breaks out in vanity.

The man who seeks advice too often is probably looking for praise rather than information.

We all admire the wisdom of people who ask us for advice.

When you think you have made your mark on the world, watch out for the guys with the erasers.

When a person is always right, there is something wrong.

The best kind of pride is that which compels a man to do his best even though no one is looking.

The problem with a perfect person—they have no room for improvement.

Some people are easily entertained. All you have to do is to sit down and listen to them.

The only thing that can keep growing without nourishment is ego.

He who stands high in his own estimation is still a long way from the top.

A man's worth is seldom the value he places on himself.

Only the truly great are humble—and only the humble are truly great.

It's all right to hold up your head, but don't turn up your nose.

An egotist is a man who thinks as much of himself as you think of yourself.

Some people know more when you try to tell them something than when you ask them something.

The bigger the man, the less he's aware of his size.

The person who knows nothing always seems to be confident in all things.

Pride is to the character like the attic to the house—the highest part and generally the most empty.

The person who takes a high place before his fellowman must take a low place before his God.

If success turns your head, you are facing in the wrong direction.

In the middle of fault is *U*.

You are always in the wrong key when you start singing your own praises.

Most people are quite happy to suffer in silence if they are sure everyone knows they are doing it.

Pride is the stone over which many people stumble.

He who blows his own horn cannot enjoy listening to the band.

Humility is like underwear—we should have it, but we should never show it.

A boaster and a liar are cousins.

Beware of anyone who falls at your feet. He may be reaching for the corner of the rug.

The bigger the person's head, the easier it is to fill his shoes.

Man is the only animal you can pat on the back and his head swells.

The trouble with blowing your own horn is it leaves no wind for climbing.

The egotist has *I* trouble.

The less a person knows, the more certain he is that he is right.

Man is made of dust, and that dust that is stuck on itself is mud.

The greatest of all faults is to imagine that you have none.

Many people might have attained wisdom had they not assumed they already possessed it.

Prayer: "Lord make me humble, and when I am humble, don't let me know it."

Every time some people look in the mirror, they take a bow.

Temper is what gets most of us into trouble—pride is what keeps us there.

Every time you turn green with envy, you are ripe for trouble.

You cannot spell sin or pride without *I* being in the middle.

Staring up to admire your own halo will give yourself a pain in the neck.

Very often, a little soap is enough to make a man slip.

Wearing a halo too tight gives others a headache.

Some people are so conceited they think that God changes his opinions to suit their needs.

When you find a person who "knows all things," take no advice from him.

About the only opinions that do not eventually change are the ones we have about ourselves.

Pride is a plant that doesn't grow well in the shadow of the cross.

Swallowing your pride will never give you indigestion.

Conceit is a form of *I* strain.

Many a person who prides himself on having an open mind merely has a vacant one.

It's strange, but a big head is the sign of a small man.

The real test of a big man is his willingness to occupy a small place in a great way.

The less some people know, the more eager they are to tell you about it.

People are seldom too busy to stop and tell you how busy they are.

Egotism is that certain something that enables a man in a rut to think he's in the groove.

Egotists are *I* specialists.

Conceit is an illness that refreshes the victim and makes others sick.

Fellows who boast of being self-made men usually have a few parts missing.

A big head is hard to keep under your hat.

The measure of a man is what he *doesn't* with power.

Most of us carry a stumbling block around—we cover it with a hat.

Flattery is something nice someone tells you about yourself that you wish were true.

Some would rather stay lost than ask for directions.

◆Principles

It's possible to do the right thing for the wrong reason.

It's never right to do wrong, and it's never wrong to do right.

Every day every Christian must choose among progression, discretion, and retrogression.

The person with small principles draws small interest.

When it comes to a solid principle, it's better to be a hardtop than a convertible.

Better to have poisoned blood than to have poisoned principles.

A man is never better than his principles.

A person without principles in one area will doubtless have principles in another.

One may be better than his reputation but never better than his principles.

When a person sells principles for popularity, he is soon bankrupt.

It is impossible to travel in the wrong direction and reach the right destination.

Be square if you want a circle of friends.

Hope of ill gain is the beginning of loss.

Many a rich bird feathers his nest by foul means.

✦Procrastination (*see also* Work)

Very few people are fast enough to keep up with all their good intentions.

On the bypass of by and by, man arrived at the conclusion of never.

Promises are like snowballs—they are easy to make but hard to keep.

Never put off until tomorrow what you feel like doing today—tomorrow it may be against the doctor's order.

Always put off until tomorrow what you should not do at all.

One reason for doing the right things today is tomorrow.

Since our task is difficult, we dare not relax; since our opportunities are brief, we dare not delay.

Sometimes it's better to put off until tomorrow what you are likely to louse up today.

Procrastination is the devil's chloroform.

Never put off until tomorrow what you should have done yesterday.

Tomorrow is the road that often leads to the house of despair.

The lazier the man, the more he plans for tomorrow.

There will always be enough for today without taking on yesterday.

Do your work today as if there were no tomorrow.

He who neglects the present moment may throw away all he has.

Tomorrow is often the busiest day of the year.

One of these days is too often none of these days.

You plan to make good some day—why not make good today?

The man who procrastinates struggles with ruin.

The devil doesn't care how much we do, as long as we don't do it today.

If you put off till tomorrow what can be done today, someone may invent a machine to do it.

A little neglect may breed mischief.

A procrastinator suffers from hardening of the oughteries.

One of the devil's most successful wiles is "Wait just a little while."

Procrastination never landed one soul in heaven, but it has doomed many to an eternal hell.

It's never too early to accept Christ, but at any moment it could be too late.

Hard work is often the piling up of the easy things you neglected to do.

Join the TNT Club—Today Not Tomorrow.

He who hesitates is last.

Putting off tough jobs makes them harder.

Live as though every day were your last—and someday you will be right.

◆Profanity

Profanity is the use of strong words by weak people.

Swearing is a lazy man's way of trying to be emphatic.

Profanity is an outward sign of stupidity.

Profanity is evidence of the lack of sufficient vocabulary and brains.

R

✦Religion

A religion not worth exporting is not worth keeping at home.

The man whose religion costs him nothing pays for what he gets.

The person who argues most about religion usually has the least of it.

Some people make a cloak out of the smallest piece of religion.

We talk a great deal about religion in this country, but we need to stop long enough to let our feet catch up with our mouths.

The religion in your heart should be visible in your life.

Some people's religion is like the Easter hat—they use it just once a year.

A religion that costs nothing is worth nothing.

Some people never get religion in their hands and feet.

Religion should have no place in your life unless it has first place.

It is a sad religion that is never strong except when its owner is sick.

Most people have some sort of religion, at least they know which church they're staying away from.

Religion is a cloak worn by some people who will be warm enough in the next world without one.

God wants man to have religion more than in his soul; he wants him to have it in his shoes.

Religion is behavior—not just belief.

✦Repentance

Repentance means not only a heart broken *for* sin but *from* sin.

Many people in mending their ways use very thin threads.

Repentance is not only saying, "I'm sorry." It is also saying, "I'm through."

Some so-called penitential crying is only hypocritical lying.

To be good, you must first look and see that you are bad.

Money will never buy repentance.

He who delays his repentance pawns his soul to the devil.

To grieve over sin is one thing; to repent is another.

Late repentance is seldom true but true repentance is never late.

✦Reputation (*see also* Character)

A company is known by the people it employs.

The most destructive acid in the world is found in our sour disposition.

No one raises his reputation by lowering others.

You cannot build reputation on what you are going to do.

Reputation is for time; character is for eternity.

Glass, china, and reputation are easily cracked and never well mended.

It is easier to acquire a good reputation than to lose a bad one.

Reputation is never completely secured—it is being continually earned.

Your hometown is where they can't figure out how you did so well.

When we live for the approval of God, we need not to be disturbed by the opinion of others.

Some get reputation and keep it; others permit reputation to keep them.

Reputation is seeming; character is being.

Reputation is manufactured; character is grown.

Reputation is what you need to get a job; character is what you need to keep one.

Reputation is what men think you are; character is what God knows you are.

Reputation is what you have when you come to town; character is what you have when you leave.

The only reputation that matters is your reputation in heaven.

An eminent reputation is as dangerous as a bad one.

The best way to gain a good reputation is to be what you desire to appear.

✦Responsibility

Plan as if Christ's return is years away, but live as if he is coming today.

Beware of the danger of allowing your rights to subordinate your responsibilities.

We have no right to complain about mistakes made by people who are doing the work we should be doing.

No job is boring if we can see God's purpose in it.

Not once has God said, "Don't call me; I'll call you."

We are immortal until our work is done.

Most of us get what we deserve, but only the successful will admit it.

Privilege and responsibility are two sides of the same coin.

It takes more time to hide one's talent than it does to use it for God.

The bread of life is never served dining-room style; it's on the cafeteria plan—you must help yourself.

A feeling of responsibility for others is the first step toward unselfishness and maturity.

The higher you go, the more dependent you become on others.

A Christian must carry something heavier on his shoulder than a chip.

Burying one's talent is a grave mistake.

So many get into the deadly trap of measuring their achievements by what others haven't done.

Three things to think of—from where you came, where you are going, and to whom you must give account.

Freedom is not a question of doing as we like but doing as we ought.

Jesus teaches that a man's attitude toward the kingdom of God is revealed by his attitude toward his property.

Our sorrows are usually the result of letting our wishes replace our duty.

When duty calls, many are not home.

If God writes *opportunity* on one side of the door, he writes *responsibility* on the other.

One way to keep your feet on the ground is to put responsibility on your shoulder.

Great trials are often necessary to prepare us for great responsibilities.

We believe in a thing when we are prepared to act as if it were true.

It does not do you any good to sit up and take notice if you just keep sitting.

Many a person has convictions for which he wants someone else to supply courage.

People may forget how fast you did the job but never how well you did it.

God holds us responsible, not for what we have, but for what we could have; not for what we are, but for what we might be.

If you are dissatisfied with your lot, perhaps you haven't taken care of it.

Things begin to look right when you stop doing wrong.

People who shirk responsibility may really be shunning success.

God often entrusts us with a little to see what we could do with our lot.

A teacher is a person charged with the responsibility of keeping a room full of live wires grounded.

I owe all my success in life to always having been a quarter hour ahead of all my appointments and responsibilities.

Being first is not as important as being right.

As Christians, our responsibility is to be faithful.

The law gives us first duty and then privilege.

Responsibility is my response to his ability.

As we must account for every idle word, so we must for every idle silence.

Many people stand for their rights but fall down on their responsibilities.

You should do your duty as *you* see it.

A lot of people go beyond the call of duty to get even farther away.

Are you willing to risk your reputation to fill your responsibility?

No snowflake in an avalanche ever feels responsible.

It is easier to do a job right than to explain why you didn't.

Having to suffer the consequences of our acts tends to develop responsibility.

A genius is a man who never puts on his thinking cap without taking off his jacket.

God's part we cannot do—our part God will not do.

There's one thing the Christian gives and still must keep—his word.

For every benefit you receive, responsibility is owed.

◆Revival

Revival is the life of Jesus poured into human hands.

The closer we come to God, the more we realize our distance.

Revival means removal.

Every generation needs a regeneration.

A recipe for revival: Draw a circle and get inside, then pray God will send revival within the circle.

We don't need the sand that Jesus walked on; we need the Jesus who walked on the sand.

It is the duty of the pastor not only to comfort the distressed but to distress the comfortable.

Some churches are so dead they don't need revival—they need resurrection.

When Christians are on fire, believers are warmed and sinners are attracted to the light.

S

✦Salvation

Jesus took our place that we might have his peace; he took our sin that we might have his salvation.

Where one goes hereafter depends on what he does after here.

The new birth is not optional—it's imperative.

Jesus came to save the lost, the last, and the least.

Of all the thousands of deceptive substitutes, a substitute for salvation is the worst.

One must be a wide-awake Christian before he can fall asleep in Jesus.

If you keep rejecting the "come" of salvation, you will have to accept the "depart" of damnation.

There are none so good that they can save themselves—none so bad that God cannot save them.

The sinner has only two options—be pardoned or be punished.

When God pardons sin, he purges the record, erases the remembrance, and empowers the recipient.

When God saves us, our sins are forgiven and forgotten forever.

Salvation causes us to step out of sin's slavery into security with Christ.

Justification means man's guilt gone and Christ's goodness given.

Salvation may come quietly, but we must not remain quiet about it.

We can be so caught up in the theology of the coming of Christ that we forget the fact of his coming.

The One who died as our substitute now lives as our Advocate.

How tragic that people pay a high price for being lost when salvation is free.

Empty cross—empty tomb—full salvation!

Calvary is never to be forgotten; and never to be repeated.

Christ believed is salvation received.

God makes us miserable through conviction to make us happy through confession.

Reformation is turning over a new leaf; regeneration is receiving a new life.

Honest restitution is a mark of honest repentance.

Better not to have been born at all than never to have been born again.

A man can go to hell in his own way, but only go to heaven God's way—through the door.

It is dangerous and fatal presumption to say "tomorrow" when God says "today."

God votes for us; Satan votes against us—we cast the deciding vote.

The church is a hospital for sinners—not a club for Christians.

Eternal life is the only life insurance you can collect after death.

Nature forms us; sin deforms us; school informs us; but only Christ can transform us.

He who is born of God should increasingly resemble his Father.

Some people have tons of religion but not one ounce of salvation.

Service can put a new coat on a man—but salvation puts a new man in the coat.

Death is more universal than life; everyone dies but not everyone lives.

Salvation is not to be analyzed but realized.

Are you on the rocks or on the Rock?

Good works are not the means of salvation but the result.

A true fear of hell has sent many souls to heaven.

Some expect to repent of their sin at the eleventh hour but die at 10:30.

Some people take up religion as an insurance against hell, then are not willing to pay the premiums.

Man is saved by believing Christ—he is lost by believing the devil.

Salvation is by atonement—not by attainment.

The thief on the cross had just one chance and accepted it.

Salvation is so simple that people overlook it; so free they do not believe it.

Christ came not to save only the "down and out" but also the "up and out."

Where will you be and what will you be doing ten years from today if you keep on doing what you are doing now?

Conversion is going into business with God.

Calvary is God's bank for a sick world.

There is a difference between religion and salvation. Religion is man trying to do something for God—salvation is God doing something for man.

Man may whitewash himself, but only God can wash him white.

Life is a one-way street; we are not coming back.

Conversion to Christ makes useful saints out of useless sinners.

Calvary knows how far man will go into sin and how far God will go for man's salvation.

God has promised forgiveness for your repentance, but he has not promised tomorrow for your procrastination.

There is a time to be born and a time to die. Where we spend eternity depends on the interval between these times.

It is never too early to decide for Christ, but the time will come when it will be too late.

An insurance agent has this slogan on his letterhead: "We insure everything except eternity."

We may travel the sea of life without Christ, but what about the landing?

Millions will miss the second coming of Christ because they fail to accept him and his first coming.

The head may seek God, but it is the heart than finds him.

No one ever got lost on the straight and narrow road.

Some day you must bow your knee to Christ—why not now?

The Christian will find satisfaction just where he found salvation.

It is impossible to drive in the wrong direction and arrive at the right destination.

Pictures of doom: Knowledge without wisdom, a ship without a port, and a man without Christ.

No reformation can ever take the place of regeneration.

Life with Christ is an endless hope; without him, life is a hopeless end.

Salvation is not something we achieve but something we receive.

Heaven and hell are in opposite directions, and no man can go both ways at the same time.

Law condemns the best man; grace saves the worst man.

A person who is almost persuaded is still completely lost.

Salvation depends upon Christ's work for us, while rewards depend upon our works for Christ.

There is a way to stay out of hell, but no way to get out of hell.

In salvation, it's who you know that counts.

What we do with Christ now determines what God will do for us later.

Salvation produces a change within that breaks the chains of sin.

Every Christian carries a key that can open the door of salvation to others.

We are saved by Christ's mediation, not by our merits.

No one is too good—nor too bad—to be a candidate for salvation.

God's grace makes new creatures out of the best and worst sinners.

Salvation changes our heritage from a living death to a deathless life.

Many who are well prepared for a rainy day are not prepared for eternity.

If you make an excuse for sin, your sin will never be excused.

We are saved by God's mercy, not by our merit—by Christ's dying, not by our doing.

You cannot repent too soon because you don't know how soon it may be too late.

If you refuse Christ because you feel you are not good enough, you are settling for less than God made you to be.

To say, "I'm not good enough to be a Christian," is a bit like saying, "I'm not healthy enough to go to the hospital."

God saves us, not for what we are, but for what he can make us.

Plan as if Christ's return were years away, but be ready as if it were today.

The old nature knows no law, the new nature needs no law.

◆Satan

Avoid Satan as a lion, dread him as a serpent, and fear him as an angel of light.

Satan's ploys are no match for the Savior's power.

The devil would rather put a long face on a saint than throw down a high church steeple.

Don't let Satan deceive you into thinking that when you plan carefully to sin secretly you will not be harmed.

When the devil brings up your past, bring up his future.

When we do wrong, the devil is tempting us; when we do nothing, we are tempting him.

The man who is fully surrendered to the Lord will never deliberately surrender to the Enemy.

When adversity is most ready to strike us, God is most ready to strengthen us.

The devil will extend plenty of credit, but think of the payment.

Christians fight evil on two fronts; sin from within and Satan from without.

You can't run with the devil and expect to reign with the Lord later.

One of the devil's temptations is to occupy our minds with the past and future so as to neglect the present.

The devil is an equal opportunity employer—all who work for him will go to hell.

Flirtation with sin can lead to romance with Satan.

Be critical of Satan, but keep in mind that he is a hustler.

It's risky when the devil is driving.

Some people desire to please God—as long as it doesn't offend the devil.

The devil doesn't bother some Christians—he joins them.

If you don't believe in the devil's existence, try working for God for a while.

The devil goes to vacation resorts, too, but you can be sure he is not on vacation.

You may be through with the devil, but the devil is never through with you.

You cannot wait on the Lord and run with the devil at the same time.

The devil promises you the whole world, but he doesn't own a grain of sand.

Some denounce the devil openly but agree with him secretly.

The devil is never too busy to rock the cradle of a sleeping backslider.

When the shepherd speaks well of the wolf, the sheep are in trouble.

As long as we tolerate even the slightest sin and inconsistency in our life, the devil has a toehold.

The devil lives in the realm of feeling, but saints live in the realm of faith.

Christ will not live in the parlor of our hearts if we entertain the devil in the cellar of our thoughts.

The Lord adds and multiplies; the devil subtracts and divides.

Don't permit Satan to remind you of what God has already forgotten.

◆Self-awareness

There are three hard things: steel, a diamond, and to know one's self.

The most difficult thing in life is to know yourself.

The easiest person to deceive is yourself.

If you are looking for perfection, don't look in the mirror.

Some people think they are in the groove when they are really only in a rut.

The worst of all frauds is to cheat oneself.

The man who goes through life looking for something soft can only find it under his hat.

Life would be so simple if our biggest problems came when we were fresh out of high school and knew everything.

You don't need to know where you are going provided you know who you are following.

Don't spend the last half of your life regretting the first half.

Confidence and respect are things you can't buy—you've got to earn them.

There is one thing for which you can be thankful—only you and God have all the facts about yourself.

Every man carries with him the world in which he lives.

◆Self-denial

To get rid of our cross is easy—die upon it.

It is not what we take up but what we give that makes us rich.

You cannot make it into heaven without bearing your cross on earth.

Joining the Red Cross will not take the place of bearing your cross.

Church members wear a cross; a Christian bears a cross.

Fellowship with Christ's suffering is the qualification for sharing his dignity.

The crosses we fear are heavier than the crosses we bear.

They who receive scars for Christ will wear stars with Christ.

What we have given up for Christ is not forfeited but transferred.

The cross is easier to him who takes it up than to him who drags it along.

✦Selfishness

Americans used to say, "Give me liberty." Today they just say, "Give me."

The perfect gift for the person who has everything—a burglar alarm.

A bore is a person who spends so much time talking about himself that you can't talk about yourself.

Too many people live cafeteria style—self-service.

No one is so empty as when he is filled with thoughts of himself.

There is little chance for people to get together as long as most of us want to be in the back of the church, the front of the bus, and the middle of the road.

A selfish heart loves for what it can get—a Christlike heart loves for what it can give.

Selfishness makes Christmas a burden; love makes it a delight.

Some people use their religion like a bus—they ride on it only when it is going their way.

A Scotsman wrote the editor of a magazine saying if they didn't quit publishing Scottish jokes, he would quit borrowing the magazine.

Some people are so narrow-minded they have to stack their prejudices vertically.

The man who has a good opinion of himself is usually a poor judge.

We might be more eager to accept advice if it didn't continually interfere with our plans.

If we want an increase of Christ, there must be a decrease of self.

The worst thing about self is that it is the smallest business in the world to be engaged in.

The man who lives for himself lives for the meanest mortal known.

Time spent pitying oneself is worse than a waste of time.

Many people do not cast their bread upon the water until it is stale.

This would be a better world if everyone were as good as he wishes his neighbor was.

People always get into trouble when they think they can handle life without God.

He who builds a fence always fences more out than he fences in.

One of the hardest things about business is minding your own.

The more you do what you like, the less you like what you do.

Some folks with a sympathetic disposition sure waste a lot of it on themselves.

It is the greatest of all mistakes to do nothing because you can do only a little.

Most of us like straightforward people who come right out and say what they think—provided, of course, they agree with us.

Most people will agree with you if you'll just keep quiet.

Jacob wrestled with an angel. Most of us wrestle with just plain self.

A miser is a person who will catch a cold just to use up the cough medicine.

We tire of those pleasures we take, but never of those we give.

Most of us prefer living in luxury to the luxury of living.

The fanatic is one who increases his speed after he loses his way.

More Christians need to say, "What must I do?" instead of saying, "I want nothing to do."

God sends no one away empty except those who are full of themselves.

He who falls in love with himself will have no rivals.

Envy provides the mud that failure throws at success.

Every time you turn green with envy, you are ripe for trouble.

How empty is a life that is filled with nothing but things.

Half of our trouble comes from wanting our way—the other half comes from having it.

Blowing out the other fellow's candle won't make yours shine any brighter.

Overstuffed bodies and underfed souls make a pretty poor combination.

Of all the four-letter words, *self* is the worst.

Selfishness is the essence of sin.

Everyone wants the world changed, but few are willing to change themselves.

When you are wrapped up in yourself, you are overdressed.

At the end of life we'll find that the only things we've lost were those we tried to keep.

We do not always see things as they are; we usually see things as we are.

The only sympathy that is wasted is when it is used on self.

We should lay aside self, or God will lay us aside.

◆Service

Want the best?—give your best.

No one can help everybody, but everybody can help someone.

God chose the poor and the few to do his work because the rich and the many, being preoccupied, refused him.

Grant that the heat in my heart will melt the lead in my feet.

God tends to use the one nearest him.

It is so much easier to tell a person what to do with his problem that to stand with him in pain.

It is better to do one thing for God than to promise to do forty things you can't do.

Service can never become slavery to one who loves.

If the world seems cold to you, kindle fires to warm it.

Many of the debts we owe are payable to man.

Forget yourself for others, and others will not forget you.

God measures our service, not by our ability, but by our willingness.

God has called us to play the game, not to keep the score.

Don't despise little things; a lantern can do what the sun can never do—shine at night.

The Christian's place is on the front line, not on the sideline.

Mend your nets with prayer, cast them in faith, and draw them in love.

Greatness lies not in trying to *be* somebody but in trying to *help* somebody.

The best way to find good in thyself is to begin to look for good in others.

Whatever you do, do it well and then some. That "then some" is what counts.

Do your best—angels can do no more.

To be successful all you need is to follow the advice you give to others.

When you dig another out of his troubles, you find a place to bury your own.

We should employ our passions in the service of life, not spend life in the service of our passions.

We are pardoned from sin, but we are not excused from service.

God didn't call you into the vineyard to eat grapes but to get busy and hoe.

Assist in all the things that need assistance, and resist all things that need resistance.

You will never become dizzy doing good turns. ,

Jesus went about doing good; many just go about.

Small deeds done are better than great deeds planned.

A dewdrop does God's will as much as a thunderstorm.

This is the true greatness: to serve unnoticed and work unseen.

Greatness is not measured by how many servants you have but by how many people you serve.

You cannot change human nature, but perhaps you can improve it.

It's hard to keep a chip on the shoulder if you take a bow from time to time.

Pray until the tears come; work till the sweat comes; give till it hurts.

Count your life by deeds—not years.

The best exercise for the heart is to bend down several times during the day to help someone.

The gospel does not shrink our lives—it expands them.

A heart enlarged by sympathy never killed anyone.

God does not comfort his people to make them comfortable but to make them comforters.

The more you do what you like, the less you like what you do.

Some folks with a sympathetic disposition sure waste a lot of it on themselves.

It is the greatest of all mistakes to do nothing because you can do only a little.

What you do for Christ is the test of your service—what we suffer for Christ is our test of love.

We've no time for muddling when we must be ministering.

Facing duty in service is easier than running away.

We make a living by getting, but we make lives by giving.

A man's reward is what he becomes—not what he gets.

Do your best—the forest would be very quiet if no birds sang except the best singers.

True wealth is the satisfaction of talent used in Christian service.

When you help a person up the hill, you find yourself closer to the top.

Ability is wonderful, but God is more interested in your availability.

It's better to attempt to do something and fail than to attempt to do nothing and succeed.

The crowns we wear in heaven must all be won on earth.

We are saved to serve; but we cannot serve to be saved.

Those who bring sunshine into the lives of others cannot keep it themselves.

Service is love dressed in work clothes.

Circumstances don't make a man—they serve him.

A person may rate himself good, if he rates himself by the things others have not done.

He who cares will share.

It is better to fill a little place right than a big place wrong.

The highest bidder for the crown of glory is the lowest wearer of the cross of self-denial.

Some people spend time counting the cost when they should consider the cost for not following him.

Satan selects his helpers from the idle—Christ from those who are busy.

You have not really lived until you have done something for someone who can never repay you.

The truly busy person is so busy that he has no time to think how busy he really is.

The only time we should look down on our neighbor is when we are bending over to help him.

Service is the rent we pay in life for the space we occupy.

A man can do more than he thinks he can, but he usually does less than he thinks he does.

True fame is founded in labors for the happiness of mankind.

It's not a shame having just one talent—the shame is not using it.

Christians should be channels, not chalices.

Every toiler who is true to his task is honorable in God's sight.

The Lord is less concerned about those who make mistakes than he is about those who don't try.

Some people cast a stale crust on the waters and expect chocolate cake in return.

It's not what you gain but what you give that measures the worth of the life you live.

The best way to forget your problems is to help someone else to solve his.

The Lord is more interested in people than in things.

It is far better that we should err in action than completely refuse to perform.

Independence is not always a virtue.

The greatest pleasure in life is to do a good turn and have it discovered by accident.

It is not the hours you put in but what you put in the hours.

We are on earth to love, to live, and to serve, not to grab, growl, and get.

Our aim should be to serve—not to be successful.

Life itself can't give you joy unless you really will it.

Life just gives you time and space—it's up to you to fill it.

Nothing worth having is secured by sin.

Nothing worth keeping is lost in serving God.

It isn't the age—it's the mileage that counts.

When you don't know what to do, do the most helpful things.

Some people spell service, "serve us."

God's requirements are met by God's enablings.

The believer's talents are not to be laid up for self—they are to be laid out for service.

A Christian can do great things for God by doing small things for others.

Your life is God's gift to you; what you do with it is your gift to God.

Our likeness of Christ is measured by our sensitivity to the sufferings of others.

The greatest joy man can experience is to be needed by just one person.

A leader does not begin to serve until he puts serving into his leadership.

Time in Christ's service requires time out for renewal.

Serving Christ under law is a duty; under love it's a delight.

People are seldom too busy to stop and tell you how busy they are.

Not where we serve but whether we serve is most important.

We have heard of many people who did little for God, but did you ever hear of anyone doing too much for God?

God doesn't measure success in units of silver, but in units of service.

Nobody really lives till he finds something big enough to give himself to.

Be of use to people and you will learn to love them.

The Lord uses those who are little in their own eyes; for the smaller we are the more room there is for God to work.

The glory of life is love—not to be loved; to give—not to get; to serve—not to be served.

A determined man with a rusty wrench can do much more than a loafer with all the tools in the machine shop.

Christian service is not optional—it's a command.

He lives not who lives not in earnest.

Ten ways to get rid of the blues: Go out and do something for someone else—then repeat nine times.

God isn't interested in how many talents we have—he's interested in how we are using the talent we have.

Rewards are usually anticlimactic—the fun is in doing.

People will be happy in about the same degree that they are helpful.

I would rather be a faithful watchdog than an indifferent shepherd.

A useful life can't be entirely peaceful and carefree.

Very few people are fast enough to keep up with all their good intentions.

Many Christians suffer from loneliness because they are sitting instead of serving.

The only way to keep the good will and high esteem of the people you work with is to deserve it.

A humble talent that is used is worth more than one of a genius that is idle.

A servant works—a king speaks.

We tire of those pleasures which we receive but never of those we give.

✦Sharing (*see also* Generosity)

It is so much easier to tell a person what to do with his problem than to stand with him in his pain.

No matter what scales we use, we can never know the weight of another person's burden.

The debt we owe to God is payable to man.

How much I'm willing to sacrifice is the measure of my love.

God's part we cannot do; our part he will not do.

Time in Christ's service requires time out for renewal.

Train your heart up to give sympathy and your hand to give help.

Nothing costs as much as caring—except not caring.

A candle loses nothing by lighting another candle.

A Christian shows what he is by what he does with what he has.

God cares for people through people.

The boy in the Bible who gave up his loaves and fishes didn't have to go hungry.

A Christian cares when the world despairs.

When it comes to doing things for others, some people stop at nothing.

One measure of our likeness to Christ is our sensitivity to the suffering of others.

It is better to suffer for the cause of Christ than for the cause of Christ to suffer.

A little encouragement can spark a great endeavor.

We show who we love by what we do with what we have.

Our job is not to see through one another but to see one another through.

The ultimate miracle of love is this—that love is given to us to give to one another.

The highest reward a man can receive for his toil is not what he gets for it but what he becomes by it.

Good received blesses much; good imparted blesses more.

We are not cisterns made for hoarding but channels made for sharing.

A blessing that is shared is not halved but doubled.

The only people you should try to get even with are those who helped you.

The best exercise on earth is to reach down and pull a person up.

When you help someone up the hill, you find yourself closer to the top.

It seems that heads, hearts, and hands would settle the world's trouble much better than arms.

The test of courage comes when we are in the minority; the test of tolerance comes when we are in the majority.

Give your best to the world and the best will come back to you.

He who receives a blessing should not forget it—he who gives it should not remember it.

Don't hoard ideas—the more you radiate the more you germinate.

There is nothing so taking as generous giving.

He who gives when he is asked has waited too long.

To touch the heart of another, use your heart.

We die by living to ourselves; we live by dying to ourselves.

The best goodness is habitual goodness.

The biggest step you can take is the one you take when you meet the other person half way.

When you help others to grow, you grow yourself.

If you wish your merit to be known, acknowledge that of others.

Money can't buy happiness—unless you spend it on somebody else.

How *much* one knows is not as important as what he *does* with what he knows.

What we give determines our wealth—not what we get.

He who sees a need and waits to be asked for help is as unkind as if he had refused it.

Realize that every material thing you have isn't owned but loaned to you from God.

The man who collects knowledge without passing it on to others is like a fruit tree in the desert.

The best way to forget your own problems is to help someone else to solve his.

If your Christianity is worth having, it's worth sharing.

A selfish heart loves for what it can get; a Christian heart loves for what it can give.

Porcupine Christians—they have many good points, but you cannot get close to them.

Those who give most are least concerned about returns.

If you share another's burden, both of you will walk straighter.

The things you do for nothing are often the most rewarding.

Everybody should have some secret sorrows; don't tell others all your troubles.

Whatever we possess becomes double value when we share it with others.

In this world it is not what we take up, but what we give up, that makes us rich.

 # Sin

The cross is a symbol of God's heartbreak over a world that has gone astray.

One may go wrong in many directions but right in only one.

Weep more for the lives of the bad than for the deaths of the good.

There are no amendments to the Ten Commandments.

Our sense of sin will always be in proportion to our nearness to God.

To sin is human; to persist in it is idiocy.

A little sin will add to your trouble, subtract from your energy, and multiply your difficulties.

You can choose your sin, but you can't choose the consequences.

Sin causes the cup of joy to spring a leak.

Think of your own sins, and you will be more understanding of the sins of others.

If we be ruled by sin, we shall inevitably be ruined by it.

True repentance means not only a heart broken *for* sin but also *from* sin.

If Christ is kept outside, something must be wrong inside.

The harvest of judgment is sure as soon as the seed of sin is sown.

Sin is not hurtful because it is forbidden—but is forbidden because it is hurtful.

Crime doesn't pay—it costs.

Christ became a curse *for* us to remove sin's curse *from* us.

Christ was delivered *for* our sins that we might be delivered *from* our sins.

He does not love what is good who does not hate what is evil.

A strong security against sin is to be shocked by it.

The sin of one person often brings tragedy to many.

We gain the victory when we give up sin's pleasure in exchange for Christ's power.

Hatred of sin should not keep us from loving the sinner.

Sin is not judged by the way we see it but by the way God sees it.

Making sin legal does not make it harmless.

Sin puts hell into the soul and the soul into hell.

No sin is little, for it is against an infinite God.

Spring is the sprouting season, but wild oats grow all year 'round.

Because Christ died *for* sin, we can die *to* sin.

You cannot put your sins behind you until you are willing to face them.

The Holy Spirit cannot apply the blood to unconfessed sin.

Prices may rise and fall, but the price of sin remains the same.

Flirtation with sin can lead to romance with Satan.

Sin is not in the deed; it is in the doer of the deed.

Sin would have few takers if its results occurred immediately.

The most expensive thing in the world is sin.

Sin is a short word, and it often makes short work of its victims.

He that thinks of sin has never thought much of God.

The pleasures of sin are "for a season," but its wages are for eternity.

The trouble with little sins is that they don't stay little.

The wages of sin have never been reduced.

He who has slight thoughts of sin never had great thoughts of God.

Sin always starts out as being fun.

Sin was once called sin—now it is a complex.

All sin springs from the taproot of self-will.

There are many new sinners, but there are no new sins.

The path of the world seems pleasant enough if you don't stop to think where you're going.

Wickedness never goes unpunished; righteousness never goes unrewarded.

Beware of the high cost of low living.

If we walk close enough to God, there will be no room for sin to come between us.

All man's problems can be traced directly or indirectly to sin, Satan, or self.

Sinners will take more pains to go to hell than saints to go to heaven.

A lot of people spend six days sowing wild oats, then go to church on Sunday praying for crop failure.

The wages of sin are paid on time.

When a man is ready to confess his sins, God is always ready to cover them with his blood.

Moderation in sin is no more possible than moderation in hanging.

The Christian has not lost the power to sin but the desire to sin.

Four words with a message: sin now, pay later.

Sin deceives, defiles, deadens, and destroys.

Some would think water tasted better if it were a sin to drink it.

A few people are led into temptation, but most are able to find their own way.

To "be angry and sin not" means to be angry only at sin.

The more a person is addicted to vice, the less he cares for advice.

The only right time to get angry is when you get angry at sin.

The only thing that is improved by breaking is the sinner's heart.

Two big sins—giving the wrong impressions and drawing wrong conclusions.

The wages of sin is death; let's quit before payday.

If you do not want the fruit of sin, stay out of the orchard.

The way of a transgressor is hard, but it is not lonely.

Wild oats need no fertilizer.

Believers are not sinless, but they should sin less.

Worldly values are a poor investment—they never pay what they promise.

We may whitewash sin, but only Jesus' blood can truly wash it white.

Grace does not offer freedom *to* sin; it offers freedom *from* sin.

Sin blinds our eyes; grace opens them.

We always pay for the pleasure of sin with the coin of sorrow.

Playing with sin is toying with judgment.

Eventually secret sins make the headlines.

Sin must be dealt with in one of two ways—punishment or pardon.

It's the sins we cover up that eventually bring us down.

Sin brings fear—confession brings freedom.

Adultery is a guilt-edged invitation to tragedy.

At Calvary, Christ *crossed* out our sins.

Confess your sins, not your neighbor's.

Not even in this world does sin pay its servant good wages.

God is not against you for your sin, but against you because of your sin.

Only fools fool with sin.

Few are willing to deny that they are sinners, but few are willing to admit they are sinning.

The chains of sin are too light to be felt until they are so strong you cannot break them.

Sinners hate Christians because they make them conscious of their sin.

Sinners who imagine they are hard-boiled are really only half-baked.

The nearer we are to God, the more conscious we become of sin.

The sinfulness of sin depends on our appreciation of what is evil and what is good.

It's remarkable the way preaching sounds personal when it begins to deal with the matter of sin.

Unconfessed sin pollutes the Christian's tongue.

Man calls sin infirmity; God calls it iniquity.

He who cannot be angry at evil lacks enthusiasm for good.

There is nothing as tragic as combining high mentality with low morality.

The curse for sin finds its only remedy in the cross of Christ.

Christ's cleansing power can remove the most stubborn stain of sin.

Sin is the greatest of all detectives—be sure your sins will find you out.

Destroy the sin in your life or it will destroy you.

The greatest sinners are those who feel sin least of all.

The most expensive thing in the world is sin.

Little sins are the pioneers of hell.

To love a small sin is a great sin.

Your hatred of sin depends upon your degree of love toward God.

No small sin is small because all sin opposes God.

◆Smiling

A smile is mightier than a grin.

Smiles never go up in price nor down in value.

People all over the world smile in the same language.

You might as well laugh at yourself once in a while; everybody else does.

If there is a smile in your heart, your face will show it.

God gives us faces; we create our own expressions.

Smiles and frowns cost nothing, but the difference in effect is enormous.

A smile is a wrinkle that shouldn't be removed.

Wear a smile and have friends; wear a scowl and have wrinkles.

Consider yourself improperly clothed unless you are wearing a smile.

You have grown up the day you have learned to laugh at yourself.

A smile is the whisper of a laugh.

When you crack a smile your personality improves.

Definition of cheerfulness: the act of concealing your true feelings.

The person who is smart enough to keep smiling usually winds up with something good enough to smile about.

Some people grin and bear it—others smile and change it.

A smile will go a long way, but you will have to start it on its journey.

Your smile is more important than anything else you wear.

A smile is the lighting system of the face and the heating system of the heart.

It is hard to tell if some people are cheerful or just proud of their teeth.

It may happen that some people are too tired to smile, so give them one of yours.

If you want to spoil the day of a chronic grouch, give him a smile.

People who smile when something goes wrong have probably just thought of someone they can blame it on.

Laughter is the shock absorber that softens and minimizes the bumps of life.

A smile is a light in the window of your face that shows that your heart is at home.

The whole world is a camera—smile please.

Laugh and the whole world laughs with you—frown and see who cares.

It always pays to smile in the morning because later in the day you may not feel like it.

You should not only smile from "ear to ear" but from "year to year."

A smile adds face value.

Never be afraid to be gracious—look what a little polish can do for scuffed shoes.

A smile is a curve that can set a lot of things straight.

A smile is a very inexpensive way to improve your looks.

You will never offend a person by returning a smile.

I would sooner wear a phony smile than a sincere frown.

Blessed is the man who can laugh at himself because he'll never cease to be amused.

No smile is as beautiful as the one that struggles through tears.

A cheerful countenance has a lot of face value.

Did you realize that laughter can be heard farther than weeping?

Smile a while and give your frown a rest.

Some people wear two-hundred-dollar suits but wear ten-cent expressions on their faces.

◆Special Days

The most important part about Christmas is the first six letters.

Unless we see the cross overshadow the cradle, we will have lost the real meaning of Christ's birth.

At Christmas consider not so much the gift of a friend but the friendship of the giver.

It is Christmas in the heart that puts Christmas in the air.

The Christmas bells some like best are on the cash registers.

Your greatest Christmas cheer comes when you dispense cheer.

Don't be so wrapped up in God's gifts that you forget the Giver.

Christmas is a time when everyone wants his past forgotten and the present remembered.

You will never truly enjoy Christmas until you look into the face of the Father and tell him you have received his Christmas Gift.

Take Christ out of Christmas and all you have is "mas."

Christmas holidays—anticipation, preparation, recreation, prostration, and recuperation.

The best news that the world ever had came from a graveyard near Jerusalem—Jesus is alive!

Some folks are like Easter eggs—ornamented on the outside and hard-boiled on the inside.

Every sunrise is God's Easter greeting.

Joseph's tomb was not a tomb at all—it was just a stopping place for Christ on his way to heaven.

Our Lord has written the promise of the Resurrection, not in books alone, but in every leaf in springtime.

A lot of people mistake Easter Sunday for Decoration Day!

The resurrection of Christ in the past gives the believer bright hope of the future.

The risen life is the best testimony to a risen Christ.

The one word that makes a difference between Christianity and all religions is the word *resurrection.*

The empty cross and the empty tomb spell a full salvation.

The Victim of Calvary became the Victor of Easter.

Christ's resurrection brightens the tomb of every believer.

The stone at Christ's tomb was a pebble to The Rock of Ages.

The Resurrection assures what Calvary secures.

Christ's resurrection is the "bud of promise"—our resurrection is the "flower of fulfillment."

What the new year brings us depends a great déal on what we bring to the new year.

A New Year's Eve party is where you meet the high and the mighty high.

New Year's resolutions are like crying babies in the church—they need to be carried out.

The worst thing about New Year's resolutions is that they come in one year and go out the other.

You can reuse last year's list of resolutions—it's probably about as good as new.

Serious trouble comes when the New Year's resolutions collide with the old year's habits.

If you kept every resolution you made last year, you would probably be skinny, smart, healthy, rich—and bored.

Let us not let the old year die without burying any old grudges.

Don't face the new year or any day without facing Christ.

Summer is the season that bugs us.

◆Stability

Some people are like fences—they run around a lot without getting anywhere.

Flowers that bend toward the sun do so even on cloudy days.

The way to endure change is to find something that never changes.

To be helped, one must be willing to be helped.

Two of the greatest personality handicaps are regret and self-reproach.

Keep both feet on the ground and you won't have far to fall.

A long life might be a good life, but a good life is certainly a long life, regardless of the number of years.

A shallow thinker never leaves a deep impression.

Mature persons take disappointments in stride.

The men who have moved the world have been men that the world could not move.

Wouldn't it be nice to be as sure of anything as some people are of everything?

He who minds his own business has a very good mind and a very good business.

A handful of common sense is worth an armload of learning.

People who are the most difficult to please are often the least worth pleasing.

The old leaves come off the tree when the new ones come in.

Most people have five senses: sight, smell, taste, touch, and hearing. The successful have two more: horse and common.

A man must be big enough to admit his mistakes, smart enough to profit from them, and strong enough to correct them.

Don't be afraid of having too many irons in the fire if the fire is hot.

To stand right with Christ, one must learn to walk with Christ.

Better be a poor man and a rich Christian than a rich man and a poor Christian.

Don't be yourself—be what you ought to be.

A fault recognized is half corrected.

People are like foghorns—they toot loudest when in fog.

Poverty is often a state of mind induced by a neighbor's new car.

You have to know the ropes in your work, or you'll get all tied up in knots.

Those who live on the mountaintop have a longer day than those who live in the valley.

A great oak is only a little nut that held its ground.

To lift others, you must be on higher ground yourself.

When you come to the end of your rope, tie a prayer-knot and hang on.

No power on earth or under earth can make a man do wrong without his consent.

When you are average, you are as close to the bottom as you are to the top.

If you feel you have no faults—that makes another one.

There are no detours along the straight and narrow path.

Being first is not as important as being right.

A cheerful loser is always a winner.

If we live up to the best in ourselves, it will be easy to find the best in others.

A good archer is not known for his arrows but for his aim.

Better to beg one's bread with Lazarus here than beg water with the rich man hereafter.

While looking for the obvious, it's easy to overlook the significant.

The glory is not in never falling but in rising every time you fall.

If we are strong enough from within, there is nothing from without that can do us harm.

Advice is like mushrooms—the wrong kind can prove fatal.

God helped to start you in life; he helped to get you where you are; he won't forsake you now.

Keep your feet on the ground even though friends flatter you.

You can tell you are on the right track—it's usually uphill.

Be like a duck—keep calm and unruffled on the surface, but paddle with all your might under the water.

Tears shed for self are tears of weakness, but tears shed for others are a sign of strength.

To be trusted is a greater compliment than to be loved.

Don't worry about knowing people—just make yourself worth knowing.

There is perfect freedom for people who do the work they want to do and live by that work.

Rough paths often lead to desirable destinations.

Many a man would reach a greater height if he had more depth.

Courage is like a kite—a contrary wind causes it to rise.

Too many Christians are pillows when the Lord wants them to be pillars.

Christ didn't take the people out of the slums—he took the slums out of the people.

A real Christian is one who can speak well of those who speak ill of him.

A hypocrite is one who is not himself on Sunday.

When two quarrel, both are in the wrong.

Horse sense naturally comes from a stable mind.

Greatness does not come from favoritism but by fitness.

No cloud could cast a dark shadow if the sun were not behind it.

Jump to conclusions and you will suffer contusions.

God can stand with us only as we stand firm.

We can only appreciate the miracle of a sunrise if we have waited in the darkness.

Prepare and prevent instead of repair and repent.

Whatever impedes a man and doesn't stop him is progress.

If you don't know where you're going, you may miss it when you get there.

Carve your name on hearts, not upon marble.

Christians may tremble on the Rock of Ages, but the Rock will never tremble under them.

The true Christian is one who is right-side-up in an upside-down world.

◆Stubbornness

To walk in our own way is to run away from God.

Some troubles come from wanting our own way; others come from being allowed to have it.

Some people are so disagreeable that after falling into a river, they insist on swimming upstream.

Some people are like the mule—awful backward about going forward.

Sometimes the best way to convince a man he is wrong is to let him have his own way.

Some people's minds are like concrete—thoroughly mixed and permanently set.

A person who can't lead and won't follow makes a dandy roadblock.

Obstinate men don't hold opinions—opinions hold them.

Some individuals insist on going through life pushing doors marked "pull."

When you close the door to God's love, sometimes he locks it.

When we are walking in our own way, we are actually running from the Lord.

✦Success

Eighty percent of success is just showing up.

It's lonesome at the top, but you do eat better.

People who say that something is impossible should not interrupt those who are managing to get it done.

Success is buying a Mercedes out of petty cash.

The only time you must not fail is the last time you try.

Few people ever carve their way to success with cutting remarks.

When we succeed, we have worked hard; when others succeed, they are lucky.

To be a success, sometimes a person must have enough courage to make a fool of himself.

The secret of success could be learning at an early age that you are not perfect.

You are only responsible to try—not to succeed.

Success is not how far you got, but the distance you traveled from where you started.

Success always covers a multitude of blunders.

Success is the ability to keep your obituary up to date.

Sometimes a noble failure serves the world as faithfully as a distinguished success.

Many a man can credit his success to the fact that he didn't have the advantages others had.

Envy provides the mud that failure throws at success.

Success is sweet, but its secret is sweat.

If at first you do succeed—try something harder.

The reason some people are successful is that they put work and plans together.

The man who is a success does more than what is necessary and keeps doing it.

A man rarely succeeds at anything unless he has fun doing it.

One of the biggest troubles with success is that its recipe is about the same as for a nervous breakdown.

The road to success is almost always under construction.

There aren't any rules for success that work unless you do.

If at first you don't succeed, try a little ardor.

The longest journey begins with a single step.

A person is successful when he has learned to live well, laugh often, and love truly.

When the elevator to success breaks down, your best bet is to take the stairs.

A successful man is the one who lays a foundation for his life with the bricks others have thrown at him.

Some people think they are successful if they can file for their social security before they file for bankruptcy.

Most people do what they are required to do; but successful people do a little more.

It is better to try to do something and fail than to try to do nothing and succeed.

Success is putting your "knows" to the grindstone.

Success does not depend on external help so much as on self-reliance.

No man has ever hurt his eyesight by looking on the successful side of life.

Success comes to those who make the greatest profit from the fewest mistakes.

An ounce of accomplishment is worth a ton of good intentions.

For success, try aspiration, inspiration, and perspiration.

Success is not an accident—it's hard earned.

No one knows what he can do until he tries.

A successful man is one with a wife to tell him what to do and a secretary who does it.

Most of us measure our success by what others haven't done.

Success is a ladder that cannot be climbed with your hands in your pockets.

Attitude makes the difference between success and failure.

The road to success is marked with many tempting parking places.

When success turns your head, you're facing failure.

The only place where success comes before work is in the dictionary.

Dissatisfaction without discouragement leads to progress.

All success is relative—the more success the more relatives.

If at first you don't succeed, you are like most people.

You can be as successful as you think and as successful as you plan to be.

Those who itch for success must keep scratching.

If man goes through life and only earns money, he is not a success.

One should never be ashamed of small beginnings; it is the small growth that disappoints.

The successful man is the one who went ahead and did the things you had planned to do.

If you have no enemies, it is a sure sign success has passed you by.

Fame needs no fanfares.

No man ever made himself a big noise by blowing his own trumpet.

If a person must announce his presence, it's a sure sign he has not yet arrived.

Some men succeed because they are destined to, but most men succeed because they are determined to.

Success is the ability to get ahead of others and to get along with some people.

You don't have to lie awake at nights to succeed—just stay awake days.

Most of us will never do great things, but we can do small things in a great way.

Success is doing what we like to do and making a living at it.

You cannot make a real success without making real enemies.

Prosperity is something created by hard-working citizens for politicians to boast about.

A man hopes that his lean years are behind him—a woman that hers are ahead.

Success is to be measured not so much by the position one has reached in life as the obstacles he has overcome while trying to succeed.

A genius is someone who aims for something no one else can see and hits it.

If a need persists, the solution exists.

Someone with a new idea is called eccentric until the idea succeeds.

You are successful when people tell you you're a lot smarter than you really are.

If you believe you have no chance to succeed, you are probably right.

Success is not judged by what we start but what we finish.

Late starters are seldom winners.

Solvency is the unanswerable argument of success.

You know a man is successful when the newspapers start quoting him on subjects he knows nothing about.

Efficiency is only another name for doing the right thing at the right time.

Success is when you are bored by people who once snubbed you.

Forget the past—no one ever backed into success.

The secret of achievement is not to let what you're doing get to you before you get to it.

A successful man is usually an average man who had a chance or took a chance.

It's better to deserve success than to attain it.

Success comes as a conquest, not as a bequest.

He who does not sacrifice is not likely to succeed.

We would all be successful if we followed the advice we gave to others.

Triumph is just *umph* added to *try*.

Past failure often furnishes the finest material from which to build future success.

Some men carve their way to success—others chisel.

The final six inches from success is between your ears.

The real opportunity for success lies within the person and not in the job.

Aim high; it is no harder on your gun to shoot the feathers off an eagle than to shoot the fur off a skunk.

◆Sunday School

We either build better Sunday schools and churches, or else we build better prison cells.

Three rules in teaching Sunday school: be sincere, be brief, be seated.

Everyone who thinks there ought to be a Sunday school ought to attend Sunday school.

The most expensive piece of furniture in Sunday school is an empty chair.

T

✦Tact

Diplomacy, at one time, consisted of giving a hand without a handout.

We are so desiring to be tactful that we are losing contact.

Tact is the art of pretending you didn't notice anything.

Tact is the unsaid part of what you think.

Tact is criticizing the mistake rather than the person who made it.

Tact is changing the subject without changing your mind.

Tact is the art of recognizing when to be big and when not to belittle.

Tact is the ability to raise the eyebrows instead of the roof.

Tact is the ability to shut your mouth before someone wants to do it for you.

Tact is the ability of making a point without making an enemy.

Tact is thinking twice before saying nothing.

Tact is the ability to think of things far enough in advance not to say them.

Tact is the ability to stand on your own two feet without stepping on anybody's toes.

People with tact have less to retract.

Tact is the ability to remove the sting from a dangerous stinger without getting stung.

Tact is the ability to give a person a shot in the arm without him feeling the needle.

Tact is the ability to hammer home a point without hitting the other fellow in the head.

✦Taxes (see also Government)

Golf is much like taxes—you drive hard to get to the green and then wind up in the hole.

One way to pay less tax—earn less.

The most permanent thing in the world is a temporary tax.

Today the earth rotates around its taxes.

Our government could raise unlimited revenue simply by taxing sin.

Tax reform is when you take the taxes off things that have been taxed in the past and put taxes on things that haven't been taxed before.

Taxes are strange; you pay this year's taxes with the money you earned last year but spent the year before.

After the government takes enough to balance the budget, the taxpayer has the job of budgeting the balance.

The taxpayer no longer fears that Congress will let him down; he just hopes it will let him up.

America is the only country where it takes more brains to make out the income tax return than it does to make the income.

A taxpayer is a government worker with no vacation, no sick leave, and no holiday.

Your money goes farther these days. In fact, a lot of it winds up in outer space.

The biggest job Congress has is to get the money from the taxpayer without disturbing the voter.

There's this to be said about taxes—if the taxpayer is alive, he's kicking.

If the world is getting smaller, why do they keep raising postal rates?

A taxpayer is one who does not have to pass the civil service exam to work for the government.

A tax collector has what it takes to get what you got.

A tax collector is "his brother's keeper."

The American taxpayer may be America's first natural resource to be exhausted.

Save for a rainy day and a new tax comes along and soaks you.

In modern day terminology a settler is one who has already paid his income tax.

Sometimes they tear down buildings to save taxes. Why not tear down taxes to save buildings?

Taxation is based on supply and demand—the government demands and we supply.

People who don't pay their taxes in due time, do time.

Taxes are a form of Capitol punishment.

As one travels down the highway of life, it becomes quickly apparent that there are far more toll roads than freeways.

We need more watchdogs at the United States Treasury and fewer bloodhounds at the Internal Revenue Service.

A lot of take-home pay is spent as foolishly as that which is withheld for taxes.

Income tax is the fine for reckless thriving.

Nowadays a dime is a dollar with all the taxes taken out.

Social security is the ingenious plan that keeps you poor all your working years, so you can be poor all your retirement years.

The purpose of the IRS is to collect the money and then pass it on to those who spend it.

A fine is a tax for having done wrong—a tax is a fine for having done well.

Invest your money in taxes—they're bound to go up.

The IRS can't tax the riches you store in your soul.

If it's such a small world, why does it take so much of our money to run it?

The advantage of being a dog: Someone else pays the taxes.

An income tax form is like a laundry list—either way you lose your shirt.

When filing income taxes, it is better to give than to deceive.

◆Television

Television has made a wonderful change in American conversation—there's less of it.

TV has gotten so bad that children are doing their homework.

Even if we don't make TV an idol, too often it makes us idle.

Some people dislike TV so much they spend many hours weekly watching it.

TV is called a medium because it's a rare show that's well done.

Television enables people with nothing to say to talk to people who aren't listening.

◆Temper

Shine like a light, but don't flash at people like lightning.

Some people do odd things to get even.

Bluntness is the art of saying nothing in a way that leaves nothing unsaid.

If salvation has done nothing for your temper, it has done nothing for your soul.

Men are like steel—when they lose their temper they are worthless.

Temper is a valuable possession—don't lose it.

The emptier the pot, the quicker it boils. Watch your temper.

A hothead has never been able to set the world on fire.

He who blows his stack adds to the world's pollution.

Those who take a grim delight in being temperamental usually are more "temper" than "mental."

The more often you lose your temper, the more you have of it.

Keep your temper—no one else wants it.

He who can bottle his temper is a real corker.

No one wants a runaway horse, yet many people have a runaway temper.

There's something that the longer you keep it the better it gets— your temper.

Hot tempers will mean cool friends.

Nothing cooks your goose more quickly than a boiling temper.

Temper is the first thing a golfer has to control. It's very bad when a ball tees you off.

The worst-tempered people are usually those who know they are wrong.

Good temper, like a shiny day, sheds a brightness over everything.

When a man's temper gets the best of him, it brings out the worst in him.

Your temper gets you into trouble—your pride keeps you there.

Temper often causes a man to speak his mind when he ought to be minding his speech.

Every time you lose your temper you advertise yourself.

Hitting the ceiling is no way to get up in the world.

If you lose your head, what is the use of the rest of your body?

Hot tempers will lead to spiritual coldness.

Your temper improves the more you don't use it.

A temper displayed in public is indecent exposure.

A person who loses his temper usually loses.

✦Temperance (see also Drinking)

A night club is a place where the tables are reserved and patrons many times are not.

Alcohol kills the living and preserves the dead.

Temperance is the nurse of chastity.

He that is a drunkard is a candidate for all vice.

Intemperance is voluntary madness.

The true worth of a man is to be measured by the objects he pursues.

An ounce of thought may prevent a pound of apology.

A person pays twice for his cigarettes—once when he gets them and second when they get him.

Always drive so that your license expires before you do.

Look before you leap and you won't limp.

A bright eye indicates curiosity—a black eye, too much.

Three ways to preserve your teeth—brush often, see a dentist twice a year, and mind your own business.

Where I go hereafter depends upon what I do after here.

The greater danger for most of us is not that our aim is too high and we miss it, but that it is too low and we reach it.

A recipe of life must contain a goodly amount of seasoning.

Some people are like wheelbarrows—they go only when pushed.

The little man is disturbed by little things.

If some people would be a little more careful where they step, those who follow wouldn't stumble.

When you argue with a fool—two fools are arguing.

Don't laugh at those who have fallen because there may be some slippery places in your own path.

The man who does as he likes is the bigger slave.

There is no paradox more tragic than a high mentality and a low morality.

Safety belts aren't as confining as wheelchairs.

Keep out of your life all that keeps Christ out of your thoughts.

All the flowers of tomorrow are seeds today.

Don't dig a grave for someone else—you may fall into it.

Some men make difficulties—some difficulties make men.

◆Temptation

He who would not eat forbidden fruit must stay away from the forbidden tree.

The best way to escape evil is to pursue good.

Anybody who thinks talk is cheap never argued with a traffic cop.

To master temptation, let Christ master you.

Don't keep your eye on temptation while praying not to be led into it.

Every temptation is an opportunity to flee to God.

By yielding to temptation one may lose in a moment what it took him a lifetime to gain.

It is better to shun the bait than to struggle on the hook.

To have control over temptation, we must allow Christ to control us.

The longer you look at temptation, the more liable you will be to fall for it.

Temptations are sure to ring your doorbell, but it is your own fault if you invite them for dinner.

If you would not fall into sin, keep away from the brink of temptation.

Temptation bothers some folks most when they can't find any.

Temptations are like bums—treat one nice and he will return with many of his friends.

Temptation usually comes in through a door that has deliberately been left open.

Few speed records are broken when people run from temptation.

When you meet temptation, turn to the right.

Nothing makes temptation so easy as being broke.

God always tests us to bring out the best; Satan tempts us to bring out the worst.

When you feel you are free from temptation, be on your guard.

Some temptations come to the industrious; all temptations come to the idle.

Each sin has its door of entrance—keep that door closed.

It is a lot easier to be virtuous when there isn't any temptation.

✦Thanks

If we pause to think, we'll have cause to thank.

God's highest gift should awaken man's deepest gratitude.

Thanksgiving is a duty before it's a feeling.

He who forgets the language of gratitude is not likely to be on speaking terms with God.

Hem your blessings with gratitude lest they unravel.

Those blessings are sweetest that are won with prayers and worn with thanks.

Gratitude shouldn't be an occasional incident but a continuous attitude.

A thankful heart enjoys blessings twice—when they're received and when they're remembered.

If you wish your merit to be known, acknowledge that of others.

Think sometimes of all that you have instead of wishing for what you don't.

If you are not thankful for what you got, it is doubtful if you'll be thankful for what you will get.

God is found in two places—one of his dwellings is heaven, and the other is in the meek and thankful heart.

It is better to appreciate things you don't have than to have things you don't appreciate.

An ungrateful person is like a hog under a tree eating acorns, but never looking up to see where they came from.

A thankful heart is not only the greatest virtue but the parent of all other virtues.

We are the objects of God's grace; let him be the object of our gratitude.

Thanksgiving is memory of the heart.

"Thank you" may be written in small letters but is a capital idea.

If you can't be thankful for what you receive, be thankful for what you escape.

If Christians praised God more, the world would doubt him less.

Appreciation and praise are the lubrication that makes life more enjoyable to us and others.

Thanksgiving is good, but "thanksliving" is better.

Thanksgiving is a college from which we never graduate.

Some count their blessings on their fingers and their miseries on an adding machine.

God's giving deserves our thanksgiving.

It is a bad moment for an atheist when he feels grateful—who does he thank?

Joy thrives in the soul of thanksgiving.

Thanking the Lord in adversity changes burdens into blessings.

I grumbled because I had to get up every morning—until one morning I couldn't get up.

Thanking God for our blessings extends them—failing to thank him will soon end them.

Appreciation is one of the rarest but one of the most beautiful virtues.

No matter how high a man may rise, he must have someone to look up to.

He who is not grateful for the good things he has would not be happy with what he wishes he had.

Anything scarce is valuable—thanks is an example.

It is better to say thank you and not mean it, than to mean it and never say it.

Thankfulness is the soil in which joy thrives.

If a man needs praise—give it to him. He cannot read his tombstone.

◆Thinking

The average man has sixty-six pounds of muscle, forty pounds of bone, and three and a half pounds of brain—which seems to explain a lot of things.

I not only use all the brains I have but all that I can borrow.

Great ideas need landing gear as well as wings.

It's the quick thinkers who become leaders—he who hesitates is bossed.

Your mind is the gateway to your heart.

Keep your mind open to the voice of God and uncluttered by unworthy thought.

The intelligent person is not only open to new ideas—he looks for them.

Those are never alone who are accompanied by noble thoughts.

The moment may be temporary, but the memory is forever.

He who will not command his thoughts will soon lose command of his actions.

A great mind is always a generous one.

The mind is a scheme machine.

The average girl needs more beauty than brains because the average man can see better than he can think.

Of all parts of man's body, the brain is used the least.

An idea that rules people inwardly will ultimately run them outwardly.

Memory is what makes you wonder what you forgot to do.

An empty head is worse than an empty heart.

Your mind is a sacred enclosure into which nothing harmful can come except by your permission.

At the start, always consider the finish.

A great many people think they are thinking when they are merely rearranging their prejudices.

An open mind is fine—but be careful what you shovel into it.

Positive thinking is the only way to produce positive results.

Mix brains with your breath—it will produce more satisfactory combustion.

Minds are like parachutes—not much good unless they are open.

The mind is like the stomach. It is not how much you put into it that counts, but how much it digests.

Ugly thoughts make ugly faces.

The man who prides himself on having courage to say what he thinks should be sure he thinks.

Ideas are like children—your own are wonderful.

A man's mind is like a car—if it gets to knocking too much, he'd better have it overhauled or change it.

A great so-called open mind should be closed for repairs.

Advice from an old carpenter: Measure twice, cut once.

The happiest person is the one who thinks the most interesting thoughts.

America is one of the few places you can say what you speak without thinking.

An empty stomach won't rest until you put something into it—too bad this isn't true with the empty head.

Watch your thoughts—they are blueprints for actions.

One should choose his thoughts with the same care as he chews his food.

Some people have gear trouble—they talk in high gear and think in low.

Which is worse—trying to talk when one's mouth is full or when one's head is empty?

Anticipation of problems is half of the battle—and the only way to anticipate is to think.

Garner pleasant thoughts in your mind, for pleasant thoughts make pleasant lives.

The art of thinking is a love affair—it gains its objective only as it is pursued.

Dreaming is much easier than thinking.

Empty lots and minds attract trash.

Keep your mind clean—change it occasionally.

It is later than we think—and some of us are not thinking.

When two people agree on everything, one of them is doing all the thinking.

Many a train of thought never reaches its station.

Nothing threatens Christian character as do impure thoughts.

Many people need to give their minds a bath.

Second thoughts are always wiser.

The mind has no garbage disposal.

Be careful of your thoughts, they may break into actions at any time.

He who cannot control his thoughts will soon lose control of his actions.

We need to be careful what we think because we are becoming what we think.

You are never alone when accompanied by noble thoughts.

Some folks get lost in thought because it's such unfamiliar territory.

Small hurts can have big imaginations.

It's not polite to talk with a full mouth or empty head.

◆Time

The longer you live, the quicker you can live a year.

A supermarket is a place where you can spend an hour trying to find instant coffee.

Nothing arrives more slowly and passes more quickly than a vacation.

When one takes time to be better, he will enjoy better times.

How time changes things—nearly every luxury eventually becomes a necessity.

A day is full of many hours just waiting for your using; and there are many ways to spend them, so be careful in your choosing.

A person with one watch knows the time. A person with two watches is never sure.

Eternity will reveal whether we have made the right use of time.

Time is never late. Some people are.

You cannot turn back the clock. But you can wind it up again.

If you could turn back the clock, where would you stop?

Use time as a tool—not as a crutch.

Lost time is never found.

When you kill time, just remember it has no resurrection.

As every thread of gold is valuable so is every moment of time.

An inch of time cannot be bought by an inch of gold.

When a man gets up against time, he is taking on an adversary who wins battles with only one pair of hands.

Leaving everything to the last minute is the surest way to make enemies of the other fifty-nine.

Taking an hour off is easy—the hard part is putting it back.

The president of the United States has no more time than you.

Wasting time is really wasting a life.

The busy person will never be too busy to attend his own funeral.

Don't just mark time; use time to make your mark.

There is only one glass that you can never refill—the hourglass.

The Lord wants our precious time—not our spare time.

Killing time isn't murder—it's suicide.

Before you try your hand at something, make sure you try your brain.

Improve your time and your time will improve you.

Millions of people live in a clock-eyed world.

The greatest use of time is to spend it for something that will outlast it.

The man of the hour never watches the clock.

Time passes quickly. We cannot buy it. We can do nothing but make good use of it.

One thing we cannot recycle is wasted time.

If you must kill time—work it to death.

An alarm clock scares the daylights out of you.

One of the worst things about retirement is that you have to drink coffee on your own time.

Time is a little chunk of eternity that God has given us.

You will never find time for anything—you must take time.

Establish your priorities before you can properly manage your time.

How you spend your time is more important than how you spend your money.

Time and words can never be recalled.

Time is not an enemy—unless you try to kill it.

I dare not waste time since I'm living for and in eternity now.

An hour lost is never found.

Counting time is not as important as making time count.

We never shall have any more time. We have, and we have always had, all the time there is.

Time is life—don't kill it.

History may be the record of the past, but more important—it is also the blueprint of the future.

Flowers that last have deep roots and bloom late—things that endure grow slowly.

Ordinary people think how they can *spend* their time; a man of intelligence tries to *use* it.

Time is the most valuable thing a man spends.

Time is the stuff between paydays.

You cannot reward anyone for lost time.

◆Tomorrow (see also Future)

Always put off until tomorrow what you should not do at all.

Never let yesterday use up too much of today.

Help others today and God will help you tomorrow.

You don't get much by starting tomorrow.

The man who does his best today will be hard to beat tomorrow.

Tomorrow is the busiest day of the year.

Today is the tomorrow you worried about yesterday.

The preparation for tomorrow is the right use for this day.

Don't let yesterday's mistakes trouble you, nor tomorrow's fears spoil your day.

Don't boast about what you are going to do tomorrow unless you can say the same thing about yesterday.

How we use today determines how tomorrow will use us.

Wisely use today and your tomorrow will be all right.

Too many things we wait for are not worth the delay.

Tomorrow will be a better day if we begin today to improve it.

I don't worry about tomorrow's problems—I'm not even acquainted with yesterday's.

Yesterday's experience plus today's action will make tomorrow a great day.

Counting time is not as important as making time count.

Time may be a great healer, but it's not a very good beauty specialist.

You can take the day off, but you cannot put it back.

Your time in this world will be short at the longest; your time in another world will be forever and ever.

The best reason for doing the right thing today is tomorrow.

The man who is waiting for something to turn up might do well to start with his own shirt sleeves.

Every tomorrow has two handles—we can take hold by the handle of anxiety or by the handle of faith.

Learn from yesterday—live for today—hope for tomorrow.

Some people are so busy planning for the rainy day that they have no time to enjoy the sunshine.

All of us are going to do better tomorrow, and we would, too, if only we started today.

Live as if Christ died yesterday, arose today, and is coming tomorrow.

Giving your best today is the best recipe for a better tomorrow.

Tomorrow is just a yesterday that hasn't arrived yet.

◆Tongue

Anybody who thinks talk is cheap never argued with a traffic cop.

Not to speak ill requires only silence.

It takes a child two years to learn to talk—it takes a man all his life to learn how to keep his mouth shut.

A bit of love is the only bit that will put a bridle on the tongue.

It would be better to leave people wondering why you didn't talk than why you did.

Profanity is the effort of a feeble mind to express itself forcefully.

A tart temper never mellows with age; and a sharp tongue is the only sharp-edged tool that grows keener with constant use.

If you wouldn't write it and sign it, don't say it.

What isn't said can't come back to hurt.

Wise men think without talking; fools talk without thinking.

Silent gratitude is ingratitude.

Man's ears aren't made to shut, but his mouth is.

By saying little, some people acquire a reputation for knowing considerable.

There are times when to say anything is to say the wrong thing.

Most people will agree with you if you just keep quiet.

No mechanical device builds up momentum quite as fast as the human tongue.

Temper often causes a man to speak his mind when he ought to be minding his speech.

By examining the tongue of a patient, physicians find out the diseases of the body and philosophers the diseases of the mind.

If you have to lose your head, at least hold your tongue.

It is usually the person with a big mouth that bites off more than he can chew.

By remaining silent you will win many arguments.

It is said the average person speaks eleven million words yearly—one-half of these are *I, my,* and *mine.*

One's heart cannot be pure whose tongue is not clean.

To speak kindly does not hurt the tongue.

It is impossible to keep your mind and mouth open at the same time.

Watch your tongue—horse sense is seldom hitched to a waggin' tongue.

Keeping your chin up also keeps your mouth closed.

I regret often that I have spoken; never that I have been silent.

Some people are cats—they lick themselves with their own tongues.

It's strange how so many people with closed minds are not able to keep their mouths shut.

A sharp tongue is no indication of a keen mind.

Lots of things are opened by mistake, but none so often as the mouth.

Long tongues will mean short friends.

Wisdom is knowing when to speak your mind and when to mind your speech.

Give your tongue more rest than your eyes or ears.

The world's most dangerous point—the tip of the tongue.

A paradox is a truth that bites its own tale.

Even a fish would stay out of trouble if he kept his mouth shut.

As a man grows older and wiser, he talks less and says more.

Think twice before you speak; and it will do no harm if you keep thinking while you speak.

If exercise makes you thin, how come there are so many people with double chins?

Your day goes the same way the corners of your mouth turn.

There's danger ahead when you throw your tongue into high gear before you get your brains going.

It is much easier for some people to say what they think than to tell what they know.

Everything that can be said can be said clearly.

The first thing some people do in the morning is to brush their teeth and sharpen their tongue.

A wise person is known for what he didn't say.

If your friends misquote you, think how much worse it might have been had they quoted you correctly.

Some people don't think before they speak—nor afterwards.

To reply to an evil word by another taunt is like trying to clean off dirt with mud.

Lord, fill my mouth with worthwhile stuff and nudge me when I've said enough.

Idle tongues can soon become busy tongues.

A person with a thick head always makes thin conversation.

A loose tongue can get into tight places.

Better to have clean hands and a pure heart than to have clever hands and a smooth tongue.

The most untamable thing in the world has its den just behind the teeth.

It is better to keep your mouth closed and let people think you are a fool than to open it and remove all doubt.

Speak when you are angry and it'll be the best speech you will ever regret.

A narrow mind and a wide mouth usually go together.

God gave man two ears and one mouth; he made the ears to always remain open, but the mouth to close.

There is a difference between free speech and cheap talk.

Two times you should keep your mouth shut—when you are swimming and when you are angry.

Speaking without thinking is like shooting without aiming.

Most people can talk by the time they are two but never learn when not to talk.

The world needs more open minds and less open mouths.

A bridle for the tongue is an excellent harness.

Some people speak from experience. Others, from experience, don't speak.

Those who jump to conclusions may land with a foot in their mouth.

Speech is the mirror of the soul—as man speaks, so is he.

The best way to save face is to keep the lower part closed.

Think twice before you speak if you intend to say what you think.

Use your head, but don't concentrate on the part that eats, drinks, and talks too much.

A person who has nothing to say spends a whole life in saying it.

What this country needs is more free speech worth listening to.

Some people talk so fast that they say things that they have not even thought.

Usually the first screw that gets loose in one's head is the one that controls the tongue.

What should not be heard by little ears should not be said by big mouths.

If you are not sure you are right, keep your mouth shut.

When you get into deep water, keep your mouth shut.

You can usually dodge a question with a long-winded answer.

Every time you open your mouth, you show what's in your heart.

More quarrels are smothered by just shutting one's mouth and holding it shut than by all the wisdom in the world.

Nature did not make your ears so they could be shut but did a perfect job on your mouth.

The teeth should be trained to bite the tongue when it talks too much.

The average person can do more harm with his tongue than with a gun.

One minute of keeping your mouth shut may be worth an hour of explanations.

He who thinks twice before he speaks says only half as much.

If there's anything we can't stand, it's people who talk while we're interrupting.

A man of words and not deeds is like a garden full of weeds.

A sharp tongue will cut your throat.

The secret of being tiresome is to tell everything.

To enjoy music, keep your ears open—to allow others to enjoy it, keep your mouth shut.

Some people never get interested in anything until it is none of their business.

Giving advice does not qualify as charity.

Not every question deserves an answer.

Tongue control requires attention to five things: To whom you speak, of whom you speak, and how and when and where.

The trouble with telling a good story is that it reminds the other fellow of a dull one.

A lot of people wouldn't speak much if they were the only listener.

If people spoke only when they had something worthwhile to say, the world would be very quiet.

It takes a wise person to know what not to say—and then not to say it.

Often the narrower the mind, the wider the mouth.

Some try to prove themselves to be right by being loud.

The two important muscles that operate the direction of the brain are the heart and the tongue.

Often those who speak less on earth are best known in heaven.

Some people say more by being quiet than those who talk all the time.

A wise man is known by the things he doesn't say.

Silence is the one of the great acts of conversation.

The only substitute for brains is silence.

Wisdom is divided into two parts—having a great deal to say, and not saying it.

If you keep your mouth shut, you can't be misquoted.

Silence is an excellent remedy against anger.

No one has to explain something he hasn't said.

If you are sure you are right—keep your mouth shut.

Think twice before saying an unkind word—then don't say it.

Some of the best preaching is done by holding your tongue.

The ability to speak several languages is valuable, but the art of keeping silent is one most precious.

Think before you speak—silent sense is better than fluent folly.

When two quarrel, there's two in the wrong.

If you take pleasure in criticism, it's time to hold your tongue.

One of the most important ingredients in a recipe for speech-making is plenty of shortening.

We cannot control the evil tongues of others, but a good life enables us to disregard them.

A closed mouth gathers no foot.

Wise men are not always silent, but they sure know when to be.

Talk is cheap because the supply is always greater than the demand.

It is better to let your foot slip than your tongue.

It's amazing how long some people can talk without mentioning what they're talking about.

A sharp tongue and a dull mind are usually found in the same head.

To say little and perform much is the characteristic of a great mind.

A person with a closed mind can get by nicely if he keeps his mouth closed too.

The other side of freedom of speech is knowing when to keep your mouth shut.

Words break no bones, but they do break hearts.

Because the tongue is wet, it sometimes slips.

Only rarely it is worth it to tell a man what you think.

He who talks without thinking runs more risks than he who thinks without talking.

Some people know *how* to say nothing but not *when*.

A slip of the foot, you may soon recover, but a slip of the tongue you may never get over.

The art of eloquence is to know when to keep still.

Freedom not to listen is sometimes even more precious than the right of freedom of speech.

What isn't said can't come back to hurt.

The folks who know the least often know it the loudest.

The only way to entertain some folks is to listen to them.

A wise man has something to say; a fool has to say something.

Let your speech be better than silence, or be silent.

"Opened by mistake" applies more often to mouths than it does the mail.

◆Trials

Often the same thing that makes one person bitter makes another better.

The same sun melts ice and hardens clay.

Disappointments are all his appointments—so put him between you and your circumstances.

God will take care of what you go through; you take care of how you go through it.

There are two ways we can meet difficulty: either we can alter the difficulty or we can alter ourselves to meet it.

Most people don't mind obstacles as long as they don't get in their way.

When God allows extraordinary trials, he gives extraordinary comfort.

As the diamond cannot be polished without friction, so the Christian cannot be perfected without trial.

To realize the worth of the anchor we need to feel the storm.

Don't be afraid of opposition—a kite rises best against the wind.

Trust God during your trials—he's had thousands of years of experience.

The sweetest songs often come from broken hearts.

Affliction can prepare ordinary Christians for extraordinary service.

Often life's greatest barriers become life's greatest blessings.

The things Satan throws in our path to defeat us can be stepping stones to victory.

Great trials often precede great triumphs.

God's chastening is never cruel, but it is corrective.

God may not shield us *from* all life's storms, but he shelters us *in* life's storms.

Don't fight your problems and setbacks—use them.

The blow most dreaded often falls to break from off our limbs a chain.

Nothing shows more accurately what we are than the way we meet trials and difficulties.

Those who bless God in their trials will be blest by God through their trials.

If it were not for the hot water, the teakettle would not sing.

If the Lord is our Shepherd, he has the right to shear us at any time, and we have no right to bleat.

With every pain that rends the heart, remember Christ had a part.

We should not be weary of the cross who are sure of the crown.

A song in the night is worth two in the day.

In the clouds of affliction, the eye of faith can always find God's rainbow.

God sends trials, not to impair us, but to improve us.

Law sentences a living man to death; grace brings a dead man to life.

Many people want to go to the promised land without going through the wilderness.

Nothing will ever be attempted if all possible objections must be first removed.

The brook would lose its song if you took away the rocks.

He who has no clouds sees no rainbows.

If life is a grind, use it to sharpen your wits.

It is only the trees that are loaded with fruit that people throw stones at.

The eagle that soars in the upper air does not worry about crossing the river.

God's love for us is not a love that exempts us from trials, but rather a love that sees us through our trials.

He who excuses himself accuses himself.

When you stop the denials, they will stop the accusations.

God's people are not without trial nor without their God amid the trial.

Prosecution is sometimes persecution in the guise of virtue.

Those who deny themselves for Christ will enjoy themselves in Christ.

In this country there is much complaint with little suffering; in some countries there is much suffering with little complaint.

A gem cannot be polished without friction, nor man perfected without the abrasive of trials.

Christians are like tea—their full strength is not drawn out until they get into hot water.

In the storm, God wants to equip us for service.

What we can do for Christ is the test of service. What we suffer for him is the test of our love.

Sorrow is fruit; God does not make it grow on limbs too weak to bear it.

Difficulties afford a platform upon which the Lord can display his power.

God sends the storms to prove he is the only real shelter.

If we didn't have rocks in the pathway, our feet would become flabby.

It is better to suffer wrongly than to do wrong.

The fruitful life results from showers as well as sunshine.

When God puts his children in the furnace, he goes with them.

A smooth sea never made a successful sailor.

Blessed are the irritations of life that bring the irrigations of God.

In the night of despair men discover the light of new hope.

We can only truly appreciate the miracle of sunrise if we have waited in the darkness.

The blue of heaven is larger than the clouds.

It is better to be pruned to grow than to be cut to burn.

There is no sunshine without some shadow.

Circumstances are just raw material out of which God makes character and strength and virtue.

Say not that this or that came to thwart you—it came only to test you.

God will not allow any problem to come to you that cannot become a learning, a turning, or earning experience.

God is more concerned about your response to a problem than he is about removing it.

Think less of the power of things over you and more of the power of Christ in you.

When God allows extraordinary trials, he gives extraordinary comfort.

If you find a path with no obstacles, it probably does not lead anywhere.

God gets his best soldiers from the highlands of affliction.

Christians lay up heavenly awards when they triumph over earthly trials.

Every irritation is an invitation to an elevation.

Clouds in our lives are sent many times to bring showers of blessing.

Sometimes the Lord calms the storm; sometimes he lets the storm rage and calms the believer.

If you take your problems to the Lord, that is natural; if you give your problems to the Lord, that is spiritual.

All sunshine and no rain makes a desert.

The man who believes in sleeping on his problems is simply adding insomnia to his other worries.

God causes many a tight place to open into the right place.

The thickest cloud brings the heaviest shower of blessing.

In every life there must be a grave, and self buried therein.

God often digs the wells of joy with the spade of sorrow.

It's harder to suffer in silence because that takes all the pleasure out of suffering.

He who has never tasted what is bitter does not know what is sweet.

All pleasures are worthless without health.

God brings people into deep water not to drown them but to cleanse them.

Trials are not bad—there's a special place reserved for those without trials—it's called a cemetery.

◆Trouble

Bearing your cross means suffering for your Savior, not for your sins.

Suffering can be like a magnet that draws the Christian closer to Christ.

The world's most disappointed people are those who get what's coming to them.

Those who never take time to mourn never have time to heal.

A toothache is a pain that drives you to extraction.

If we would enlarge upon our blessings as we exaggerate our troubles, our troubles would be lessened.

Look at your blessings with both eyes—at your troubles with one.

In times like these, it helps to remember there have always been times like these.

Be grateful for a few problems—they make a job interesting.

What would some people think about if they didn't have troubles?

If you find a pathway with no obstacles, it probably doesn't lead anywhere.

Your attitude toward your trouble often hurts you more than the trouble.

For the Christian, dark clouds of trouble are but the shadow of God's wing.

When troubles call on you, call God.

It takes tough seas to make good sailors and great captains.

One always pays interest on borrowed trouble.

Obstacles are what you see when you take your eyes off the goal.

Today's gloom may be only a passing cloud veiling the radiance of tomorrow's joys.

When trouble comes, a man's true quality is revealed.

Ulcers are a direct result of mountain climbing over molehills.

Trouble will drive you to prayer, but prayer will drive away trouble.

Some problems in life are meant to be lived with.

Adversity is the diamond dust heaven polishes its jewels with.

The troubles hardest to bear are those that never come.

When the way seems blocked, use the blocks to mount on.

How you handle your problems by day determines how you sleep by night.

Too often trouble starts out by being fun.

You can save yourself a lot of trouble by not borrowing any.

It's not the liberty we have, but the liberties we take that cause most of the trouble in the world today.

Those who bless God in their trials will be blest by God through their trials.

Think less of the power of things *over* you and more of the power of Christ *in* you.

God gives us strength to face our problems, not to flee from them.

It is not the load that breaks you down; it is the way you carry it.

The person who persists in courting trouble soon will find himself married to it.

When we put our cares in God's hands, he puts his peace in our hearts.

We realize the strength of the anchor when we feel the stress of the storm.

God is with us in the night just as surely as he is with us in the light.

When you brood over your trouble, you hatch despair.

Man was made for trouble—if he doesn't get it, he will make it.

You cannot keep trouble from coming into your home, but you don't have to give it a chair to sit on.

Frustration is not having anyone to blame but yourself.

The most trouble is produced by those who don't produce anything else.

You don't need a reference to borrow trouble.

Progress begins with getting a clear view of the obstacles.

The troubles of yesterday added to the worries of tomorrow are too heavy to be carried today.

Most people are more comfortable with old problems than with new solutions.

To stop big trouble, begin stopping the small ones.

He who seeks trouble will have no trouble in finding it.

Telling your troubles is like swelling your troubles.

If you cannot make light of your troubles, keep them in the dark.

There's no such thing as the perfect solution—every solution, no matter how good, creates new problems.

A good way to forget your troubles is to help others to forget theirs.

If only half of our wishes came true, then we would have twice as many troubles.

If you are looking for the meaning of life, it may be in the trouble God is sending your way.

There are two ways we can meet difficulty: either we can alter the difficulty or we can alter ourselves to meet it.

The difficulties of life are intended to make us better, not bitter.

To avoid trouble, breathe through your nose; it keeps your mouth shut.

Some neighbors borrow everything from you except your trouble.

When you invite trouble, it usually accepts.

Perhaps the Lord allows some people to get into trouble because this is the only time they ever think of him.

When you turn green with envy, you're getting ripe for trouble.

The average person brings most of his troubles on himself and uses poor judgment in choosing them.

God has a solution planned before we even know we have a problem.

One thing about trouble, it gives you something to talk about.

If you want problems to pile up, never seek a solution for them.

The only things some people are willing to share are their troubles.

◆Truth

Beware of the half-truth—you may have gotten the wrong half.

Beauty is mind deep.

A lot of stuff that passes for food for thought these days is nothing but the baloney of propaganda.

He who says he enjoys a cold shower in the morning will also lie about other things.

Christianity helps us face the music, even when we don't like the tune.

Most things too good to be true, aren't.

A fish seems to grow daily after the day it was caught.

Integrity needs no rules.

Nothing increases the size of the fish like fishing by yourself.

When in doubt, tell the truth.

You may not be what you think you are, but what you think, you are.

Truth wins every argument if it is stuck to long enough.

The worst lies are those that most resemble truth.

People cannot change truth, but truth can change people.

Your promises to God should be as binding as your signature on the mortgage.

You won't get scriptural harmony if you play only one string of truth.

The ignorant are always deaf to the truth.

It is better to be square than go around in the wrong circles.

One thing you can give and still keep is your word.

Too many Christians keep the truth on ice instead of on fire.

A shady business never yields a sunny life.

The teeth may be false, but be sure the tongue is true.

People called President Lincoln "Honest Abe." What do they call you?

It's twice as hard to crush a half-truth as a whole lie.

The biggest and worst thief of all is the one who will rob you of truth.

Be sure the goods in the window represent correctly the products on the counter.

Why are the apples always much larger on the top than those in the bottom of the basket?

The man who deserts truth in trifles cannot be trusted in matters of importance.

Truth is stranger than fiction—and it's cleaner.

The truth is so hard to see because we are standing in front of it.

Golf is a game in which the ball lies poorly and the player lies as well.

Infidelity never wrote a line that was comforting on a deathbed.

Speaking of truth—we should have regular checkups to avoid truth-decay.

The cloak of a false profession will make an awful blaze when God burns up the stubble.

Jumping to conclusions is not nearly as good a mental exercise as digging for facts.

Never stretch the truth—it may snap back in your face.

If truth stands in your way, you're headed in the wrong direction.

Ananias wouldn't attract attention today in this age of specialized prevarication.

When you tell the truth, you don't have to remember what you said.

As stretching a rubber band weakens the rubber, so stretching the truth weakens the truth.

Sometimes nothing is harder to see than the naked truth.

Some people handle the truth carelessly; others never touch it at all.

When playing golf, nothing counts like your opponent.

A photographer couldn't make a living if he made pictures of people as they really are.

Always be truthful—it takes a fantastic memory to be a successful liar.

Many people don't actually lie; they merely present the truth in such a way that nobody recognizes it.

The truth of a matter is not determined by how many people believe it.

Never be diverted from the truth by what you would like to believe.

If any man seeks *greatness*, let him forget *greatness* and ask for *truth* and he will find both.

Truth is like a torch—the more it is shaken the more it shines.

If you won't admit you've been wrong, you love yourself more than truth.

Some folks we know don't mean to exaggerate—they just remember big.

Goodness is a special kind of truth and beauty—it is truth and beauty in human behavior.

There's no limit to the heights a man can attain by remaining on the level.

Nothing ruins truth like stretching it.

Truth that is out of balance is heresy.

Truth needs no defense—it only needs witnesses.

Error is often dressed in the garb of truth.

A lie can travel halfway around the world while the truth is putting on its shoes.

No man ever got lost on a straight road.

All who cry are not truly sorry.

U

✦Understanding

The best way to keep from stepping on other people's toes is to put yourself in their shoes.

Some of the best arguments are spoiled by people who know what they are talking about.

The important thing is not how fast you are going, but where you are going.

It is always easier to hate something than it is to understand it.

We are not to see through people; we are to see them through.

Suffering in silence is sweet if everyone knows about it.

Horse sense keeps you from sowing wild oats.

Diplomacy is thinking twice before saying nothing.

We cannot really be for something we don't understand.

The biggest step you can take is the one you take when you meet the other person halfway.

Instead of putting others in their place, try putting yourself in their place occasionally.

The man who has a true Christian spirit never takes delight in the faults of others.

Don't pray for rain unless you are willing to put up with a little mud.

It is better to see a few things vividly than to remember a lot of things vaguely.

Before you can dry another's tears, you must learn to weep.

When God puts a tear in your eye, it's because he wants to put a rainbow in your heart.

We may not always see eye to eye, but we should walk hand in hand.

Smart is when you believe only half of what you hear—brilliant is when you know which half.

Sooner or later you must learn that God makes no deals.

Speed is not everything—direction counts.

No matter what scales we use, we can never know the weight of another person's burdens.

Many complain of their money, few of their judgment.

In heaven, God will reveal what on earth he chose to conceal.

You must look into people as well as at them.

No one is always wrong—even the stopped clock is right twice each day.

When rejecting the ideas of another, make sure you reject only the idea and not the person.

You have heard of Murphy's Law. I follow Morton's Law—taking everything with a grain of salt.

✦Unstable People

If envy were a fever, all the world would be ill.

When some people run into a telephone pole, they blame it on the pole.

Confusion is the enemy of all comfort.

It's hard for any empty sack to stand erect.

Some people fall for everything and stand for nothing.

The surest way to mishandle a problem is to avoid facing up to it.

It is inconsistent Christians who help the devil the most.

Some people think they are busy when they are only confused.

Some people are like gamblers—they don't have sense enough to quit when they're ahead.

People who don't know whether they are coming or going are usually in the biggest hurry to get there.

If you say what you think, don't expect to hear only what you like.

Some people are like fences; they run around a lot without getting anywhere.

One reason so many people are not reaching the top is that they never start at the bottom.

Some people are so busy learning the tricks of the trade that they never learn the trade.

He is a fool who fawns over strangers, feuds with his friends, and fails his own family.

V

◆Victory

Win when you can—but when you lose, act as if you enjoyed it for a change.

There are some defeats more triumphant than victories.

No one is tired on the day of victory.

Triumph of wrong is never final victory.

Victory will make us sing, shine, and surrender.

Though each step to the cross was a step of agony, it was also a step to victory.

For the Christian, to *trust* is to *triumph.*

The Christian finds victory only as he starves the old nature and feeds the new.

God wants you to be a victor—not a victim.

If there were no enemies, there would be no battles; if no battles, no victory; if no victory, no crown.

◆Wisdom

Specialization is the art of learning more and more about less and less.

Keep God's *truth* in your head and his *love* in your heart.

Advice is like snow—the softer it falls, the deeper it goes.

Discretion too often marks the end of discovery.

Thinking well is wise, planning well is wiser, but doing well is wisest.

A right attitude toward others will help keep God's truth in our head and his love in our heart.

Some folks may live and learn, but by the time they've learned it's usually too late to live.

A stiff neck usually supports an empty head.

It is better to know some of the questions than all of the answers.

A person is not necessarily smart just because he says things that are smart.

It is surprising how many know how to make a good living, yet do not know how to live good.

Learning is the preface of doing, and if it is done well, it results in wisdom.

The middle of the road may not be the most exciting place to be, but at least you will be farther from the ditch—on either side.

Biting off more than you can chew is the way to cut some wisdom teeth.

An expert knows all the right answers if you ask him all the right questions.

Don't forget in the *darkness* what you learned in the *light*.

Why can't life's problems hit us when we're eighteen and know everything?

If we should lock up all the feebleminded, who would write all our hit songs?

The good lawyer knows the law—the clever one knows the judge.

The best night spot is a comfortable bed.

If you don't learn from your mistakes, there's no sense in making them.

Diplomacy is the art of letting someone else have your way.

Buying cheap merchandise to save money is like stopping a clock to save time.

It is a wise man who knows that he isn't.

People with good horse sense know when to say nay.

Wisdom comes more from living than from studying.

Wisdom consists of passing up nonessentials.

A wise man always prepares for the inevitable.

A diplomat is anyone who thinks before saying nothing.

A word to the wise isn't as good as a word from the wise.

Wisdom is the reward you get for a lifetime of listening when you'd have preferred to talk.

Common sense is genius in homespun.

Do not ask for perfection in all you do but for the wisdom not to repeat mistakes.

Wisdom? Knowing as much at thirty-six as you thought you knew at eighteen.

Common sense is instinct; enough of it is genius.

Right reason is stronger than force.

A wise man knows more than he tells, but a fool often tells more than he knows.

A born diplomat is someone who remembers your birthday but forgets how many.

Knowledge comes by taking things apart; wisdom comes by putting them together.

The door of wisdom swings on the hinges of common sense and uncommon ignorance.

Being brilliant is not making a simple subject complicated; it is making the complicated subject simple.

True wisdom starts with a heart full of faith, not a head full of facts.

Luck is nothing but good planning properly executed.

Some people are wise—some are otherwise.

Muhammad said, "Trust Allah but tie your camels."

Wisdom is the ability to discover the alternatives.

Fools fight one another, but wise men agree together.

The peoples of the world wouldn't have to resort to arms if they'd use their heads.

No man really becomes a fool until he stops asking questions.

A clever person is one who put his problems away for a brainy day.

Learn from the nail—its head keeps it from going too far.

Good judgment comes from experience—experience comes from bad judgment.

A good deal of trouble has been caused in the world by too much intelligence and too little wisdom.

It's what we learn after we know it all that really counts.

Common sense is seeing things as they are and doing things as they should be done.

Greatness lies not in being strong, but in the right use of strength.

You don't have to be listed in *Who's Who* to know what's what.

This is judgment day—use plenty of it.

It is unfortunate to have more dollars than sense.

Great ability without discretion usually comes to a tragic end.

There is just as much horse sense as ever, but it seems like the horses have it.

A wise man thinks all he says; a fool says all he thinks.

An efficiency expert is one who is smart enough to tell you how to run your business and too smart to start one of his own.

There are few things more difficult than the art of making advice agreeable.

Many things can give me wisdom, but only love can make me wise.

To profit from good advice requires more wisdom than to give it.

The beginning of wisdom is silence—the second is listening.

It is wise to act wise unless you are otherwise.

Diplomacy is the art of telling your friends they have "open minds" instead of "holes in their heads."

True wisdom lies in gathering the precious things provided by each day as it goes by.

Wisdom is knowing what to do; skill is knowing how to do it; virtue is doing it well.

True wisdom is the accurate perception of what is really important.

A proverb is a short sentence based on long experience.

Wisdom is the ability to discover alternatives.

Two things to avoid—knowledge on ice and ignorance on fire.

The start of wisdom is silence—the second step is listening.

A man doesn't begin to attain wisdom until he recognizes that he is not indispensable.

A wise man will desire no more than he may get justly, use soberly, distribute cheerfully, and leave contentedly.

Learning is the preface of doing, and if it is done well, it results in wisdom.

A wise man is one who is never afraid to ask the shopkeeper to show him something cheaper.

Horse sense behind the steering wheel is more important than horsepower under the hood.

Wisdom is divided into two parts—having a great deal to say and not saying it.

Wisdom is only an uncommon amount of common sense.

A handful of common sense is worth a bushel of learning.

It's a shame that nature did not provide everyone with two additional senses—horse and common.

You can easily judge the character of a man by how he treats those who can do nothing for him or to him.

The simpler solution may not be the right one, but it's usually the one to consider first.

Our judgment can be no better than our information.

Disillusionment is the first step toward wisdom.

What a fool does in the end the wise man does in the beginning.

The fellow with horse sense doesn't trot with the crowd.

◆Witnessing (see also Missions)

Something is fishy if we aren't fishing for men.

The rewards of witnessing are well worth the risks.

Those on the road to heaven will not be content to go there alone.

Two things should happen to the Christian—something happens in us and something happens through us.

No tears for the lost will mean no rainbows for the soul.

There's enough Bread of Life to supply the whole world, but are there enough volunteers to distribute it?

It's easier to love humanity as a whole than to love one's neighbor.

Personal soul winners get more results with tears in their eyes than arguments on their lips.

The gospel is not something we go to church to hear; it is something we go from the church to tell.

When Christians live the gospel, sinners will listen to the gospel.

Let's reach out to a world in need with the Word it needs.

It is good to be a Christian and know it—it's better to be a Christian and show it.

To really enjoy religion, one must first have it, then use it.

The only way to "preach the gospel to every creature" is to go to every creature.

Too many times we care more for a person's feelings than we do for his soul.

Do I value those for whom Christ died—do I also value those in whom Christ lives?

A passion for Jesus soon becomes a passion for telling others about Jesus.

We who know the need must be willing to sow the seed.

Hospitality is evangelism's greatest tool.

Christ never told his disciples to stay at home and wait for sinners to come to them.

The secret of evangelism is allowing the love of Christ to overflow in every word, every action, and every thought.

The church must go into the world because the world won't come into the church.

Your mission field is the next unsaved person you meet.

In witnessing, behaving the gospel must go hand-in-hand with believing it.

Don't expect God to use you as a lighthouse somewhere if God cannot use you as a candle where you are.

You cannot witness to the wrong person about Christ.

Keep your light shining—God will place it where it will do the most good.

God hasn't made many of us lawyers, but he has done something for all us Christians. He has subpoenaed all of us as witnesses.

Souls cost soles.

We must have Christ revealed to us if we are to reveal him to others.

Talk to the Lord about sinners, then talk to sinners about the Lord.

If, like the shepherds, you have heard and seen, then, like the shepherds, go and tell.

There isn't enough darkness in all the world to put out a single candle.

A church is no stronger than its fellowship and no bigger than its visitation.

If you are on the rocks, don't despair; be a lighthouse.

Before going to the moon, how about visiting your neighbor next door?

Every Christian occupies some kind of a pulpit and preaches some kind of a sermon every day.

The best bell to call people to church is a good example.

There are some who will never know Christ unless you introduce him to them.

A Christian is a living sermon whether or not he preaches a word.

A saint is like a window—he lets the light shine through.

You can never win to Christ a soul that you do not love.

If you refuse to serve the Lord, he may one day refuse to let you.

Lighthouses don't make noises—they just shine.

You are the salt of the earth, but remember, the earth needs some sugar, too.

Some very effective sermons are delivered when one man is the preacher and one man is the congregation.

We are ringing church bells instead of ringing doorbells.

Anyone can go door-to-door, but only you can witness where God has placed you.

Do you have a burden for the lost, or have you lost the burden?

If every Christian visited like you do, would anyone ever know your church is concerned about them?

Christianity is like chicken pox—if you have it, you will give it to others.

Remember, to be a witness means to live in such a way that one's life would not make sense if God did not exist.

Trim your lamp more often so that it will give more light and less smoke.

The pastor's job is to fill the pulpit—the member's job is to fill the church.

The tact needed for evangelism is contact.

We will either give the gospel out or we will give the gospel up.

The only way to get others to God is first to get to him yourself.

A soul winner is one who never gets used to the sound of marching feet on the way to a lost eternity.

A living Christ in a living man is a living sermon.

Everybody wants a harvest, but few want to plow.

All people cannot witness the *same way*, but all people can witness *some way*.

He who lives like Christ wins men to Christ.

◆Women

The best thing for a cold shoulder is a mink.

Just why is it that you *convince* a man, but must *persuade* a woman?

Most women don't mind Yule shopping—they charge right ahead.

The best years of a woman's life are between twenty-eight and twenty-nine.

Some women work at changing a man, and when they have changed him, they don't like him.

The best cookbooks are no substitute for good cooks.

A young beautiful woman is the act of nature—a beautiful old lady is the work of art.

A good secretary is a woman that usually does the work that some man gets credit for.

The best man for the job—a woman!

A woman's age is like the speedometer on a used car—you know it's been set back, but you don't know how far.

It takes a smart woman to decide if a man is too old to be considered eligible, or too eligible to be considered old.

When a woman lowers her voice, it's a sign she wants something. When she raises it, it's a sign she didn't get it.

The difference between a soldier and a woman is that one faces the powder—the other powders her face.

They say that every man needs two women—a secretary to take everything down and a wife to pick everything up.

The better a woman looks, the longer the man does.

The average women would rather dye than have gray hair.

We speak about the equality of the sexes, but whoever saw a retired housewife?

Many a woman who goes on a diet finds that she is a poor loser.

No wonder women live longer than men. Look how long they are girls.

A lady is a woman who makes a man behave like a gentlemen.

Women without principle draw considerable interest.

A large woman stood in church and sang, "Love Lifted Me." A skinny man stood next to her and sang, "It Took a Miracle."

Flirting is the gentle art of making a man feel pleased with himself.

A woman's beauty lasts only as long as her disposition stays sweet.

American women are the best *yessed* women anywhere.

Women's lib: Too many plots and plans and not enough pots and pans.

The modern kitchen can never replace the old-fashioned cook.

The European wife is a servant; the American wife works her husband to death, and then takes a cruise on the insurance.

The smart girl who searches too long for a smart cookie is apt to wind up with a crumb.

An intelligent girl is one who knows how to refuse a kiss without being deprived of it.

Cosmetics are a woman's way of keeping a man from reading between the lines.

Too many women think they are improving on Mother Nature when they're fooling Father Time.

The proportion of females arrested for burglary is on the rise. First equal rights, then equal wrongs.

Most men believe that a woman's place is in the home; they expect to find her there immediately after she gets off work.

The upkeep of women is the downfall of man.

Kissing a girl is like opening a bottle of olives—if you get one, the rest comes easy.

The idealist puts a woman on a pedestal—and the practical man comes right along with a ladder.

Some men marry poor girls to settle down, and others marry rich ones to settle up.

A girl strings along with a guy only to see if he's fit to be tied.

Many a woman has started out playing with fire and has ended up cooking over it.

Most women know the value of love—only men the cost.

A beautiful woman is the one you notice. A charming woman is the one who notices you.

Some women make a fool out of a man—but many a godly woman has made a man out of a fool.

Women live longer than men because they need the time to finish all they started to say.

About the only time a woman really succeeds in changing a male is when he's a baby.

A man is judged by the company he keeps—a woman by how late she keeps company.

Women prefer husbands with a will of their own, provided it's made out in the wife's name.

It's better to be an old maid than to wish you were one.

Strange but true—you never heard an Englishman telling a woman, "You look like a million pounds."

Men say women can't be trusted too far—women say men can't be trusted too near.

Diamonds don't grow on trees, but you will find them on certain limbs.

Women's lib, someone said: "It's Adam's rib and Satan's fib."

Spring is the time of the year when women pay clothes attention to each other.

Women's fashions may change each year but their designs remain the same.

The girl who has many men on the string will soon get into a tangle.

A modern girl: screams at the sight of a mouse, but climbs into a car with a wolf.

◆Words

Sign in veterinarian's office: Doctor will be with you shortly. Sit! Stay!

Sign in music shop: Gone Chopin. Bach in a Minuet.

Energy crisis: when you can't fuel all the people all the time.

Our language is funny—a fat chance and a slim chance mean the same thing.

Some things not worth saying are now put into songs.

An argument is two people trying to get in the last word.

I don't mind freedom of speech in the nation, providing we don't have to listen to it.

The strongest words are usually used in the weakest arguments.

Those who say the least often say the most.

A good word is as easily said as a bad one.

Talk about others the same way you want others to talk about you.

If you have nothing to say, say it.

One great use of words is to hide our thoughts.

Those who have the most to say usually say it with fewest words.

A great anecdote is worth a volume of biography.

Too often a word to the wise is just enough to start an argument.

As a man grows wiser, he talks less and says more.

A major part of self-control is mouth-control.

It's easier to save face if you keep the lower half shut.

Sparkling conversation is made by filling the mouth with gems of thought.

Evil talk is the devil's halitosis—keep silent and it will die a natural breath.

Kind words do not wear out the tongue.

Our words may hide our thoughts, but our actions will reveal them.

It would be better to leave people wondering why you didn't talk than why you did.

If your foot slips, you may recover your balance, but if your tongue slips, you cannot recall your words.

Some people know *how* to say nothing, but few know *when*.

Don't speak unless you can improve on the silence.

The speech most winning has its end close to the beginning.

It isn't so much what we say as the number of times we say it that makes us boring.

Courage is sometimes mistaken for fear that remained silent.

It's a great pity the right of free speech isn't based on the obligation to say something sensible.

The best evidence that one has a fine command of language is his ability to keep his mouth closed.

The popular speaker is one who knows all the advantages of stopping sooner than his audience expects him to.

All minds face a world full of ideas, but only a great mind knows how to relate them constructively.

A person who constantly puts his foot in his mouth finally throws his whole body out of balance.

The words we say will teach if we practice what we preach.

Some measure their generosity by the abundance of advice they give.

Strange, but it appears those with the biggest mouths always have the least to say.

God does more than hear words; he reads hearts.

If it goes without saying, do not insist on repeating it.

Most entanglements are caused by vocal cords.

When at a loss for the right word to say, try silence.

God's Word tells us of his love; our words should tell him of our love.

It is wiser to choose what you say than to say what you choose.

Silence is the best and surest way to hide ignorance.

One way to store up knowledge is to keep your mouth shut.

Have you noticed that people who are not smart say things that do?

Every time you speak, your mind is on parade.

Well-timed silence has more eloquence than speech.

What many speakers lack in depth, they give in length.

You can never exercise an open mind and an open mouth at the same time.

It's difficult to put your foot in your mouth when it is closed.

When you have nothing to say, never say it out loud.

There is no substitute for brains—but silence sometimes helps.

Holding a conversation is good, but sometimes you should let go of it.

Many a man who is proud of his right to say what he pleases wishes he had the courage to do so.

You cannot judge an auto by the sound of the horn—nor a man.

When you cannot get people to listen any other way, tell them it is confidential.

The words you speak today were yesterday's thoughts.

It is more important to get the thoughts than the last word.

Keep your words sweet—you may have to eat them.

Waste of words and time are two of the greatest expenses of life.

The kindly word that falls today may bear its fruit tomorrow.

The most acute indigestion is sometimes caused by the words we've eaten.

Better that your heart should have no words than your words have no heart.

Apology is often the best way to have the last word.

Spend not your money before it be got; speak not your mind before you have thought.

America needs more free speech that is worth something.

If you think little of a person, you ought to say as little as you think.

Kind words are short to speak, but their echoes are endless.

A lot of trouble in this world arises from the combination of a narrow mind and a wide mouth.

Great talkers are usually little doers.

Language has three important uses—it expresses thought, conceals thought, and takes the place of thought.

The fact that silence is golden may explain why there is so little of it.

Evil words cut more deeply than a sword.

Knowing what to say is not enough; we must know how to say it.

Words break no bones, but they do break hearts.

Gentle words fall lightly, but they have great weight.

Speech is silver, but silence is golden.

There are two types who say very little: the quiet type and the gabby type.

Blessed is the man who abstains from giving windy evidence of the fact that he has nothing to say.

Talk is cheap because the supply has always exceeded the demand.

People will pay more attention to what you say if you pay more attention to what they say.

If you are a person of few words, you won't have as many to take back.

A person is not necessarily smart because he says smart things.

When someone doesn't speak to you, he's trying to tell you something.

Karate is chop talk.

◆Work (see also Ambition)

An executive is one who never puts off until tomorrow what he can get someone else to do today.

Pray to God, but row for shore.

Housework is something you do that nobody notices unless you don't do it.

To be effective in God's work is quite different than to be active in God's work.

An executive is one who hires others to do what he is hired to do.

Somehow or other, as we get older, work seems a lot less fun, and fun seems a lot more work.

Variety may be the spice of life, but it's monotony that brings home the groceries.

The average American is a guy who was born in the country, worked hard so he could live in the city, then worked even harder to get back to the country.

The word *easy* appears only once in the New Testament, and then in connection with the *yoke*.

If a man does only what is required of him, he is a slave. If he does more than is required of him he is a free man.

We never hear anything about the resolutions of the apostles, but a great deal of the Acts of the Apostles.

Stealing the initiative is the one form of theft that always pays.

No one needs a vacation as much as the person who just had one.

Maintain your motivational therapy. Add to your smarts.

Meet the success twins—cultivation and conversation.

Want to percolate? Then circulate.

We spend thousands of dollars on time-saving devices; then work overtime to pay for them.

Learn to labor and to wait; but be careful how you start, lest you learn to wait so well, you overlook the labor part.

The hen is the only one who can lay around and still be a producer.

What we need is not a forty-hour week but a forty-day week.

Labor Day is so named because it's the only day when nobody does any.

It takes just as much energy to wish as it does to plan.

It's not the ability to kick that makes a mule such a valuable animal but his ability to pull.

Dreaming has its values, but never should it become a substitute for work that needs to be done.

Stop at the bottom and wake up.

A person does not grow old through work—but through rusting.

The idle man does not know what it is to enjoy rest.

Our nation became big by starting things.

People may not remember how fast you did your work, but they will remember how well you did it.

Some people pray for more than they are willing to work for.

If you're rich and have two jobs, you are diversified—if you are poor, you are moonlighting.

You may be on the right track, but if you sit there, you'll be run over.

It is easier to do a job right than to explain why you didn't.

It is quite possible to work without results, but never will there be results without work.

The best incentive plan: Get busy, or you're fired.

Work is the price of success.

If you want to be successful, start working on the job before you have to.

The man with push will pass the man with pull.

Times are hard for folks hunting soft jobs.

Man invented work as an easy way to escape boredom.

The highest reward one can get for good work is the ability to do even better work.

Everything comes to those who wait, as long as those who wait work like mad while they are doing so.

If the devil can find a man who is idle, he will send him to work.

It is better to wear out than to rust out.

You can't climb the ladder of success with your hands in your pockets.

We don't need to change the work week so much as we need to change the weak work.

Nobody ever got his mind dirty doing hard work.

A laborer is ready to work when the work is ready.

Genius is seldom recognized for what it is—a great capacity for hard work.

The world does not pay for what a person knows, but it pays for what a person does with what he knows.

Being idle isn't necessarily doing nothing—it's being free to do anything.

The father of success is work; the mother of achievement is ambition.

There may be luck in getting a good job, but there is no luck in keeping it.

God put work into your life; he expects you to put life into your work.

Weeds grow themselves—flowers need cultivation.

It's better to lose sleep on what you plan to do than to be kept awake by what you have done.

Don't just entertain ideas—put them to work.

Before you say you cannot, give it a try.

A good worker does not make the same mistake twice.

Today's preparation determines tomorrow's achievement.

The more steam you put into your work, the louder you can whistle when the job is done.

Nothing ruins a neighborhood for the average husband like having an enthusiastic gardener move in.

The surest way of establishing your credit is to work so hard that you won't need it.

Grandma said they wore exercise outfits in her day, too, but they called them housedresses.

Unless a man undertakes more than he can possibly do, he will never do all that he possibly can.

Good intentions die unless they are executed.

The best medicine is to love your work and your enemies.

No race can prosper until it learns that there is as much dignity in tilling a field as there is in writing a poem.

A true humanitarian has one simple rule at the office: If you have enough strength to call in sick, you should be at work.

There are two kinds of people; those who do the work and those who take the credit. Try to be in the first group; there is much less competition there.

There is something fascinating in the prospect of getting by without working, but all the joy is taken out of it by the fierce competition.

While we can't cross a bridge until we come to it, it just might be smart to lay down a pontoon ahead of time.

We will never be challenged by seeing through our task till we recognize the challenge of seeing our task through.

You cannot clean up this old world with soft soap—it takes grit.

The reward of a thing well done is to have done it.

The man who never does more than he gets paid for seldom gets paid for more than he does.

The more you sweat in peace, the less you bleed in war.

People don't care about their work unless they feel appreciated.

Even back in Grandpa's time there was something to make you sleep—they called it work.

Great things are done when men and mountains meet.

The world owes you a living only after you have earned it.

Two ways to get to the top of an oak tree—climb it or sit on an acorn.

You will never lose your shirt if you keep your sleeves rolled up.

A clean mouth and an honest hand will take a man through any circumstance.

Most men who get to the top quickly start by rising early.

Christians are not called to merely endure change, nor to profit by it, but to cause it.

Work isn't work if you enjoy it.

It takes an honest man to tell whether he's tired or just lazy.

Nothing would be done at all if a man waited until he could do it so well that no one could find fault with him.

To gain success, do not merely stare up the steps—step up the stairs.

Rewards are usually anticlimatic—the fun is in the doing.

The best time to look for work is after you get the job.

Most of us can do more than we think we can but usually do less than we think we have.

The difference between a career and a job is about twenty or more hours per week.

Unless a job means more than money, it will seldom return more than money.

A boss is a person who is always early when you're late and late when you're early.

The best investment you can make in life is hard work.

Some who are not paid what they are worth ought to be glad.

Don't itch for something you're not willing to scratch for.

For keeping busy, the bee is praised; the mosquito is swatted—it's a matter of give and take.

A lot of people look for employment—very few look for work.

Don't let the fact that you can't do it all keep you from doing what you can.

The number of people who are unemployed isn't as great as the number who aren't working.

If some employees were paid what they are worth, the employer might be in violation of the minimum wage law.

As a man grows wiser, he talks less and says more.

They who work hardest watch best for the Lord's return.

You don't have to lie awake at nights to succeed—just stay awake.

If you ever expect to have any pull, you'll have to push for it.

Too many Americans believe it's easier to vote for something than to work for it.

There is perfect freedom for people who do the work they want to do and live by that work.

Industry can do anything that a genius can do and many things that it cannot.

The best way to keep from being unemployed is to work at it.

People rarely succeed at anything unless they have fun doing it.

If you make your job important, it's quite likely to return that favor.

If you do not make more of your job than the average man, then the average man can hold your job.

He that teaches not his son to do some trade makes him a thief.

He who cannot speak well of his trade does not understand it.

Footprints in the sands of time can never be made by sitting down.

The cards you hold in the game of life have little meaning if they are never played.

If you want a place in the sun, you must expect some blisters.

If at first you don't succeed, try a little harder.

Sign on a private detective's office: We pry harder.

The best oil you can use in life is elbow grease.

Be quick to work and slow to talk.

No man can be a workman for God until he is a workmanship of God.

To do nothing is tiresome; one can never stop and take a rest.

The price of mastery in any field is thorough preparation.

The key to willpower is want-power. Those wanting something badly enough will find the willpower to do it.

It is not enough to put your shoulder to the wheel—you must remember to push.

Work, wait, win. Start at the bottom and there is one way to work—up.

Work smarter instead of longer.

Ideas are funny things; they do not work unless we do.

The best way to erase bad conditions is to use the hard work eraser.

Sitting and wishing will not change your course. What good is a wagon without a horse?

We don't need to change the work week—we need to get the weak to work.

Nobody ever drowned in sweat.

The wishbone will never take the place of the backbone.

The reward of doing a good job is more work.

Dodging work is the hardest work of all and yields the poorest returns.

The best way to move mountains is to begin with molehills and work your way up.

A generation ago most men finished a day's work and needed a rest—now they need exercise.

Most people who wake up famous haven't been asleep.

Remember the clock: it passes the time by keeping its hands busy.

Good ideas are perishable—if you don't use them they won't keep.

Starting on the right road and facing the right direction pays few dividends unless you keep moving.

Most jobs are carried out best by committees of one.

The only people who are criticized are the people who do something.

If you worked for your employer as you serve God, how long would you hold your job?

All that stands between you and the top of the ladder is the ladder.

Have your tools ready—God will find work for you.

Everything worthwhile is upgrade.

The time God allows us is just enough for the work he allots us.

Some people work themselves to death by labor-saving devices.

A man is not paid for having hands and head but for using them.

To some people, the ideal occupation is one that doesn't keep them occupied.

A press agent is a man who hitches his braggin' to a star.

The best kind of pride is that which compels a man to do his best work even though no one is looking.

The mosquito never waits for an opening—he makes one.

Work is not meant to be a penalty for living.

Let not your motto be "get by" but "get on."

I am a great believer in luck, and I find the harder I work, the more I have it.

The mosquito doesn't get slapped on the back until he starts to work.

Sign in unemployment office: Don't underestimate yourself—let us do it for you.

Pray for a good crop, but don't forget to hoe.

A job well done is a job well planned.

It doesn't matter whose payroll you are on; you work for yourself.

If you don't put a shoulder to the wheel, you may find your back to the wall.

Instead of giving yourself a pat on the back, try giving yourself a shove.

There is only one man better than the man who gets behind and pushes, and that is the man who stays ahead and pulls.

Rule for success: work your tongue little, your hands much, and your brain much.

Inspiration is presentation—a job well done is well planned.

The man who just watches the clock will always remain one of the hands.

Your work is an excellent commentary on your character.

◆Worry

God is our help in trouble; if you worry, you are on your own.

Don't lie awake at nights worrying about how to succeed; just stay awake days.

Don't worry about knowing people; just make yourself worth knowing.

Don't worry what the world is coming to; be concerned what it has already come to.

Worrying doesn't give you anything but wrinkles; something else to worry about.

The best cure for worry is to go deliberately forth and try to lift the gloom off somebody else.

Worry is *fear-thought,* not *fore-thought.* It is cured by *prayer-thought.*

If God attends the funeral of a sparrow, do you think he does not care for me?

When we worry, we believe more in our problems than in God's promises.

If we fill our hours with regrets of yesterday and with worries of tomorrow, we have no today in which to be thankful.

To worry about what we cannot help is useless. To worry about what we can help is stupid.

The hardest wart to remove is the worry wart.

Worry give small things big shadows.

Worry is a thin stream of fear trickling through the mind. If encouraged, it cuts a channel into which all thoughts drain.

A person who is too busy to worry in the daytime and too tired to lie awake at night need not worry about being able to grow gracefully.

Worry is useless, senseless, and worthless.

Worry doesn't do any good, I know; most of the things I worried about didn't happen.

What you say in hurry may cost you much worry.

Why worry when you can pray?

The letter *I* is always found in the middle of anxiety.

Ulcers are not caused so much by what you eat as what you allow to eat you.

Sing your troubles away—who ever saw a bird worry?

The man yesterday who worried about tomorrow isn't here today.

There is a difference between *worry* and *concern*. A worried person sees the problem; the concerned person solves the problem.

Worry pulls tomorrow's cloud over today's sunshine.

Why let yourself be consumed by what's eating you?

The nice thing about a college education is that it enables us to worry about things all over the world.

Why worry about the shadows of life? Turn your face to the sun and you won't see them.

If you want to test your memory, try to remember the things that worried you yesterday.

Worry is the advance interest you pay on troubles that seldom come.

Life lived in worry invites death in a hurry.

If a care is too small to be made into prayer, it is too small to be made into a burden.

You cannot change the past, but you can ruin a perfectly good present by worrying over the future.

A day of worry is more exhausting than a week of work.

Worry is as useless as saving sawdust.

Worry is the interest paid on trouble before it is due.

Anxiety does not empty tomorrow of its sorrow; it empties today of its strength.

Worry is a circle of inefficient thought whirling about a pivot of fear.

Worry comes through human interference in the divine plan.

Worry is wasting today's time to clutter up tomorrow's opportunities with yesterday's troubles.

The person looking back with worry will bump into troubles ahead.

A psychiatrist is a man who doesn't worry so long as others do.

The reason worry kills more people than work is that more people worry than work.

You wouldn't worry about what people think of you if you knew how seldom they do.

There are two days in one's life about which no one should worry—yesterday and tomorrow.

At night turn all your worries over to God; he's going to be up all night anyway.

Some people waste a lot of energy climbing mountains before they are even in sight.

Prayer is an acknowledgment of faith; worry is a denial of faith.

Worrying is praying to the wrong God.

◆Worship

Did you ever hear anyone say, "We're not going to the lake this afternoon; Sunday is the only day we have to rest"?

Since we fight for the liberty to worship, should we not make more use of that liberty?

When we recognize Jesus' kingship, we'll give him our worship.

A person may be worthy of admiration, but Christ alone is worthy of adoration.

When we submit to Jesus' lordship, we'll give him our worship.

It is possible to be so active in the service of Christ as to forget to love him.

The word *worship* is a shortened form of the old word *worthship*, which means showing God the worth he holds in your life.

Fellowship with a holy God will produce holy living.

Some people think Sunday is Funday.

He who lives a life of love and charity is constantly at worship.

Emotion without devotion is nothing more than commotion.

Active worship requires active involvement.

For God's people, *worship* must come before *work*.

Y

✦Youth

Say what you will about rock and roll, you have to admit it's opened up a whole new field of expression for kids who can't sing.

It isn't what a teenager knows that worries his parents; it's how he finds out.

One way for a girl to whip up a boy's interest is to give him a good eye-lashing.

The best safeguard for the younger generation are the prayers of the older generation.

Don't worry about the teenager who hates vegetables. He also used to dislike girls.

No wonder the youth are confused—many adults are telling them to find themselves and others are telling them to get lost.

When a youth starts sowing his wild oats, it's time to start the thrashing machine.

It seldom occurs to teenagers that someday they will know as little as their parents.

Teenagers are people who demand to be different, yet they dress exactly alike.

He who controls not his youth will not enjoy his old age.

The flower of youth is most beautiful when it bends toward the Son of righteousness.

The worst thing that I can find with the younger generation is that I don't belong to it.

To keep young, associate with young people. To get old in a hurry, try keeping up with them.

There is nothing wrong with the younger generation that the older generation didn't outgrow.

You save an old man and you save a unit, but save a boy and you save a multiplication table.

If you want to stay youthful—stay useful.

Young people's favorite books—Mom's cookbook and Dad's checkbook.

Adolescence is when boys discover girls, and girls discover they have been discovered.

Youth is not only a time of life; it's a state of mind.

The young and old have all the answers; those in between are stuck with the questions.

Don't spoil your teenagers; you have a right to the car at least one night a week.

The foundation of every state is the education of its youth.

Teenagers need to learn that "No" is a complete sentence.

Z

✦Zeal

Zeal without knowledge is a fire without control.

Kindness has converted more sinners than either zeal, eloquence, or learning.

The apostles turned the world upside-down because their hearts had been turned right-side up.

Don't let the best you have ever done be the standard for the rest of your life.

INDEX